MARGARET
Atwood

Twayne's World Authors Series

Canadian Literature

Robert Lecker, Editor
McGill University

TWAS 740

MARGARET
Atwood

Jerome H. Rosenberg
Miami University

Twayne Publishers • Boston

For Lana Kay
and
For Shana Eden . . .

Margaret Atwood

Jerome H. Rosenberg

Copyright © 1984 by G. K. Hall & Company
All Rights Reserved
Published by Twayne Publishers
A Division of G. K. Hall & Company
70 Lincoln Street
Boston, Massachusetts 02111

Frontispiece photograph courtesy of Graeme Gibson

Book Production by Elizabeth Todesco
Book Design by Barbara Anderson

Printed on permanent/durable acid-free
paper and bound in the United States of
America.

Library of Congress Cataloging in Publication Data.

Rosenberg, Jerome H., 1943—
    Margaret Atwood.

    (Twayne's world authors series
Canadian literature ; TWAS 740)
    Bibliography: p. 171
    Includes index.
    1. Atwood, Margaret Eleanor, 1939–
—Criticism in interpretation.
I. Title. II. Series.
PR9199.3.A8Z85   1984   818'.5409   84-4672
ISBN 0-8057-6586-7
ISBN 0-8057-6599-9 (pbk.)

Contents

About the Author

Dr. Jerome H. Rosenberg first met Margaret Atwood in 1975, during a summer visit to her rural home in Alliston, Ontario, a few months after he had begun to contemplate a book-length commentary on her work. His interest in Atwood, and in Canadian literature generally, derived from his initial excitement with Atwood's craft, from her encouragement during that first and subsequent visits with her, and from his previous scholarly work in the literature of another Commonwealth country, Australia.

Trained primarily as a student of American literature, Dr. Rosenberg was introduced to Australian literature by Professor Joseph J. Jones of the University of Texas at Austin, where Rosenberg earned his doctorate under Professor Jones's guidance, completing in 1971 a dissertation on comparative patterns of development in American and Australian literature. Since that time Rosenberg has published several articles on American, Australian, and Canadian literature, including essays on Margaret Atwood and Australia's Rolf Boldrewood.

In 1979 Rosenberg was elected to membership on the executive committee of the Modern Language Association division on English Literature other than British and American, serving in 1982 as secretary and in 1983 as chair of that division. Currently Professor of English at Miami University, Oxford, Ohio, he has been teaching there since 1968.

Preface

In constructing this study of the works of Margaret Atwood I have taken to heart an admonition she awarded me in an April 1976 letter: an author's life, she wrote, is "best handled after the writer is dead." She added cryptically, about herself, "not dead yet." Partly because of that succinct counsel and partly because Atwood, now only in her mid-forties, is at the prime of her life and career, I long ago decided that any prolonged biographical study in this book would be inappropriate. A biographical survey, which should legitimately deal with decade-long epochs in an author's life, awaits another time, another place, and perhaps another writer. Atwood may be flattered to be considered "worthy of Twaynification" (as she put it in a 1975 letter); but I agree with her that her writing, and not her life, should be central to the study. I have thus put my own efforts toward intensive critical investigation of Atwood's works, dealing with particular texts and with the overall development of her craft. Those biographical details that have crept past the barricades are ones that I felt would contribute to the reader's general impression of Atwood as poet, novelist, short-story writer, and literary and social critic.

It is with the facts of Atwood's childhood and early professional growth, and with the controversies (literary, cultural, and political) surrounding her role as critic, that biography most intrudes in this study. One must know where an author has begun to comprehend where she has gone: Atwood's early experiences in the bush country of northern Ontario and Quebec certainly have contributed to both the imagery and the vision of her works; and the maneuverings that led to the publication of her first major volume, *The Circle Game,* amplify the transition from literary nonentity to winner of the Governor-General's Award, an honor that catapulted Atwood to almost overnight fame (preceded, of course, by years of struggle and growth that most critics ignored). Since that time, for more than a decade, Atwood has been recognized as a major Canadian literary figure; and she has, for something less than a decade, been attracting an increasingly large and generally admiring audience in the United States, England, and continental Europe. Her success has made her a public figure and invited upon her a critical scrutiny that (to her expressed dismay) involves her public image as much as her skill as a writer. Variously scorned and admired by Canadian nationalists, adopted by adherents of the women's movement, and castigated by some Canadian literati who believe she has threatened Canadian writers by somehow circumscribing their creativity, Atwood has consistently risen above these parochial concerns. Yet to ignore them completely would be to neglect a significant facet of her career.

Accordingly, in chapter 1, I have presented a capsule biography of Atwood's earlier years, interspersed with a consideration of her earliest experiments with the written word, leading eventually to the crafted images and central concerns of *The Circle Game.* In chapter 6, which places Atwood in Canadian and world literature and ascertains her role in the surging growth of Canadian literature during the years in which she was first making her mark, I've commented on several of the more notorious events in her professional life. Chapter 5, which investigates Atwood's nonfiction prose, also contributes somewhat to our understanding of her image, since it involves, particularly, her controversial critical work, *Survival,* in which she laid out, to the joy of some and chagrin of others, her view of what constituted an essential Canadian literary tradition.

The bulk of this study, however, is contained in chapters 2 through 4, which are largely devoid of biographical detail. Chapters 2 and 3 investigate Atwood's poetry, book by book, beginning with *The Circle Game* and concluding with *True Stories,* published in 1981. Although Atwood's poetry could be abstracted into several dominant themes, each individually and reductively examined, I felt this organic, synthetic study of each book would more effectively reveal the scope and shifting winds of her achievement through the years. Lengthier than the remaining chapters, chapter 2 is particularly detailed in its examination of Atwood's first four major collections of poetry. It thus provides an elaborate though hardly exhaustive indication of the significant trends in her writing, and it offers an index against which her later poems and her prose writings—less expansively treated—may be evaluated.

In both chapters on Atwood's poetry I have deliberately avoided any elaborate reference to *Survival,* which many reviewers have accurately labeled a guidebook to Atwood's earlier concerns as a poet and novelist. I prefer that her poems reveal their own qualities, both formal and thematic, rather than let my commentary be dictated by the narrow thematic niches that *Survival* carves for itself. There is, of course, a relationship between *Survival* and Atwood's other works, but I have reserved my explicit remarks about *Survival* for chapter 5. Similar *caveats* apply to chapter 4, which examines each of Atwood's five novels and her first collection of short stories.

One difficulty a critic faces in writing about a prolific living author is that, while the critic is silently contemplating the author's already-published works, the author continues to produce, gleefully exhorting the critic (as Atwood did me in 1981) to "hurry up before I publish MORE," and reminding him that it "serves you right for choosing an undead author!" With these thoughts in mind, I momentarily cease my contemplation and here offer what must be viewed as a preliminary, though by no means premature, study of this significant contemporary writer.

Jerome H. Rosenberg

Miami University

Acknowledgments

To Margaret Atwood and Graeme Gibson and their daughter Jess, for several pleasant and enlightening visits to their Alliston farm. To Atwood for generously allowing me to quote from letters and other unpublished materials, for reading and commenting on sections of a draft manuscript of this study, and for her encouragement.

To Alan Horne, of the University of Toronto's Robarts Library, for his bibliographic expertise; and to Richard Landon, Katherine Martyn, and the staff of the Thomas Fisher Rare Book Library, for their easing my way into the Atwood manuscript papers. To the staff of Miami University's Edgar Weld King Library, and especially William Wortman, Sarah Barr, Susan Berry, and Karen Clift for processing more interlibrary loan requests than one might reasonably expect, or deserve.

To Provost David Brown and Miami University for a research leave in 1978; to the Miami University Faculty Research Committee for a summer research appointment that same year; and to the Research Office, the Faculty Research Committee, C. K. Williamson, Gary Knock, Marjorie Cook, Douglas Wilson, Robert Johnson, and Britton Harwood, who—in various capacities—provided financial support for travel and occasional expenses.

To Joseph Jones for starting it all; to my editor, Robert Lecker, and to Twayne Publishers for their advice and patience; to William Gracie and Robert Kettler, Miami University colleagues, for reading portions of the manuscript and helping me trim both babble and excess; to Dennis Lee and Diane Bessai for insights on Atwood; to Bennett Rafoth and Daniel Giancola for bibliographic footwork; to Nan Talese, William Toye, and Phoebe Larmore for help along the way; to Linda Sandler and others interested in Atwood, both near and far, for intellectual companionship; and to Sharon Jahns, Donna Shackelford, and Molly Fort for typing drafts of this study.

Brief portions of this study have been adapted, with permission, from articles that originally appeared in *Essays on Canadian Writing* and *Studies in Canadian Literature*. Frontispiece photograph, used with his permission, is by Graeme Gibson.

Acknowledgments

Permission for general quotation from her work granted by Margaret Atwood. Grateful acknowledgment is made to the following publishers for allowing me to quote from Atwood's poems:

In Canada:
Margaret Atwood, *The Circle Game* (Toronto: House of Anansi Press, 1967).
From *The Animals in That Country* by Margaret Atwood © Margaret Atwood by permission of Oxford University Press Canada.
From *The Journals of Susanna Moodie* by Margaret Atwood © Oxford University Press Canada.
From *Procedures for Underground* by Margaret Atwood © Oxford University Press Canada.
Margaret Atwood, *Power Politics* (Toronto: House of Anansi Press, 1971).
From *You Are Happy* by Margaret Atwood © Margaret Atwood by permission of Oxford University Press Canada.
From *Two-Headed Poems* by Margaret Atwood © Margaret Atwood by permission of Oxford University Press Canada.
From *True Stories* by Margaret Atwood © Margaret Atwood by permission of Oxford University Press Canada.

In the United States:
Poems from *The Animals in That Country* are reprinted by permission of Little, Brown and Company in association with the Atlantic Monthly Press. Copyright © 1968 by Oxford University Press (Canadian Branch).
Poems from *Procedures for Underground* are reprinted by permission of Little, Brown and Company in association with the Atlantic Monthly Press. Copyright © 1970 by Oxford University Press (Canadian Branch).
From *You Are Happy* by Margaret Atwood. Copyright © 1974 by Margaret Atwood. Reprinted by permission of Harper & Row, Publishers, Inc.
From *Two-Headed Poems,* copyright © 1978 by Margaret Atwood. Reprinted by permission of Simon & Schuster, a division of Gulf & Western Corporation.

Chronology

1939   Margaret Eleanor Atwood born 18 November 1939 in Ottawa, Ontario, Canada, to Carl Edmund Atwood and Margaret Killam Atwood, the second of three children; older brother, Harold, born 1937; younger sister, Ruth, born 1951.

1939–1945   Lives in Ottawa until 1945, then in Sault Ste. Marie; spends spring, summer, and fall of these years with parents in Quebec north bush, where father does insect research.

1945   Writes juvenile poems, "Rhyming Cats."

1946–1961   Moves with family to Toronto, where father has position on University of Toronto faculty; spends spring, summer, and fall months in northern Ontario and Quebec bush.

1952–1957   Attends Leaside High School in Toronto; writes for literary magazine *Clan Call.*

1957–1961   Attends Victoria College, University of Toronto; meets Dennis Lee; writes for *Acta Victoriana* and *The Strand*; begins reading poetry in public at Bohemian Embassy; graduates with honors in English language and literature.

1959   Works as crafts counselor at Camp White Pine, Haliburton, Ontario, where she meets artist Charles Pachter; "Fruition," her first poem in a major journal, appears in *The Canadian Forum.*

1961   Publishes *Double Persephone*; awarded E. J. Pratt Medal for Poetry.

1961–1962   Graduate study at Radcliffe College, Harvard University, on a Woodrow Wilson Fellowship; receives master's degree in English.

1962–1963   Continues graduate study at Harvard University; meets first husband James Polk.

1963–1964   Returns to Toronto and works for market research company; poems appear in *Poésie/Poetry 64*; writes libretto for John Beckwith's music, *The Trumpets of Summer,* broadcast on the CBC.

1964–1965 Teaches literature and composition at University of British Columbia in Vancouver; poetry sequence "The Circle Game," accompanied by Charles Pachter's lithographs, published in limited edition, the first of several such collaborations with Pachter.

1965–1967 Returns to Harvard, with aid from Canada Council grant, to continue doctoral study; begins dissertation on the English metaphysical romance, concerning the works of Rider Haggard and others.

1966 President's Medal for Poetry, University of Western Ontario; first major collection of poems, *The Circle Game,* published by Contact Press.

1967 Governor-General's Award for Poetry for *The Circle Game*; first prize in Centennial Commission Poetry Competition for *The Animals in That Country; The Circle Game* republished by House of Anansi Press; marries James Polk.

1967–1968 Teaches literature at Sir George Williams University in Montreal.

1968 *The Animals in That Country.*

1968–1970 Resides in Edmonton, Alberta; teaches creative writing at University of Alberta, 1969–70 academic year.

1969 *The Edible Woman*; Union Poetry Prize (*Poetry,* Chicago).

1970 *The Journals of Susanna Moodie* and *Procedures for Underground*; meets novelist Graeme Gibson.

1970–1971 Travels in England, Italy, and France.

1971 *Power Politics*; returns to Toronto.

1971–1972 Teaches literature and creative writing as Writer-in-Residence at York University, Toronto.

1971–1973 Serves as editor and member of board of directors of House of Anansi Press.

1972 *Surfacing* and *Survival.*

1972–1973 Teaches as Writer-in-Residence, University of Toronto.

1973   D. Litt. from Trent University; invited to tour Soviet Union as part of cultural exchange program—subsequently cancels trip in protest of U.S.S.R. expulsion of Alexander Solzhenitsyn; divorces James Polk; moves, in September, to farm near Alliston, Ontario, with Graeme Gibson.

1974   *You Are Happy*; LL.D. from Queen's University; Bess Hopkins Prize (*Poetry*, Chicago); drama, *The Servant Girl*, televised by the CBC.

1976   Gives birth, in May, to daughter, Eleanor Jess Atwood Gibson; *Selected Poems* and *Lady Oracle*; translation of *The Edible Woman*—first of many continental editions—published in Italy.

1977   *Dancing Girls* and *Days of the Rebels*; City of Toronto Book Award and Canadian Bookseller's Association Award for *Lady Oracle*; award of the Periodical Distributors of Canada Short Fiction.

1978   *Two-Headed Poems* and *Up in the Tree*; St. Lawrence Award for Fiction; travels to Afghanistan and Australia.

1978–1979   Resides for winter in Scotland.

1979   *Life Before Man.*

1980   Moves from Alliston to Toronto; D. Litt. from Concordia University; Radcliffe Graduate Medal.

1981   Serves as chairman of the Writers' Union of Canada; *True Stories* and *Bodily Harm.*

1982   *Anna's Pet* and *Second Words.*

1983   *Murder in the Dark* and *Bluebeard's Egg.*

Chapter One
Journey to the Interior

When Margaret Atwood was five years old she put together a book of poems called "Rhyming Cats." Bound and illustrated by Atwood herself—among her first experiments as a "bookmaker," she later said[1]—this childhood project might well be considered merely a trivial bit of personal memorabilia. Composed of assorted "found" poems and more original ones built upon what Peggy Atwood could spell and what seemed to her to be pretty rhyming words, "Rhyming Cats" is just the sort of exercise any moderately creative child interested in writing might produce. Had its author, in later life, continued with one of her several nonliterary careers—remained perhaps (like her character Marian MacAlpin in *The Edible Woman*) a writer for a market research firm, or become (as her father might have preferred) a scientist like himself or her older brother—it would today be sitting in an attic trunk rather than in the manuscript collection of the University of Toronto's Thomas Fisher Rare Book Library. Not a significant augury of things to come, it is valuable today only as an intriguing footnote to the development of Atwood's art. But it does suggest, within its lines of juvenile verse, certain echoes of its author's later concerns as an established, prolific, and sometimes controversial writer of poems, novels, short stories, and criticism.

Of Hooks and Eyes and Fairy Tales

One of the twenty-two poems in "Rhyming Cats" is entitled "Fairies":

> Fairies come at magic times.
> And they make such magic
> chimes.
> This rymes.[2]

Set among other poems about "the very first bunny" she has "ever seen" and a spring landscape with birds singing and laying eggs while "baby calves tremble on tiny legs," "Fairies" suggests the child's attention to the magic of life; and it foreshadows, even if inarticulately, the future writer's knowledge of the ordering quality of poetic art, of rhyme, to make life hold together. "My Picture Book," another poem in the sequence, provides substance for Atwood's adult assertion that *"Grimm's Fairy Tales* was the most influential book I ever read":[3]

> I look into my picture book
> and see all kinds of things
> Like bears and moths and things
> like that, and pretty things
> Like kings.

The catalog continues, with images of "dragons" and armor-bedecked knights, and with "stories of pretty queens" that the child reads "at night." It concludes with a look toward the future:

> But when I grow too big
> for my nice picture book,
> I'll always think about those
> tales (the ones about the
> cook.)

Going beyond the young writer's precocious use of rhyme, rhythm, and verbal repetition in these lines, and ignoring the non sequitur about the cook (provided obviously for the sake of the rhyme scheme), here is some hint at least of those tales of protean changes in shape from frogs to princes and from household drudges to enchanting objects of a prince's desire, those magical potions and yet more magical kisses that awaken sleeping maidens from metaphorical death. And here, too, is some sense that these are images Atwood would remember.

But it is the darker side of Grimm's tales that affected Atwood most acutely. As she expressed it in 1981, "Grimm's, yes. But take a look at Grimm's. . . . Some of the stories are gruesome in the extreme. . . . It was not the sleeping princess element that attracted me." Among the things she remembered from childhood was "Snow White, viewed at some too-early age (5?) Mother thought I was being very quiet because I was enjoying it. Actually I was [riveted] with fear. The transformation of the evil queen into the witch did me in forever." Another childhood memory involved the tales from the "dark period" of Beatrix Potter.[4]

"Rhyming Cats," though only by coincidence, looks toward this darker note in Atwood's work as an accomplished writer. The aesthetic ordering of the rhyming mind of the artist, even the self-conscious concern of the artist with rhyme and other transformative devices of poetic craft, has profound implications. As Atwood later exhibits with both wit and terror, language is subtle, even dangerous, in its ambiguous ability both to clarify and obscure the chaotic possibilities of life under the surface. To manipulate language is to alter one's impression of reality. She begins her fifth volume of poems, *Power Politics* (1971), with this now-notorious, delightfully grotesque image:

> you fit into me
> like a hook into an eye
>
> a fish hook
> an open eye[5]

The equivocal meanings of "hook" and "eye" operate with subtle yet unyielding pressure to force readers, as one writer has suggested in another context, into "uncomfortable mental confrontations that most people would obviously prefer to avoid."[6] It is, of course, coincidental that, searching for the rhyming words of another of the poems in her little volume, the child would settle on an image familiar to those who grew up during World War II and engaged in games of imagined battles. The linking of a quest for knowledge with violence, surely a matter of rhyme more than reason, is thus accidental; but it is intriguing as well:

> Teacher, Teacher number one,
> She and I we had such fun.
> When we came in we had a
> bun.
> When we went out we
> found a gun.

The mundane life of games and fun—yet underneath, barely below the surface, lies the everpresent threat of inevitable chaos, what Atwood in a mature poem refers to as "the unnamed/whale"[7] that invades our being and destroys our nice attempts to provide ourselves with calm, ordered lives.

"This Is a Photograph of Me"

Atwood's own life would, on the surface, seem to belie such perception of chaos. Writing in 1965 to Peter Miller of Contact Press (which was about to publish her first major collection of poems, *The Circle Game*), she observed that she had "had unfortunately a happy childhood."[8] Hers was a close-knit family, with a Nova Scotian background that stressed intellectual development and viewed the wasting of resources—whether of the mind or of the environment—as a cardinal sin. Storytelling and creative activity, like "Rhyming Cats," were encouraged; and the children—Margaret, her older brother Harold, and eventually a younger sister, Ruth—were included in their parents' activities. One feature of this childhood, however, was something other than ordinary. From infancy into late adolescence Atwood spent six or seven months of every year in the bush of northern Ontario and Quebec, where her entomologist father conducted research. These family trips north, pulling her rhythmically every year away from her various city homes in Ottawa, Sault Ste. Marie, and finally Toronto, provided Atwood with an early and extensive knowledge of life in the woods, evident in imagery that runs throughout her works.

A more profound effect of these journeys was that her years in the bush allowed her to confront life in its primitive, elemental forms, freed from the comforting but artificial costuming of urban, contemporary life. The near-drowning of the protagonist's brother in the novel *Surfacing,* for example, was drawn from an experience Atwood's own brother once faced. The bush provided her not only with knowledge but also with a kind of wisdom, a way of seeing. One writer has observed, perhaps overdramatically, that the journeys from bush to city and back were a shock to Atwood's sensibilities: "what alarmed her most was the way people changed their appearances; especially her mother, who put on nylons and dresses and hats and gloves and make-up when they came south. They had one identity for the city and one for the bush." Atwood's own recollection is that she did not find her experience "that unusual . . . children do not find anything that happens to them unusual"; rather than causing alarm, her nomadic experience "meant . . . that there were . . . two environments that I could feel comfortable in." They enabled her to confront and adjust to two distinct yet interacting worlds.[9]

These two worlds emerge throughout Atwood's works and become one of the pronounced features of her writing. The title poem of her second collection, *The Animals in That Country* (1968), suggests a

value judgment about the two worlds it describes. At the same time
it captures some of the doubleness of vision provoked by the alternating states of Atwood's early life:

> In that country the animals
> have the faces of people:
>
> the ceremonial
> cats possessing the streets
>
> the fox run
> politely to earth, the huntsmen
> standing around him, fixed
> in their tapestry of manners
>
> the bull, embroidered
> with blood and given
> an elegant death, trumpets, his name
> stamped on him, heraldic brand
>
> . . .
>
> In this country the animals
> have the faces of
> animals.
>
> Their eyes
> flash once in car headlights
> and are gone.
>
> Their deaths are not elegant.
>
> They have the faces of
> no-one.
> [2-3]

Here, intermixed with Atwood's more political concerns regarding
technology and waste, is a pungent acceptance of reality, stripped of
the fictions that humans impose on nature in their attempt to evade
turmoil. Atwood's double vision is heightened by her precise diction:
her "embroidered" blood and "elegant" deaths, the emotionless, "polite" destruction of the fox, provide a baroque context of macabre insights. Man's ritualized activities, his attempts to order and

anthropomorphize elemental nature, are seen as a futile means of evading his own physical mortality, as a way of encasing himself, like the characters of Iris Murdoch's *The Unicorn,* for example, in the textured and protected fabric of spiritual sleep. Yet, as one of those characters accurately notes and as the action of that novel bears out, the time must come when "the figures so strangely woven into the quiet tapestry would . . . jerk into unpredictable life" and indeed, too, into unpredictable death.[10] Such is the world that Atwood constructs for us. Against the comforting aesthetic distance and bloodless violence of myth, she places her perception of bare reality; our mythic scenarios, need them as we may, must be seen for the evasions and the lies that they are.

Double Persephone

Atwood's attempts to deal with this double vision and its implications are reflected in an unpretentious pamphlet of seven poems which came out of her years at the University of Toronto's Victoria College, where she began undergraduate studies in 1957. She now regards *Double Persephone,* published the year she received her baccalaureate degree (1961), as merely "a bibliographical curiosity" that she printed, glued, stapled, and distributed herself.[11] Still, the formal, tightly structured metrics of these poems, and their overt use of classical mythology, illustrate certain literary impressions that she encountered at Victoria College.

Always a voracious and eclectic reader, Atwood during this period discovered the poems of Jay Macpherson and—through Macpherson's personal library—many other Canadian poets, including Margaret Avison, George Johnston, P. K. Page, and James Reaney. Already well-versed in classical mythology, she also read Robert Graves's *The White Goddess,* whose commentary on the female poet made an especially deep impression on her. And she studied, although only in one or two courses, under Northrop Frye. It is from this varied background that the poems of *Double Persephone* emerge; and they represent a point of departure in Atwood's development of a distinct poetic voice.

Frye's contribution toward this development is as much a matter of debate as is his effect generally on Canadian poets of the late 1950s and early 1960s. Such writers as James Reaney, Jay Macpherson, Eli Mandel, and others are often considered to be part of a school of mythopoeic poets that allegedly arose under Frye's aegis in the 1950s. Atwood, among others, has questioned Frye's influence on these poets, however, and she has suggested on several occasions that the most important effect Frye had on her was that "he recommended at some point that I not run away to England and become a waitress."[12] Even so, Frye's perceptions about the nature of Canadian poetry during the time of Atwood's apprenticeship do provide some insight into her early technique.

Commenting on Macpherson's *The Boatman,* which won the Governor-General's Award in 1958, Frye noted that it exemplified Canadian poets' growing concern with the craft of poetry and in particular with its formal elements, "myth, metaphor, symbol, image, even metrics." He defined mythopoeic poetry as formal rather than representational: "When it is formal, the poet seeks metaphor, the language of pure identification that he shares with the lunatic and the lover; he seeks myth, the stories of gods whose actions are not limited by reality . . . ; and he seeks apocalyptic imagery, the vision of a universe which is humanly as well as divinely intelligible. The representational tendency in poetry is sophisticated and civilized: the formal tendency is primitive, oracular, close to the riddle and the spell."[13] One thinks, perhaps, of Coleridge's "Kubla Khan" and the artist's descent into the underworld, or of "Procedures for Underground,"Atwood's thematically similar poem, derived from a Bella Coola Indian myth.

But formal elements must be tied to life. The poet, says Frye, must resolve "the perennial technical problem of transmuting the substance of myth into the form of immediate experience," must create poems that become "a kind of reservoir of feeling in which one's literary and personal associations mingle and are held in the kind of variable emotional contemplation that it is one of the primary functions of poetry to provide." Frye says of Macpherson's work, her "myths, like her allusions, flow into the poems: the poems do not point to them."[14] Myth as mere ornament is not the point.

Although Atwood throughout her poetry retains the mythopoeic qualities that Frye describes and shapes them to her own needs, it is primarily in her early work that we see these mythic impulses tied to tight rhythms similar to those Macpherson constructs. But Macpherson's craft is not Atwood's. And in *Double Persephone* Atwood's rigidly structured poems are often wooden, both in rhythm and in the overly static, artificial imposition of myth upon experience. The formal met-

rics of one poem, for example, are stiff, creating a rhythm that, for
all its regular metre, seems prose-like:

> The twisted paths are hidden; the lost mother
> Listens for a sound she cannot hear,
> A deadened child's-cry; sister and brother
> Cover their lips with wild-strawberry leaves

Another poem, though revealing a flash of the wit that is also typical
of the mythopoeic poets and, eventually, a hallmark of most of Atwood's work, seems rhythmically monotonous, its images too stylized
and forced:

> The shepherdess with giddy glance
> Makes the amorous shepherd dance,
> While sheep hurtle the stiles for love
> And clouds pile featherbeds above

Delightful though this mock-mythological debunking of ritual may
be, its effect diminishes by the end of the poem. As one reviewer
observed at the time of *Double Persephone*'s publication, "Miss Atwood
borrows too much, or not enough; her archetypal menagerie, and
meditations on the lost garden and love-in-death, tend to be more
contrived at than composed."[15]

But if stylistic artificiality is a weakness in the poems of *Double
Persephone* it is also a component of Atwood's poetics that sustains her
double vision and the tensions it produces. Emerging from a pervasive formalism in rhythm and language, this artificiality has thematic
significance, providing a link between Atwood's style and her controlling ideas. We see the process in "Iconic Landscape":

> The girl with the gorgon touch
> Stretches a glad hand to each
> New piper peddling beds of roses
> Hoping to find within her reach
>
> At last, a living wrist and arm
> Petals that will crush and fade
> But always she meets a marbled flesh
> A fixing eye, a stiffened form
> Where leaves turn spears along the glade

> Behind, a line of statues stands
> All with the same white oval face
> And attitude of outstretched hands
> Curved in an all-too-perfect grace.

The girl's desire for living flesh and human passion is understandable, but what is interesting is that this longing for life is tied equally to a desire for "petals that will crush and fade." If we wish to live, we must face both decay and death, as well as imperfection. Love cannot be achieved in an encounter with stone faces and "hands/Curved in an all-too-perfect grace." Influenced by Graves's vision of the female poet as destructive White Goddess, the poem's ultimate irony is that the seeker, she who "stretches a glad hand to each" potential lover, is also the destroyer of that which she seeks, turning the promising pipers into "stiffened forms" inhabiting and enhancing the very formal garden she wishes to escape. As in Amy Lowell's "Patterns," a poem in which the speaker (also in a garden) is incapable of doing more at the end than cry out in despair, here too the persona is trapped. The rhythms of life lived by ritual, like the rhythms of the poem itself, prevent escape.

In *Double Persephone* Atwood implicitly questions the ability of poetry to create life when by necessity it fixes emotion in static language, in patterns and conventions that, once writ, are carved in stone. Her concern is exactly that presented in the underlying paradox of Keats's "Ode on a Grecian Urn": the perfect, eternal, yet never-to-be-climaxed love pictured on the urn, this "Cold Pastoral," posed against the mortal, mutable, living passion of earthly, imperfect love. "There are two kinds of death," says Atwood in "Chthonic Love,"

> One rots the breath
> From the urgent bone
> And burns the soul to a slim leaf
> Spring before the storm;
> The other folds life up
> And slides it through the door
> To the lost garden, where
> Depend transparent tapestries,
> Candles of light, and cups of air.

> Love, you must choose
> Between two immortalities:
> One of earth lake trees
> Feathers of a nameless bird
> The other of a world of glass,
> Hard marble, carven word.

There is little doubt where Atwood's sympathies lie. The rush of images of life in the second stanza, unconfined by conventional punctuation, assert (with their mysterious "nameless bird") a magic that somehow makes the rotting and burning, the decay and death—and uncertainty—of mortal love worthwhile. The poet sets this magic against images of death-in-art: insubstantial "transparent tapestries," "cups of air" suggesting encirclement and enclosure, even suffocation, a folded-up life, neatly packaged, sent to a "lost garden"—the adjective is significant—of "hard marble" permanence. In its final image, however, the poem asserts its inherent failure. For what is "Chthonic Love," this poem, but a "carven word" that, as a work of art, defeats the very vitality of its message?

It is this question that Atwood would return to constantly as her career developed, and it may explain in part the freer rhythmic and syntactic structures that identify her poetry after *Double Persephone*. It is true, in any event, that a year after its publication she wrote, on a scrap of paper entitled "My Poetic Principles on Oct. 29 1962," these and other scribbled injunctions: with regard to line length and the appearance of the poem on the page, "One shd not be *too* vertical; but its an escape from the (now) stilted horizontal line. . . . Random . . . rhyme—to control a poem without making it *look* controlled. . . . anyway a pox on regular end-rhyme; a pox also on *no*-rhyme. . . . arbitrary stanza: refers only to the *no.* of lines in a stanza. Another method of controlling a poem without making it seem boxed or fitted. . . . The stanza division need not have any relation to the development of thought i.e.—there can be run-ons. Uneven numbers of lines give open effects, evens give closed ones. Five & seven are good numbers." Apparently, Atwood took her own advice. By 1964 Milton Wilson was able to point to her poems in *Poésie/Poetry 64* and comment on her "remarkably varied work, in form, subject, and tone." To some extent at least, Atwood had broken away from the tailored poetics of *Double Persephone*.[16]

"ALL is Well"

The 1966 publication of *The Circle Game* culminated this first phase of Atwood's creative life. But it was a pursuit that began even before *Double Persephone* appeared. "I've always written all kinds of things," she says. "When I was in high school and college I was writing borderline literary material that people don't usually associate with me—musical comedies, commercial jingles, various things under pseudonyms. I even wrote an opera about synthetic fabrics for my Home Economics class. It was about that time I realized I didn't want to be a home economist, I wanted to be a writer." Although she has referred to her years from age eight through sixteen as "my sterile period," Atwood wrote several poems and essays for the Leaside (Toronto) High School *Clan Call;* and, upon entering Victoria College, she began publishing her work in *Acta Victoriana,* the college journal, and *The Strand,* a college literary magazine. She also contributed to *The Sheet,* published by the Bohemian Embassy, a Toronto coffeehouse where, during 1960–61, she gave poetry readings, cryptically advertised in one program as presenting a poet who "writes a clear subtly imaged poetry of mutational experience." Among her works for *Acta Victoriana* and *The Strand* was a jointly authored satirical piece written, under the pseudonym Shakesbeat Latweed, by Atwood and fellow English literature student Dennis Lee, whom Atwood met at Victoria College. Lee was to become Atwood's close friend and literary confidant, offering her his suggestions during the manuscript stages of some of her most important works.[17]

Atwood's creative development was rounded out by her involvement in college dramatic productions, an echo of such teen-age activities as her performing highly sought-after neighborhood puppet shows. She also continued her work in art, a craft she would eventually put to professional use in illustrating such volumes as *The Journals of Susanna Moodie* and her first children's book, *Up in the Tree,* and in providing political cartoons for *This Magazine* under the name "Bart Gerrard." Her first publication in a major journal was a poem entitled "Fruition," which appeared in *The Canadian Forum* in September 1959. Very much in the style of *Double Persephone,* it showed little promise of what was to come. Between 1959 and 1964, the year she was commissioned by the Canadian Broadcasting Corporation (CBC) to write the libretto to accompany John Beckwith's music in the choral composition *The Trumpets of Summer,* Atwood's work had appeared in John Robert Colombo's *Poésie/Poetry 64,* in such journals as *Queen's Quarterly, Alphabet,* and *The Tamarack Review,* and on the CBC radio programs *Anthology* and *New Canadian Writing.*

The publishing history of *The Circle Game* captures both the difficulties and the joys Atwood encountered as she tried, in the early 1960s, to publish a volume that would build upon her earlier work and establish her career in the Canadian literary world. By a circuitous route, the story of *The Circle Game* goes back in part to the summer of 1959, when Atwood was working as a nature instructor and crafts counselor at Camp White Pine, a Jewish summer camp in Haliburton, Ontario. There she met Charles Pachter, then 16, the Toronto artist who was to become a close friend and eventually produce several limited editions of her poems, illustrated by prints he had designed. The first of these collaborations was inspired by a sequence of poems entitled "The Circle Game." In 1964, the year after Contact Press had disappointed Atwood by accepting, then rejecting, a volume of poems she had submitted, Pachter was studying at the Cranbrook Academy of Art in Bloomfield Hills, Michigan, where he was planning his initial project. He wrote to Atwood, then beginning a year of teaching in the English Department at the University of British Columbia, and asked her to send some poems that could be developed into a folio of lithographs. On 23 September Atwood mailed Pachter the poems, "2 things, both of which abound in pictorial images; one a longish single poem which could be broken into verses, and the other a series of 7 (The Circle Game) in which 2 scenes alternate & are then pulled together in the final poem. I'd probably lean towards the latter. . . . If neither really does things for you I have piles more."[18]

While Pachter, over the next several months, experimented with different typefaces for the poems and tentative lithographs to illustrate them—Atwood at one point writing to him that she was "ecstatic. About yr. prints"—she was "writing like absolute bloody hell. So much that I can't sit down to go over some of`the old stuff . . . without immediately producing a new poem." She was also at this time writing short stories and beginning the novel that would eventually become *The Edible Woman.* But if there was ecstasy over Pachter's illustrations and excitement over her own productivity, there was depression as well. Between 16 November 1964, and 5 March

1965, Atwood had received a total of four rejection notices from three publishers for two major works, an early and never-to-be-published novel entitled "Up in the Air So Blue" and a collection of poems entitled "Places, Migrations."

On 24 June Atwood wrote to Raymond Souster, renewing her correspondence with Contact Press, and sent a reassembled collection of poems. She suggested two titles, *The Winter Sleepers* and *Journey to the Interior*. Despite some initial conflict between Souster, Louis Dudek, and Peter Miller, who together constituted the editorial board of Contact Press, they agreed to publish the book, rejecting Atwood's titles and substituting *The Circle Game,* suggested by Miller. On 29 September he wrote to Atwood, telling her of their decision and confirming an earlier note sent her by Souster.

Thus began what was to become a breakthrough event in Atwood's career. Though Pachter's initial lithographs as such were not related to Contact's decision to publish, he was involved in the ferment of the next several months, as the layout for the physical book was being constructed. Atwood had written to Miller that she wanted to produce the cover design herself; and he eventually agreed after she observed that Pachter could design the cover at no additional cost. But when Pachter sent her a scaled-down version of one of the original lithographs he had already designed and especially liked, Atwood's notion that it resembled female genitalia signaled the beginning of an awkward turn of events. By the time Pachter had sent her another design, it was the end of October, Atwood had finished composing her new novel and entitled it *The Edible Woman,* and she had sent to Miller various bits of information for the book's cover blurb, acknowledgments, and dedication ("For J. . . . this is handy, as everyone I know begins with J."). By February the question of the cover design had become a major issue; and what had begun as a friendly gesture was growing into a seriocomic impasse, with Atwood feeling that she was "leaving a trail of carnage . . . wherever I go." In March, after Miller had sent the coverless manuscript to the printer and had offered several illustrations of his own to Atwood, she finally designed two covers herself, one of which Miller accepted, thus ending the intrigue. The ecstasy of things coming together was expressed by a letter, composed mostly of a large sunburst "ALL is Well," that Atwood sent Miller on March 9.

In May 1966 "The Settlers," originally published in *Prism Inter-*

national and serving as the final poem of *The Circle Game,* was awarded the President's Medal of the University of Western Ontario; and, by October, *The Circle Game* was finally published. In 1967, the centennial year of Canadian confederation, Margaret Atwood's book of poems won the Governor-General's Award over the collections of such established writers as Earle Birney and F. R. Scott.

Chapter Two
Thoughts from Underground

The Circle Game

Reviewers of Atwood's work have attempted to place her in many different categories: she has been called a feminist writer, for her incisive commentaries on sex roles; a religious writer, for her visions of spiritual ecstasy; a gothic writer, for her images of grotesques, misfits, and surreal disorientations of the psyche; a writer of the Canadian wilderness; a nationalist writer; a regionalist. Atwood herself has noted, however, that "I never describe myself . . . self-definition is a kind of prison."[1] *The Circle Game,* filled with images of enclosure and attempted escape, reflects her insistence that we not be bound by prisons of any kind. Its poems are concerned with oppositions and transformations—from one state to another; from innocence to knowledge; from sterile love-games to passionate relationships between people; from stagnant object-oriented lives, defined by seemingly encrusted but potentially fragile myths, to lives that recognize chaos, pain, and even death, not only as inevitable but also, in some Whitmanesque way, as a pathway to knowledge. The very texture of the poems dissolves from one mood into another, as Atwood declares her aversion to the patterns of myth that hold sway over us and as she creates new scenarios that are perhaps more protean, more capable of transformation.

To emphasize these broad themes is not to ignore the Canadian scene that is the milieu of these poems. The images of the Canadian wilderness that Atwood employs—the pervasive, wintry, and abundantly water-filled northern landscape—serve to evoke the Canadian environment. They explain and contemplate its mysteries. And they convey Canada's distinct and emerging identity, as reflected in the social, cultural, and political movements of the 1960s and 1970s. They evoke, too, that troubled "garrison mentality" that both Northrop Frye and Atwood, in her critical book *Survival* (1972), see as a characteristic Canadian trait.[2] But metaphorically Atwood's landscape imagery depicts the fragility and tenuousness of life for all of us. She gives us a land that "flows like a/sluggish current," into whose quicksand solidity we may at any moment sink; and she builds for us cities that "are only outposts," architectural deceptions sitting on a "crust of ice that/easily might break" and suck us down into physical and spiritual chaos. If this downward journey is frightening, she suggests, it may also be necessary. In the commonplace world of "too many foregrounds . . . we have lost something," a vision "that informs, holds together/this confusion, this largeness/and dissolving."[3] It is a vision that we may partially discover if we are sufficiently persistent, a vision that provides the key to once-known but long-forgotten racial memories and primitive assertions of immortal life.

The camera eye. Atwood establishes this idea early in *The Circle Game:* "if you look long enough," says the persona of the first poem in the collection, "eventually/you will be able to see me." Structured like so many of Atwood's poems, "This Is a Photograph of Me" (11) posits two worlds, one in which reality is obscured and made distant by romantic descriptive images ("in the background there is a lake,/and beyond that, some low hills") and another that conveys the facts of the matter, that this "photograph of me" does not seem to contain me because it "was taken/the day after I drowned."

The tension between these two worlds is initiated and enriched, at the beginning of the poem, by the persona's seemingly innocent commentary on the quality of the photographic image. The picture "was taken some time ago" and "at first it seems to be/a smeared/print: blurred lines and grey flecks/blended with the paper." Such blurring cannot be tolerated by the rage of the human mind for order, however, and so the mind imposes discernible images in a detached, aesthetic manner, creating an effect similar to the casual, emotionless description that one encounters in such a Robbe-Grillet story as "The Secret Room." Atwood's language, like Robbe-Grillet's, becomes that of the museum tourguide describing a painting:

> then, as you scan
> it, you see in the left-hand corner
> a thing that is like a branch: part of a tree
> (balsam or spruce) emerging
> and, to the right, halfway up
> what ought to be a gentle
> slope, a small frame house.
> [11]

The tension between photographic image and reality is present even within these lines of clarified description: we see an undefined *"thing that is like a branch,"* its indistinctness further emphasized by the ironic, because irrelevant, qualifying description "(balsam or spruce)." As the poem proceeds, in the next two lines, to a further aesthetic distance in which the background of lake and hills is described, Atwood immediately asserts a deeper level of reality, the more incisive truth that the persona drowned the day before the picture was taken; she cannot be seen, not because of the poor quality of the photograph, but because she is dead.

Yet, the persona almost simultaneously asserts, "I am in the lake, in the center/of the picture, just under the surface." We are thus thrust into the middle of a phenomenological paradox, in which the landscape reveals two mutually exclusive events. The photograph contains the persona, but the timing of the photograph necessarily obscures the fact that she is there. Time thus works, curiously, in this poem in two ways: "taken some time ago," the photograph is, by time, decayed; the supposed ability of photographic technology to preserve an instant of time has been ravaged by time itself and the photograph transformed into an incomprehensible mass of dark and light shadows. Yet the rhythms of time provide, also, an ironic, cautiously optimistic tone for the poem. For the empty photograph does not deny the presence of the speaker—it denies only her visibility at the moment the picture was snapped. The speaker is dead, caught up by the fate time demands of all mortal creatures; but the photograph remains, after all, a picture "of me," present in the space captured by the camera. In some future time, "eventually," if we but "look long enough," she will reappear. In an early manuscript version of the poem, Atwood had substituted the word "long" for the original, scratched-out alternative "hard," a shift that signals her deliberate decision to emphasize the process of time. Time, rather than the intensity of the viewer's perception, would bring about the speaker's return.[4]

To accept time, however, to participate in the real world, is to accept also the chaos, decay, and death that are part of life. This, psychologically, we cannot always do. And in this poem linguistic tensions—typical of Atwood's poetry—reflect our dilemma. The casual language, the static verbs, the passive constructions, and the predominant imagery of space rather than of time contend against the poem's assertion that the persona will eventually reappear. Even that assertion is ambiguously phrased: *"if* you look long enough." The speaker's return is only a contingency, dependent upon the endurance of the viewer. It may well be, as Atwood says in "A Place: Fragments," that truth is "something too huge and simple/for us to see" (76). Or the problem may be our inherent inability to grasp, simultaneously, both the concrete facts that constitute reality and the broader truths that these facts suggest: "a cliff," she says in "Journey to the Interior," "is not known/as rough except by hand, and is/therefore inaccessible" (57). We may feel the texture of a cliff if we come close enough to it; but, at that close range, it is no longer a cliff, merely a wall before our eyes. We may, from a distance, see a cliff in all its abstract enormity, or we may feel its concrete roughness, but not at the same time. Dreams may permit us to transcend these conscious limitations. In "A Descent Through the Carpet" the floral-patterned rug upon which the speaker stretches "makes the sea/accessible." But such a descent entails a journey to truths that we may not wish to encounter: "to be aware," she says, "is/to know total/fear" (21–22). What *will* we see when the drowned speaker rises from the depths of the lake? Or is Atwood far more subtle, presenting us with an idea that is indeed "too huge and simple?" Does she mean merely that if we "look long enough," we will join the speaker in death and only then "be able to see" her? That essential truth may be more than we wish to acknowledge.

For all the linguistic ambiguity and irresolution of "This Is a Photograph of Me," it is just such an acknowledgment that Atwood often demands. Our attempts to capture and enclose an instant of time, to postulate an unalterable identity, are doomed to failure. Visions of immortality may be captured only in the romantic conceit of a glass-enclosed paperweight snowstorm through which two lovers walk holding hands, or under a bell jar encapsulating a peaceful pastoral scene, sealing it and transforming it into an illusory eternal moment. Such illusions help us endure; but Atwood would seem to agree with Ralph Ellison's observation in *Invisible Man* that "the mind that has conceived a plan of living must never lose sight of the chaos against which that pattern was conceived."[5]

In "Camera" (45–46) Atwood re-creates such chaos. Here, in a typically Atwoodian mixture of closely viewed empirical details, surreal imagery, and essential truth, the writer suggests that we cannot, without serious dislocation of sensibility, separate ourselves from the often-destructive rhythms of time and nature. Even within the photographic print the seasons move on inexorably from "nearly spring" to "the last of autumn." The photograph becomes, like Oscar Wilde's fantastic picture of Dorian Gray, not merely "a smeared/print" but an ever-changing emblem of our inability to stop time and conceal decay: "You want this instant:/nearly spring, both of us walking,/ wind blowing," says the speaker to her lover; "you want to have it and so/you arrange us . . . you insist . . . the sun hold still in the sky." But, she also admonishes him, "look again/at your souvenir,/ your glossy square of paper/before it dissolves completely." The poet's subtle use of qualifying adverbs as she addresses her "camera man" ("wherever you partly are/now") also insists on the temporality of our existence. We may accept that truth or not. But if we wish to experience love, the speaker emphasizes with her climactically poised juxtaposition of emotion and technological grotesqueness ("how can I love your glass eye?"), then we must accept nature's cycle, including death and possible return.

The return, however, is not so clearly delineated in "Camera" as it is in "This Is a Photograph of Me." Atwood's voice here expresses skepticism at the transit from death back to life. That renewal is only implied by the archetypal cycle of seasons controlling the poem's structure. In the bare, realistic imagery of decay, dissolution, and death Atwood illustrates the problem we face: that it is easier to perceive concrete evidence of time's destructive power than to conceive of its more metaphysical ability to bring about radical transformations and rebirths of the spirit. We may marvel at the seemingly miraculous metamorphosis of the caterpillar into a radically different creature, but such magical changes can be explained in nonspiritual terms. And what we are left with, still, is the fact that the splendid butterfly's life is a brief one indeed.

Chaos as a way to revelation and immortality becomes only a possibility; and Atwood's subtle wit operates in the poem to undercut even that idea. She seems to evade the images of decay by turning them into a joke: her accretion of concrete details—"muddy rubble," "scattered" clothing, "bare tree"—develops toward a humorous exaggeration, in the line "there has been a hurricane." Tonally subdued but made emphatic by its isolation from surrounding images, the line provides an essentially realistic explanation for the debris; it also effectively summarizes the power that nature brings to bear upon our egocentric notion that we can "insist/that the clouds stop moving." But it seems incongruous: we do not really need a hurricane, too, yet Atwood forces one upon us, exaggerating to reinforce her skepticism.

The psychic chaos symbolized by the hurricane initiates the per-

sona's journey, but it seems to lead nowhere; the surreal imagery at
the end of the poem denies return. The "small black speck" that the
speaker's photographic image has become is infinitely far away, "trav-
elling towards the horizon/at almost the speed of light." And the
ability of a journey through time to reveal truth and to make all
things well seems as questionable a notion as the photographer's belief that he can stop time altogether. A compromise is possible: the
photographer could accept time's movement and travel with the persona through life's shifting and uncertain weather. Yet such a compromise seems elusive for Atwood. The persona's lover in "After the
Flood, We," for example, merely saunters beside her, "talking/of the
beauty of the morning,/not even knowing/that there has been a
flood" (12); he remains with her, yet she travels alone.

"**Against still life.**" This physically outward, psychologically
inward, mostly solitary journey that suffuses Atwood's poetic landscape in *The Circle Game* takes many forms. In "Migration: C.P.R."
she exploits the traditional new-world myth that traveling westward
can free the soul: the physical journey across the continent becomes
an attempt to escape "from allegories/in the misty east, where inher-
ited events/barnacle on the mind." Yet one finds "inescapable mists"
in the West also, and the attempt to evade them becomes problematic: "There are more secondhand/stores here than we expected:/
though we brought nothing with us/(we thought)/we have begun to
unpack." The atavistic desire to find "a place of absolute/unformed
beginning" seems little more than a romantic dream (52–56). Yet the
need to quest inward remains. Evolution, Atwood observes in "Eventual Proteus," has brought us irretrievably to a loveless world where
"we keep/our weary distances" and flinch beneath "caustic" kisses
(31–32). Thus, we continue to "journey to the interior," into dangerous exotic landscapes, to places where "many have been" but from
which "only/some have returned safely" (57).

The relationship of the inward and backward journey and an outward quest for community and love is developed in the poem
"Against Still Life" (65–67). Here the speaker addresses her lover and
asks that he communicate to her the knowledge he has gained from
his own interior speculations. A mirror-image of "This Is a Photograph of Me," this poem reverses the roles of that earlier work: now
it is the lover who is submerged below the surface, hidden, his "smile
contained," his voice silent; and it is the speaker who impatiently
waits for the eventual awakening that will reveal the mysteries of the
drowned and silent world. As he sits opposite her, like an "orange in

the middle of a table," she becomes passionate and violent: "These orange silences . . . make me want to . . . crack your skull . . . to make you talk, or get/a look inside." To be "against still life" is to confront experience and to be human, to ascertain what there is in our racial and personal memories that makes us what we are and allows us to relate to one another. Yet the all-too-human tendency for violent action revealed in the speaker's voice reminds us of the violence that is contained, along with knowledge, by "these orange silences" we wrap around ourselves. And so the poem dissolves into a call for patience and deliberation. "If I watch/quietly enough/and long enough," the persona says, perhaps "at last, you will say . . . all I need to know." But to know all remains dangerous. The "mountains/inside [the lover's] skull/garden and chaos, ocean/and hurricane," are inner forces reflecting outer storms (like the hurricane in "Camera") that destroy our flimsy dreams of order and contentment. Though we cannot understand and love one another without facing such violence, we had best approach it circumspectly. As the persona says, we must "take the orange/with care enough and hold it/gently," lest its infuriatingly silent skin explode.

The violence is enclosed, of course, by more than the orange's skin. Just as the lover sits distant from the persona, a table's width between them, so too is the orange set "in the middle of [the] table," circumscribed by the table's rectilinear shape and distant from the precarious edges where it may topple off into chaos. Atwood reproduces the image in a poem several pages later. In the second section of "A Place: Fragments" (73–74) the orange is replaced by a snowstorm paperweight, an image that Atwood also uses in *Power Politics* to suggest, if ambiguously, the containment of a beautiful, romantic moment. Here, however, the glass skin of the paperweight encloses violence. The paperweight belongs to an "old woman" who "had a neat/house" and "a clean parlour," where she kept various items of well-ordered bric-a-brac. Set off "in the center/of the table," the object becomes an icon, drawing our eyes to a part of our being that we cannot escape. It is only a "hollow glass globe/filled with water, and/a house, a man, a snowstorm." But Atwood perceives a significance in its surroundings:

> The room was as
> dustless as possible
> and free of spiders.

                              I
              stood in the door-
              way, at the fulcrum where

              this trivial but
              stringent inner order
              held its delicate balance
              with the random scattering or
              clogged merging of
              things: ditch by the road; dried
              reeds in the wind; flat
              wet bush, grey sky
              sweeping away outside.
              [74]

The picture Atwood draws is ironic, even to the fine touch about the
spiders, as she expresses the futility of our building houses against
the outer storm when that storm is merely an emblem of the violence
within us, the snowstorm in the glass globe contained by a skin that
is as fragile as the walls of the house that enclose and protect its "inner order" from the "wet bush" and "grey sky" outside. It is this
mundane attempt at order that Atwood attacks in "The City Planners," earlier in the volume. "What offends us," she says, "is/the
sanities:/the houses in pedantic rows, the planted/sanitary trees."
There is "no shouting here, or/shatter of glass"; yet "certain things"
reveal "the future cracks in the plaster/when the houses, capsized,
will slide/obliquely into the clay seas, gradual as glaciers/that right
now nobody notices" (27).

It is not so much our building cities (or imprisoning our emotions,
or holding firm to commonplace reality, or taking photographs) to
which Atwood objects; rather, it is our forgetting what we are building them against. Atwood's balance is exquisite, her philosophic position elusive. We must build our cities to protect ourselves from
elemental nature, yet if we build them too well we will delude ourselves and fail to notice their inevitable disintegration; we must handle our passions carefully to stave off our own violent and
unpredictable natures, yet if we control them too well we will lead
sterile lives; we must prevent our spirits from traveling too deeply on
interior journeys, lest we become lost and confused, yet we must allow them to travel enough that we are acquainted with the dark
night of our souls, the mysterious key to what we are and how we
came to be; we must create myths to evade our mortality, lest we

despair, yet if we create too well we will isolate ourselves from the world, and for all our efforts we will die anyway. Like the speaker in "A Place: Fragments," we must position ourselves in the doorway, between order and chaos, anxiously poised for action.

"The circle game." The need for action is explored most fully in the title poem of the collection. The characters in the alternating cycle of seven segments which make up "The Circle Game" (35–44) are the speaker, her lover, and a group of children playing a singing, dancing, and frighteningly trance-like game on the lawn outside. Atwood reinforces the game's emotionally imprisoning ritual through her hauntingly repetitious style, in which certain threatening phrases reecho and quicken to produce an increasingly unbearable tension that demands release. The release comes, but only at the end. Then the tension breaks through the cool, restrained surface of the poem, and the speaker cries out for deliverance from all the circle games by which we are imprisoned.

The poem's first section introduces us to the children playing ring-around-the-rosie "on the lawn / joined hand to hand,"

> each arm going into
> the next arm, around
> full circle
> until it comes
> back into each of the single
> bodies again
> [35]

Here, in the synechdochic language of disembodied arms and depersonalized bodies, Atwood has already suggested the dehumanizing effects of the circle game in which the children are engaged, their bodiless arms somehow acting independently, their bodies moving grotesquely, like automatons. The speaker observes that "we might mistake this / tranced moving for joy / but there is no joy in it." There is instead discordance, an out-of-focus quality in the children's actions: they are concentrating, but "their feet move" only "almost in time to the singing" and "their eyes" are "fixed," hypnotic, "on the empty / moving spaces just in / front of them"; they are "intent," again only "almost / studious," but in their intentness they ignore each other ("they are singing, but / not to each other"). They ignore as well the realities ("the grass / underfoot," "the trees / circling the lawn," "the lake") that surround them. Concluding this section with

a ritual repetition of phrasing that comments, both aurally and se-
mantically, on the pointlessness and the danger of the game, the
speaker notes that, for the children, "the whole point . . . of going
round and round / is (faster / slower) / going round and round" (35–36).
The scene shifts in the second section to a room occupied by the
speaker and her lover, whom she is addressing. Yet we sense that,
like the singing children, she is speaking more to herself and her private distress, conducting an interior monologue rather than a sincere
act of communication. He, in any event, peering narcissistically into
a mirror, seems not to be listening.

The room's many mirrors ("even / the back of the door / has one")
may distort and deaden, but they also insulate the lovers from the
dangers of reality. The couple become like Tennyson's Lady of Shalott, who dare not view Camelot, except in the shadows of her own
mirror, lest she be cursed with mortality. Like the mirror, which
holds the lovers' emotions in a lifeless stasis, the room itself is a protective enclosure that isolates the lovers from the threat of chaos.
Even that protection may be fragile. The "walls," observes the
speaker, are after all "thin"; and, ominously, "there is always . . .
someone in the next room" (36–37). The room, it seems, has become
a garrison, a refuge protecting the lovers from imminent disaster.

This theme is picked up, obliquely, in section 3, which seems
merely to comment further on the apparent pointlessness of the children's games. "However," it begins, "in all their games / there seems /
to be some reason." The speaker expresses surprise that, "when we
read them legends / in the evening / of monstrous battles, and secret /
betrayals in the forest / and brutal deaths, / they scarcely listened" (37–
38). Yet we know that the children disregard these tales of violence
for the very reason they play their vacuous circle game and ignore the
lake, the trees, the landscape surrounding them: to isolate themselves
from reality.

At the same time, Atwood develops, tonally, an opposing reason
for the children's unconcern: these chivalric, "monstrous battles"
smack of the postured, elegant deaths of "The Animals in That Country." Atwood's ironic undercutting is evident as she juxtaposes,
against these battles and deaths, the mundane details of childhood
concentration, the yawning, fidgeting, and chewing of unsavory articles that make up our remarkably commonplace existence. Thus is
mythic grandeur deflated. And "a slight cut" on the youngest child's
toe becomes a comment on the ritual stories of unreal bloody battle:

for all its slightness, it is a violence more vital than "the final sword" sliding "through/the dying hero." It points to the dangers that do in fact lie about us. The children see these dangers, as they build trenches on the beach,

> fortified with pointed sticks
> driven into the sides
> of their sand moats
>
> and a lake-enclosed island
> with no bridges:
>
> a last attempt
> (however
> eroded by the water
> in an hour)
> to make
> maybe, a refuge human
> and secure from the reach
>
> of whatever walks along
> (sword hearted)
> these night beaches.
> [38]

The bridgeless lake, encircling the island, like the circle of arms with which the poem begins, is a device of exclusion, something to keep out danger, something to secure the island (each of us) "from the reach/of whatever" lurks in the dark. But, again, if our circle games are strong, they are also fragile, "eroded by the water/in an hour." There is always someone outside the room and the walls are thin.

Section 4 returns us, in the alternating rhythm which is the poem's own enclosing circle game, to the room. Here, the speaker elaborates on the nature of the game of love, the game of relationships denied, hinted at in section 2 and related to the attempts at security fabricated by the children in section 3. "I notice," she says, "how/all your word-/plays" and other rituals of love "are now/attempts to keep me/at a certain distance/and (at length) avoid/admitting I am here." Atwood treats us to her own word games, the parenthetical "at length" evoking, ambiguously, both temporal eventuality and spatial distance. But the main point emphasized in this section is the objective I-it relationship demanded by the mythologizing lover, who fears the

speaker as an invading reality and regards her with analytic curiosity
rather than with love:

> I watch you
> watching my face
> indifferently
> yet with the same taut curiosity
> with which you might regard
> a suddenly discovered part
> of your own body:
> a wart perhaps
> [39]

The difficulty with these lines (if we are meant to sympathize with
the speaker) is that they smack of projection, the speaker passively
observing her lover as he passively observes her, his detachment her
own, as they each act, regressively, the mirror for the other.

The wart becomes an object of exploration and the lover, in a dissolving of image into image, becomes the explorer, not of the interior, but of the superficial geography which is the speaker's body.
He, who was "a tracer of maps" in his childhood, becomes the car-
tographer of her surface landscape: "So now you trace me/like a country's boundary/or a strange new wrinkle in/your own wellknown
skin" (39).

The tone, at this point, shifts to a subdued rage similar to that of
T. S. Eliot's Prufrock, when he speaks of "the eyes that fix you in a
formulated phrase" and pin you "wriggling on the wall." Both the
intent and imagery of Atwood's metaphors recall that earlier poem
about the vacuity of modern life and about our fear of breaking the
circle of lies that holds things "in their proper places": "I am fixed,"
says the speaker, "stuck/down on the outspread map/of this room,
. . . transfixed/by your eyes'/cold blue thumbtacks" (40). In what
seems to be another apt borrowing from Eliot, the speaker refers to
"the voices through the wall" and thus reminds us of Prufrock's lingering in the trance-like sleep which is the landscape of Eliot's
poem—but lingering (in Eliot's words) only until "human voices
wake us, and we drown."

Section 5 carries us to a "block/of grey stone that was once a fort/
but now is a museum" being visited by the speaker, her lover, and
the children who, the speaker (wistfully?) observes, are not "our children." Here, in a scene where Atwood has already begun to draw the

disparate characters together, they still are separated: "While they explore/the cannons" in the museum, "we walk outside." The children admire "the guns/and the armour," while the speaker wonders why, within "the careful moulding/round the stonework archways," the weapons are preserved, away from the crumbling earthworks outside, where they once sharpened "themselves on war," and "are now indoors/there, in the fortress,/fragile/in glass cases" (40–41). The weapon imagery, carried over from section 3, is ambiguous: the weapons represent those chaotic forces of violence and passion that we both desire as an escape from the circle game and fear for their danger. The guns are, as antiques, protected from the outer weather by structures (the fort, the glass cases) that cannot last; we are protected from the guns, icons of violence, by these same fragile structures.

The sixth section defines further our narcissistic games, the fantasies we create to give significance to our lives without really confronting the essential problems of those lives. The speaker, who accuses her lover of playing these games, sees the fault in herself as well, "although" (she says) "I tend to pose/in other seasons/outside other windows." Her remark leads directly to section 7, which begins "Summer again," as if to suggest that it is now the speaker's turn to pose (42).

Here Atwood brings together, dramatically, the various strands of imagery encountered in the preceding six sections. The room in which the lovers lie seems to parallel the "four gray walls, and four gray towers" of the Lady of Shalott, who weaves a "magic web" out of the "shadows of the world" she perceives in her mirror. The lovers, too, perceive their world obliquely, the mirrors of their room becoming a bridge to the outside where the children, still playing their trance-like circle game, are now seen in the room's reflecting glass surfaces. In those mirrors natural objects become manufactured ones ("this casual bed . . . is/their grassy lawn," "these scuffed walls/contain their circling trees,/that low clogged sink/their lake"). And manufactured objects become the tools of the lover's manipulation, as Atwood intensifies the nightmarish perceptions of her persona. When Tennyson's Lady of Shalott looks beyond her mirror and views Camelot, she breaks the magic spell of art, her mirror cracks, and she is thrust into her doom, of reality and death. Here, the mirrors do not crack; and the speaker, in a surreal recognition of the inextricable interweaving of art and life, sees all the most trivial, random items of nature become part of the careful design of her antagonist-lover: "a

wasp comes,/drawn by the piece of sandwich/left on the nearby
beach/(how carefully you do/such details)" (42–43).

As section 7 accelerates in its ritual repetition of images introduced
earlier in the poem, the world reflected in the mirrors becomes increasingly regressive, collapsing into the universe created by the
lover's solipsistic imagination. No longer people, the reflected children become mannequins, manipulated like the speaker for the lover's
own grim pleasure: "You make them/turn and turn, according to/
the closed rules of your games." The speaker sees ever more clearly
in such images her own entrapment, and in desperation she finally
cries out for "the circle" to be "broken" (43–44).

At the heart of the speaker's violent desire to break the circle is a
wish to deny the kinds of knowledge that have defined human culture
and consciousness since Adam and Eve ate of the apple in Eden. It is
a wish to destroy the rational and constricting world of "glass cases"
and "prisoning rhythms," of language and myth, of history and progress. And it is a desire to return to the primitive, irrational roots of
human existence, to assert a more anarchic vision, a psychic landcape
from which the artificiality of form has been banished. But if the
speaker's outcry is a necessary result of the poem's inner logic, it is
also a futile one. A wish born of frustration, it seeks to deny that
precise human need to build systems that the images of the poem
have demonstrated to be an inescapable part of the human condition.
In this poem at least, the circle remains unbroken.

"All the edges."   In "The Settlers" (79–80), the final poem in
this volume, Atwood does seem finally to break the circle. Her persona, joined in death by her partner and forming with him a single,
"inarticulate/skeleton," becomes the landscape itself. Buried by the
invading, unapprehending settlers, "our bones grew flesh again,/came
up trees and/grass." Thus absorbed into the earth, the bones emerge
as part of an affirmative vision of life renewed, a territory where
"horses graze . . . and/children run . . . across/the fields of our open
hands." Here, the promise of "This Is a Photograph of Me" is realized; the drowned persona has emerged from the depths. And love,
too, becomes possible, the bones of the persona and her lover "so/
intermixed" that they become "one/carcass," joined and inseparable,
part of each other and the land which spawned them. But the cost is
great. For this harmony, presented as an exultant final vision, still
demands the annihilation of individual identity, a loss that runs
counter to conscious human desire. Death, even if viewed as a pre-

condition of renewal, continues to be a leap into the unknown, and the transformation of "open hands" into "fields" can be sustained only as metaphor. The conflict remains unresolved. "The Circle Game" ends with the cry, "I want the circle/broken." And the final poem presents a vision of that wish fulfilled. Yet in a poem earlier in the collection Atwood describes what may well be her more characteristic attitude. In "Evening Trainstation Before Departure" her persona defines her existence as one involving constant movement, metamorphosis, change. Life becomes a delicate balancing act, between enclosure and freedom, between involvement and detachment, between form that provides order and the recognition that order alone is both meaningless and futile. In her movement Atwood's persona, like the persona in "A Place: Fragments," stands on the threshold and lives "on the edges/(what edges)/I live/on all the edges there are" (16). It is this essentially realistic and moderating position, poised between alternative extremes, that Atwood exploits throughout her works.

The Animals in That Country

With the imminent demise of Contact Press in 1967, *The Circle Game* was out of print even before it had been awarded the Governor-General's Award. In April 1967 Dennis Lee wrote to Atwood on behalf of himself and Dave Godfrey, proposing that their newly formed House of Anansi Press reissue *The Circle Game*. Atwood agreed, and the Anansi edition came out in autumn 1967. It was followed, only a few months later, by the 1968 Oxford University Press publication of Atwood's second collection, *The Animals in That Country*, a book that had resulted from Oxford's inviting her, in late 1966, to submit a manuscript. The poems in this collection had been written in 1965–66, during the ferment of pre-publication activities involving *The Circle Game* and while Atwood was in the doctoral program at Harvard University for the first year of her second two-year sojourn in Cambridge, Massachusetts. By the time the volume came out in 1968 she was at Sir George Williams University in Montreal teaching English; by then, also, many of the individual poems had appeared in various journals or been read on the CBC, and the manuscript of the collection had won first prize in the Centennial Commission Poetry Competition.

Atwood had returned to the United States in 1965 to complete her graduate work at Harvard, but her feelings toward America were not completely cordial. She was repelled by the planned obsolescence and waste of America's consumer society; and the mid-decade escalation of the Vietnam war effort did little to make her more content. In "It Is Dangerous to Read Newspapers," a poem midway through *The Animals in That Country,* Atwood attacks the waste and brutality of war. The speaker begins with vague references to her innocent childhood during the period of World War II: "While I was building neat/ castles in the sandbox,/the hasty pits were/filling with bulldozed corpses." What she dreads more, however, as she brings us up to date into the era of Vietnam's flaming jungles, is the futility of her own "good intentions" and her helpless complicity in the slaughter: "Each time I hit a key/on my electric typewriter,/speaking of peaceful trees/another village explodes."⁶ Opposed to the Vietnam war, yet residing in the country that was pursuing it, Atwood may have been projecting her own frustration with what might have seemed a morally equivocal position.

Whatever her reasons—and at least some of them were financial rather than philosophic—her desire to leave the United States was intense. Writing to Wynne Francis in September 1966 about the possibility of a teaching position at Sir George Williams, she commented that "I really have to get out of this rather horrible country next year, and back to Canada."⁷ *The Animals in That Country,* which contains some of her most overtly political early poems, captures her emotions about American culture—its rampant commercialism, its Faustian technology, its imposition of these evils on Canada, and its Americanization of the Canadian mind.

An "abstract hunger."   The book opens with a tone of irony more intense than what appears anywhere in *The Circle Game.* Again thrust into a journey, we contemplate the "Provisions" (1) we should have taken along with us. But, standing "on the disastrous ice, the wind rising," we find that we are unprepared:

> nothing in our pockets
>
> but a pencil stub, two oranges
> four toronto streetcar tickets
>
> and an elastic band, holding a bundle
> of small white filing-cards
> printed with important facts.

The words we use to formulate and explain our lives, those "important facts" we collect and record, neither guarantee survival nor elucidate the mysteries of life and death. Held together by a fragile "elastic band," they are as feeble against the wind and ice, nature's assertion of power, as all our attempts to contain, to explain, to abstract, to survey, and to map our world. Atwood pursues this idea in "The Surveyors," where nature is assaulted by the chainsaw and marking instruments of land developers, who blaze "their trail of single reason" and attempt to impose order on "a land where geometries are multiple." But the earth is too strong, and these "painted assertions" of the surveyors are transformed "to signs without motion, red arrows/pointing in no direction; faint ritual/markings leached by time/of any meaning" (4).

In "The Green Giant Murder" Atwood presents the alternate possibility, that our ecological ravages upon the earth may result in its untimely death. Yet Atwood's deeper attack is on the fact that, even then, man's abstracting, emotionless, measuring mind will see little loss and the earth will remain merely an object of study. Personified as the Green Giant—an allusion, in part, to the commercial myth figure popularized by a food canning company—the earth has died or been killed. The men walking its surface, caricatured as monomaniacal detectives morbidly obsessed by the circumstance of death, swarm "over the victim, . . . their magnifying glasses" twittering "with excitement/in the clear light." The detectives, disputing among themselves, do not know how the giant died. Some suggest that "he did it/himself." Those who thus blame the earth for its own demise are absurd; far more corrupt, suggests Atwood, are those who "say he is blameless," praising "him/for being what he is:/a . . . corpse," and therefore the "essential/fact for the practice of their/art, these cool/dissections" (32–33).

In the interconnected world of Atwood's metaphors man's inability to see himself in relation to the earth is merely a symptom of his general inability to sustain relationships: with other humans, with the animals who are our counterparts in the natural world from which we have separated ourselves, and between the separate yet complementary parts of our divided selves. In "The Trappers" (34–35) she develops more fully our relationship with animals. The circle games of her first book become the veritable "steel circles" of the traps that restrain and kill the trappers' prey; and the steel circles become, in turn, metaphors for that which entraps the trappers: "the steel jaws

of their answerless/dilemma." In this poem Atwood asserts a truth
that becomes a comprehensive subject of her novel *Surfacing:* that,
because we are both one with nature and distinct from it, our attitudes toward ourselves are influenced by our victimization of animals.
The poet says of the trappers: "I can understand/the guilt they feel
because/they are not animals/the guilt they feel/because they are."

For all this guilt, the trappers need to subdue nature, need to give
it an order, however ironically violent that order may be. Atwood
shows the killing to be real; her powerfully concrete images ("the
dead thing, the/almost-dead that must be/bludgeoned") pungently
express the vivid cruelty enacted on the snow-covered landscape. Yet,
simultaneously, there is in this killing an abstract ritual, "a repeti-
tion/of red on white, the footprints, the inevitable/blood. . . . The
chain, the/steel circles." It is not accidental, this image of the circle
formed of steel; it solidifies the more abstract significance of her other
circle-game symbols that represent all those ploys we invent to comprehend and combat what we perceive to be the chaotic existence that
surrounds us. In this poem the game is our playing out of an "abstract hunger/to trap and smash/the creature" and "to mark the snow
with feral/knowledge . . . to make each/tree and season an owned/
territory." But it is a futile ritual, Atwood suggests; the very need to
repeat it becomes a token of defeat. And we are left with our "recurring fear/of warm fur," the nightmare envisioned by the deranged
persona of "Arctic Syndrome: Dream Fox" who has become the
hunted animal itself: "In the neck/of the sleeping hunter/my teeth
meet" (49). We may litter and "desecrate" the earth as we pass
through it, says Atwood in "Backdrop Addresses Cowboy," leaving
behind "a heroic/trail of desolation," but we cannot, finally, conquer
it. Says the mocking landscape to the cowboy: "I am the horizon/you
ride towards, the thing you can never lasso" (50–51).

   "Whose dream is this?"   Our need to understand and thus
control the space we inhabit—and our inability to do so—is treated
somewhat differently in "At the Tourist Centre in Boston" (18–19).
Here Atwood employs color imagery, much as Wallace Stevens does,
to question the ability of our dreamlike blue abstractions to capture
the green, fecund reality of concrete nature. The speaker is in the
tourist centre and sees a map of Canada, "my country under glass,"
somehow "reduced to the size of a wall." Next to the map are "10
blownup snapshots/one for each province, . . . the green of the trees
dulled;/all blues however/of an assertive purity." These photographic

images of life in the various provinces are only partial and therefore unrealistic ("Quebec is a restaurant and Ontario the empty/interior of the parliament buildings"); the people, such few as are pictured in the photographs, are plastic, posed models, their "teeth white as detergent." The speaker asserts and at the same time questions her own experience, her own memories: "I seem to remember people,/at least in the cities, also slush,/machines and assorted garbage. Perhaps/that was my private mirage." But she still asks: "Whose dream is this . . ./is this a manufactured/hallucination, a cynical fiction, a lure/for export only?"

Atwood is attacking the false perceptions that are encouraged about Canada, by Canadians, particularly among Americans; but she blends this political, nationalistic attitude into an evocation of her persistent themes of fear and isolation, of the self's alternating attraction to the landscape and repulsion from it. The poem ends on one of her disconcertingly ambiguous and ominous notes. The speaker asks the "unsuspecting/window lady" whether she sees anything "watching you from under the water"; and she wonders aloud, "Who really lives there?" As if in answer, we are led once again, in the very next poem, on a backward journey toward roots that are at once compelling and fearful.

"Who locked me/into this crazed man-made/stone brain," asks the speaker of "A Night in the Royal Ontario Museum" (20–21). Though "man-made," the museum contains relics that transform it into an emblem of our own inescapable psyches: "fragments of gods, tarnished/coins, embalmed gestures"—the mythic and historic images of civilization that have brought us to our present confounded state. The speaker wanders, in this maze of "chronologically arranged" pieces of the past, "looking for the EXIT sign." But there is no exit: "in spite of the diagrams/at every corner, labelled/in red: YOU ARE HERE/the labyrinth holds me."

The museum's orientation diagrams operate on two levels: as guides to museum locations, certainly, but also as metaphorical guideposts on the speaker's journey through history and culture. That journey is in part a Canadian one, as the speaker in effect asks Northrop Frye's question—"Where is here?"[8]—and finds that there is no answer, that not even the Royal Ontario Museum in Toronto can give a truer picture of Canada than the Tourist Centre in Boston. But Atwood's universal message is present also: that the purely human journey on earth does not betray answers to the important questions of

life; and that the attempt to rediscover primitive roots has dangers
that are not balanced by the quality of the answers given:

> I say I am far
> enough,   stop here   please
> no more
>
> but the perverse museum, corridor
> by corridor, an idiot
> voice jogged by a pushed
> button, repeats its memories
>
> and I am dragged to the mind's
> deadend, the roar of the bone-
> yard, I am lost
> among the mastodons
> and beyond . . .
> [21]

The atavistic, mystic journey to beginnings, paradoxically captured
in the technologically created recordings of the museum and its misleading signs, is a dead end that reduces us to mere stone once again.
The speaker, identifying with the exhibits, becomes herself "a fossil/
shell, then/samples of rocks/and minerals." Our racial memories, en-
cased in our brains, as in the metaphorical museum, fail us.

Atwood asserts a more optimistic vision in the final poem of the
collection. Modifying an idea expressed earlier (in "Notes From Various Pasts"), that in evolving from sea to land creatures we have
"lost/an/electric wisdom/in the thin marooning air" (10–11), she
suggests in "Axiom" that the imponderable and chaotic sea will
"soon . . . be/all earth: a known/land, a country" (69). This idea
works well as a nationalistic hope for a Canada that is more than
imagined lakes and moose roaming the countryside, or noble
mounted police in red coats always getting their man. But the quest
of the explorer to conquer and give meaning to the elemental chaos
that surrounds us and inhabits our very beings is more problematic.
The artist-explorer may populate the wilderness, may make the sea-
land a solid reality; but, as Atwood observes in *Survival*, "the attempts to impose this kind of order . . . may . . . be a form of
madness."9

"**Progressive insanities.**"   Such madness is the subject of several poems related by their assertion that the unknown landscape re-

veals itself in our romantic relationships with others and in our discoveries about ourselves. The scenario presented in "A Pursuit" involves two lovers, whose bodies become veritable landscapes. Each hunts for the other "through the wilderness of the flesh/across the mind's ice/expanses." The speaker fears that she will find her counterpart "dead in the snow," and she suggests that the hunt (in fact a searching for the self) is futile: "These expeditions/have no end./Through the tangle of each other/we hunt ourselves" (66–67). In "Astral Traveller" Atwood sees the soul as separated from the body, seeking reconnection: "Getting away was easy./Coming back is an exacting theory." The speaker tells herself, "I will never get there," and she is probably correct; the only redemption is in the attempt (68).

In "An Icon" Atwood asserts the role of the artist attempting to circumscribe chaos and give definition to random objective data. Again the goal is realization of one's identity; again it is formulated in terms of an other self being made subject to the artist's machinations; but again, too, the other becomes an alter ego, a mirror-image double of the self. And art, the attempt to circumscribe, becomes a weapon of grotesque intentions: "You are/the lines I draw around you;/with this cleaver of a pencil/I hack off your aureole./I can make you armless, legless." The artist wishes through these maneuvers to "seize" the person, but he is "slipperier than clumsy colour," and he evades her, breaks "the cages/of black circumferences/by which I would surround you." And, turning on the artist, "whistling and destructive . . . as a hurricane," the alter ego takes control, scrolling her "up like a map" (60). The artist, somehow drawn into the pages of her sketching pad, thus becomes her own victim.

In part, Atwood is exploiting the Faustian motif, the extraordinary sin of mere mortals attempting, through a pact with evil or the devil, to comprehend divine knowledge, to create anew rather than merely live within the natural, vague limits of God's creation. In an era in which such Faustian control is within technological grasp, when scientists, with computers, can literally chart the terrain of the human brain and manufacture protean life in test tubes, Atwood's use of the motif is not a journey into the unreal and fantastic. It is instead an accurate depiction of our potential for good and evil in the latter half of the twentieth century. In "Speeches for Dr Frankenstein" (42–47) she employs Mary Shelley's gothic thriller as a point of departure for her own variations on the theme. Atwood emphasizes the grotesqueness of Frankenstein's undertaking in ways that are conventionally gothic and typical of her incisive imagery.

In the first section of the poem she disconnects the tools of Faustian creation from the agent Frankenstein and in so doing suggests his lack of control: it is not Frankenstein who acts; rather, amidst "an ether of cheers," it is his "wrist" that extends "a scalpel." Sections 2 and 3 are presented as a battle, in which Frankenstein discovers that the secrets he wishes to grapple with are his own secrets, the material he wishes to mold is his own body: "a living/skeleton, mine, round,/ that lies on the plate before me." "The thing," at first, "refuses to be shaped." The good doctor thrusts; "the thing fights back." But finally Frankenstein wields the scalpel "with delicate precision" and cries out in triumph, "O secret/form of the heart, now I have you" (42–43).

Not content with the mere conquering, however, the artist takes over from the scientist, contemplating ornaments: "Baroque scrolls on your ankles?/A silver navel?" But the scrollwork of the artist, in its pretensions toward skill and knowledge, is not natural, is in fact a sign of dementia: "I was insane with skill:/I made you perfect." And what should have been a work of love becomes instead an object of fear. Frankenstein deserts his creation and questions his "ravenous motive" in making the monster, his "reflection" who has "stolen/ everything you needed:/my joy, my ability/to suffer." The creature, once a part of Frankenstein, has taken over: "You have transmuted/ yourself to me: I am/a vestige, I am numb." And the doctor, to be whole, must recapture that part of himself that the creature has become, "must pursue/that animal I once denied/was mine." The doctor seeks to reassimilate the creature he has cut from himself, thus healing the division between head and heart that, in his attempt to deal with "impious wonders," he has created. The creature, however, has his own thoughts on the matter: "you would like to heal/that chasm in your side," he says to Frankenstein, "but I recede . . ./I will not come when you call." Like the artist of "An Icon," Frankenstein has become the victim of his own game (43–47).

Being victimized by one's preconceptions is the primary concern of "Progressive Insanities of a Pioneer" (36–39). In its explicit commentary on the inherent chaos of man's rage for order, this poem is central to the volume. It begins with a paradox typical of Atwood's poetic perception. The pioneer, standing in the middle of an interminable green wilderness, "a point/on a sheet of green paper," proclaims himself, in a commonplace act of human arrogance and conceit, "the centre." Yet there are no points of focus: "no walls, no borders/anywhere; the sky no height/above him, totally un-/enclosed." Unlike the artist's white paper filled with lines and margins in "The Icon," nature's green paper is limitless. It is for the pioneer a suffocating fullness; and he shouts, incongruously, yet appropriately too, "Let me out!" With this spare introduction Atwood sends us into the maze of the pioneer's experience, as, attempting to settle the Canadian wilderness, he discovers the frailty of his ill-conceived design (36).

The pioneer, attempting to structure the space around him, asserts that he is "not random," that he has purpose. He tries to till the soil, to cultivate it, to change its seeming chaos, its wildness, into pastoral order. But the green sheet has its own language, its own symbols, and it replies to the pioneer's assertions "with aphorisms:/a tree-sprout, a nameless/weed, words" that "he couldn't understand." In a parable of Canadian settlement the pioneer encases himself within a garrison environment; he builds a house, with its geometric straight lines and its surrounding fences, and thus tries to escape the apparently nebulous order of nature, to deny that he is a part of it. But the house cannot evade "the idea of an animal" that "patters across the roof"; and the fences defend the fields "in vain:/everything/is getting in" (36–37).

In the poem's sixth section Atwood asserts that the pioneer might have saved his sanity, such as it is, if he had (could have?) assimilated nature, recognized its natural order, "stocked his log house-/boat with all the animals/even the wolves." Then, like Noah on the ark, "he might have floated" on the waterlike land that is Canada and the world. Instead, he stamps his foot on what he asserts is solid land, and watches it "sink/down through stone/up to the knee." The poem becomes a reversal of the story of Genesis, as the pioneer becomes an Adam unable to name the beasts: "Things/refused to name themselves; refused/to let him name them." And thus that first requirement of symbolic thought, that which allows us to create fictions to order our environment—language—is disallowed. The pioneer foresees "disintegration," the tension overcomes him, and "the green/vision, the unnamed/whale" invades his being. Nature triumphs over unregenerate man, who is incapable of accepting the landscape on its own terms (38–39).

For all its philosophic certainty, however, the message of "Pro-

gressive Insanities of a Pioneer" seems unsatisfying, seems—particularly in the ambiguous context of Atwood's other work—mere
dogmatic idealism. As we have seen elsewhere, an attempt to assimilate nature or to allow nature to enfold us is, in Atwood's poetic
landscape, often an emotional or intellectual cul-de-sac. Our evolution effectively precludes any significant re-engagement with external
nature or with inner instinct. If we suffer as a result, we must simply
do the best we can. Such seems to have been Atwood's initial impulse
in the creation of "Progressive Insanities," which in a manuscript version was originally—and more mildly—entitled "Some Difficulties of
a Pioneer," and which concluded on a more flippant note: "In the
end/he gave up on things with roots/and planted a crop of rocks./
expecting little profit."[10] In the published poem Atwood changed the
ending to one more ominous and thus more consistent with the images that precede it; but the manuscript version reveals the potentially less doctrinaire statement the author might well have presented
to public scrutiny.

   "I touch you."   It is when Atwood moves away from the discussion of philosophic problems that her poems become, both aes-
thetically and emotionally, most satisfying. Often freer in rhythm
and more evocatively phrased, such poems transport us beyond the
chasm separating head and heart to a region beyond. In "I Was Reading a Scientific Article" (64–65), for example, she looks ahead to the
kind of intensely affective language that increasingly and happily intrudes into her later collections. The poem begins with a comment
on a technological achievement, the very kind of analysis that elsewhere Atwood criticizes: "They have photographed the brain/and
here is the picture." Expecting an attack on technological cannibalism, we are instead led into an exultation at the infinite capacities for
love and wonder in the human mind: "I touch you, I am created in
you/somewhere as a complex/filament of light."

   The speaker cannot "excavate" the inextricable secrets of her lover's
"heavy unbelievable/skull," but here that fact no longer seems to
matter. Atwood takes us into the world of Keats's nightingale, yet
unlike the creator of that essentially more pessimistic reverie, she
does not ring any bells to wake us up:

>   my hands trace the contours of a total
>   universe, its different
>   colours, flowers, its undiscovered
>   animals, violent or serene

its other air
its claws

its paradise rivers
[65]

David Helwig has written of this poem that, unlike most of the collection, where Atwood presents alternating hells of unstructured space and imprisoning form, "here the senses and emotions reach out, undeterred by chaos or inhibiting form. The mind expresses feeling rather than interfering with it."[11] Though the thematic emphasis of "Progressive Insanities of a Pioneer" is taken up in larger scope in Atwood's next volume of poems, it is this warmer, more personal attachment to her material that may be the larger achievement foreshadowed, in the long run, by *The Animals in That Country*.

The Journals of Susanna Moodie

In 1970 Atwood published two collections of poems, *The Journals of Susanna Moodie,* which relates, through a modern persona's vision, the experience of a mid-nineteenth-century English settler in Canada, and *Procedures for Underground,* a less significant volume that nevertheless offers several extremely evocative poems. The Moodie collection is derived from two books, *Roughing It in the Bush* (1852) and *Life in the Clearings* (1853), written by Mrs. Moodie, about her sojourn in the Canadian wilderness and settlement areas. It is Atwood's most cohesive group of poems, developing a single character throughout and elaborating on the themes expressed in "Progressive Insanities of a Pioneer." Structurally, the book follows Mrs. Moodie's life, beginning with her immigration to Canada and ending with her death and spiritual resurrection in the latter half of the twentieth century. Now fully linked to the land she both loved and despised, she comments on the futility of man's attempts to conquer the wildness of nature.

"Violent duality." In an afterword following the poems Atwood observes that Mrs. Moodie's memoirs show her to have been "divided down the middle: she praises the Canadian landscape but accuses it of destroying her; she dislikes the people already in Canada but finds in people her only refuge from the land itself; she preaches progress and the march of civilization while brooding elegiacally upon the destruction of the wilderness. . . . She claims to be an ardent Canadian patriot while all the time she is standing back from the country and criticizing it as though she were a detached observer, a stranger." Atwood believes that Moodie's "violent duality" is the prototypical Canadian attitude: "even if we were born here," she says, "we are all immigrants to this place." Although she feels that Mrs. Moodie's books are mere "collections of disconnected anecdotes," Atwood abstracts from these miscellanies of settlement trivia Moodie's essential voice, her deeply divided sensibility that appears only under the surface of her otherwise "discursive and ornamental" prose. This "other voice," says Atwood, "running like a counterpoint through her work," reveals a conflict between her mind and heart that Mrs. Moodie only barely comprehends.[12]

It takes a skilled reader or a perceptive poet to discern Moodie's "other voice." Much of the narrator's doubleness in *Roughing It in the Bush* results from the passing of time: the narrator sees that her experiences since a given event have altered her outlook on the event. Even so, there is a remarkable absence of tension in her observations. At one point, for example, Mrs. Moodie comments on the fears she had held when she and her family first came to Canada in 1832. She notes, "Now, when not only reconciled to Canada, but loving it, and feeling a deep interest in its present welfare, and the fair prospect of its future greatness, I often look back and laugh at the feelings with which I then regarded this noble country."[13]

Such turgid prose lacks conviction. It ignores the dangers of disease, fire, and starvation that legitimately motivated Moodie's highly unlaughable feelings when such events occurred. More compelling, yet rare, are those instances in which the narrator reflects inwardly on the significance of her life in the bush: following her tale of a forest fire that nearly destroyed her home and family, surrounding the house on all sides until a providential rain extinguished it, Moodie notes that, "for a long time after," that fire "haunted me in my dreams. I would awake with a start, imagining myself fighting with the flames, and endeavouring to carry my little children through them to the top of the clearing, when invariably their garments and my own took fire just as I was within reach of a place of safety." Yet more significant in its revelation of Moodie's "other voice" is her comment, as she and her family are about to depart from the woods, on how seven years in the bush had affected her, not only physically, but spiritually as well: "For seven years I had lived out of the world entirely; my person had been rendered coarse by hard work and exposure to the weather. I looked double the age I really was, and my hair was already thickly sprinkled with grey. I clung to my solitude. I did not like to be dragged from it to mingle in gay scenes, in a busy town, and with gaily dressed people. I was no longer fit for the world."[14]

It is this more reflective Moodie that Atwood exploits in her collection of poems, developing a persona who attempts to become spiritually a part of the very land she fears, a secluded soul who is indeed "no longer fit for the world" of social manners and progress. It is the journey from repugnance and fear toward acceptance and eventual assimilation that the journals recount.

"Journal I." The first journal begins with Moodie's "Disembarking at Quebec" (11) and finding, as does the speaker in Atwood's earlier poem "Provisions," that what we bring with us to the new world is usually an incongruity: "the things I carry in my hand/—a book, a bag with knitting—/the incongruous pink of my shawl/this space cannot hear." The problem of the explorer or the settler is an epistemological one, a puzzling out of the ways by which we can know the reality that surrounds us and thus accommodate ourselves to something totally alien. But for Moodie, at first, there is mere absence: "The moving water will not show me/my reflection./The rocks ignore./I am a word/in a foreign language." In the second poem, "Further Arrivals" (12–13), she refuses "to look in a mirror" for fear she will see nothing. Questioning reality, she observes that "whether the wilderness is/real or not/depends on who lives there."

Yet this first journal is largely a tale of Moodie's growing awareness; and by the fourth poem in the sequence, "The Planters" (16–17), she is able to see beyond the delusions of the other characters. Unlike the insane pioneer, whose denial of reality is his defeat, the settlers' illusions do sustain their vision of the pastoral possibilities of the wilderness—to ignore the "unnamed/whale" seems for them to hold it off. The illusion is, as always, a fragile one, but for the time it works. "They are right," says Moodie. And she continues:

> . . . If they let go
> of that illusion solid to them as a shovel,
>
> open their eyes even for a moment
> to these trees, to this particular sun
> they would be surrounded, stormed, broken
>
> in upon by branches, roots, tendrils, the dark
> side of light
> as I am.
> [17]

For Moodie, however, the truth is necessary; and her ability to perceive the darker side of knowledge—"the dark/side of light"—is an essential part of her quest for survival in the new world, even if such dark knowledge may thrust her into a disordered nightmare.

The nightmare Moodie undergoes in "Journal I" is indeed chaotic, but it is also enlightening. Filled with images of disease and disaster, it is yet a pathway to knowledge and an escape from old despairs— "the long illness" of her ocean crossing, "the cities rotting with cholera" (12). The empty darkness that she enters is, at least, a fresh beginning. Until vision comes, however, reality is nebulous. In "The Wereman" (19) Moodie's "husband walks in the frosted field/an X, a concept/defined against a blank"; entering the forest, he "is blotted out." Though "he will/return" at noon, Moodie is uncertain what it is he will return as, what shape he will have turned into, even what shape he will see her as "when he opens the door." For Moodie, in "Paths and Thingscape" (20–21), the land becomes an enemy watching her "like an invader/who knows hostility but/not where."

Her paranoia is justified when she is, in fact, attacked. "The Two Fires" (22–23) threaten Moodie and her family with annihilation. In "the summer fire," the trees melt, "returning/to their first red elements/on all sides, cutting me off/from escape or the saving/lake." Here, in a poetic transmutation of the fire episode from *Roughing It in the Bush,* Atwood has Moodie sit "in the house" like "a charm," protecting her "sleeping children" from "that shapeless raging" outdoors and concentrating on the fragile "logic of windows," the straight lines and geometric shapes that dispute chaos. In "the winter/fire inside," such logic is questioned: "the carefully-/made structure" shrivels in the flames and becomes itself a threat, an imprisoning "cage of blazing/bars." Now it is the snow-laden open air that becomes, ironically, the protective garrison: "each refuge fails/us," says Moodie, "each danger/becomes a haven." And more. For, as Moodie notes, the "two fires in-/formed me"—gave me knowledge and "formed me" fresh—"left charred marks/now around which I/try to grow."

In the next poem we find Moodie finally "Looking in a Mirror" and seeing that, seven years after entering the wilderness, she has been transformed into an ugly hag, her "heirloom face . . . a crushed eggshell/among other debris" (24). Her civilized veneer has been erased and she is nearly ready to accommodate herself to the bush. But she has taken too long, and (in "Departure From the Bush," 26–27) it is time for her to move to a less remote area. She recalls how, while in the wilderness, "the animals/arrived to inhabit me," to make her a part of their world; but she also observes that "I was not ready/altogether to be moved into"; the animals, entering her "two/by two," could tell that, unlike Noah's ark, she could not accept them all, that she "might/capsize." And so, when her husband writes that she must leave the bush, she does so without having been "completed." As the sleigh rounds "the first hill" on her journey "towards the city," she "was/(instantaneous)/unlived in." The animals inhabiting her soul leave her, and Moodie knows that "there was something they almost taught me/I came away not having learned."

"**Journal II.**"   "Journal II" covers Moodie's life from 1840 to 1871. Composed of social commentary, haunting memories of bush life, and apocalyptic dreams, it carries Moodie from a tentative acceptance of the new world's savagery to an understanding of "The Double Voice" that controls her perceptions of the Canadian landscape. Atwood has gone beyond the strictly chronological structure of "Journal I" to produce in "Journal II" a more complex interweaving of poems. Nestled between two crucial poems concerning the deaths of Moodie's children are Moodie's comments on society ("The Immigrants," "1837 War in Retrospect," "Charivari") and her dreams ("Dream 1: The Bush Garden," "Dream 2: Brian the Still-Hunter," "Dream 3: Night Bear Which Frightened Cattle"). Atwood alternates these poems so that each dream seems subtly to comment on the preceding social event that Moodie describes. Taken together, the two sets of poems contribute to Moodie's growing vision and acceptance of her fate.

In "The Immigrants" (32–33) Moodie observes how the new settlers, envisioning the receding "old countries" as "perfect, thumbnail castles preserved/like gallstones in a glass bottle," believe that in the new world "they will make an order/like the old one." But, as Moodie notes, the immigrants "are too poor" to sustain their aspirations, and the land itself conspires against them, as "the green fruit shrivels/in the prairie sun." Moodie sees in the immigrants her earlier self, attempting to make the new world flourish, inevitably failing, and continually "riding across an ocean of unknown/land to an unknown land." She dreams, finding herself back in "The Bush Garden," where she had attempted to cultivate the soil. The fruit does not shrivel in the dream. Rather, far worse, her attempt to impose order on the land reveals itself as a terrifying nightmare. The vegetables, large and luxuriant, become animals, whose flesh is torn violently by the human hand as it pulls them, "red and wet," from the earth. "I should have known," says Moodie in the dream, that "anything planted here/ would come up blood" (34).

The image of blood and violence leads directly into Moodie's contemplation of the "1837 War in Retrospect." The colonial-era rebellion becomes for Moodie a pointed example of the foolishness of human behavior. History, of which this rebellion is a part, is composed of accidental circumstances that are essentially mere excuses for action, "flukes" and "mistakes" that we clutch "like parachutes" as if to deny gravity. "This war," says Moodie, "will soon be among/ those tiny ancestral figures/flickering dull white through the back of your skull." The reasons for the war will be forgotten, she implies, and the warriors will take on the caricatured features of toy soldiers in a child's crayoned "diagram of a fort" (35).

The second of Moodie's dreams, "Brian the Still-Hunter" (36), incorporates her memory of an episode during the bush years, when a silent, solitary warrior of another sort visited her home. Brian's killing is both more essential and more paradoxical than that of the toy soldiers of the rebellion. He hunts animals, yet like "The Trappers" of *The Animals in That Country* he identifies with them. "I kill," he says, "because I have to/but every time I aim, I feel/my skin grow fur." He becomes the prey at which he shoots and questions God's justice toward the creatures of the wild. Having tried once "to cut his throat," and bearing yet "the white scar made by the hunting knife/around his neck," Brian understands both the strength of the wilderness and his own human weakness. His hunting, tragic and guilt-ridden though it is, evokes compassion and ties him to the animals he kills: "I die more often than many," he says to Moodie. His gloomy acceptance of nature's chaotic order and of his part in it parallels Moodie's own growing accommodation. Yet, at the poem's end, he is like the soldiers of the rebellion—one who has become lost to time. Moodie awakens from her dream and remembers: Brian "has been gone/twenty years and not heard from." The message he might have communicated is buried in the past.

In "Charivari" (37) Atwood shifts her emphasis somewhat to ask how we might become truly "human" and avoid the killing that has marked our existence on the earth. Moodie is listening to a tale about a charivari in which young idlers, disguised as Indians and otherwise fantastically arrayed, heckled a marriage between a black man and a white woman and inadvertently killed the groom, "pretending to each other/it was a joke, until/they killed him." The joviality of the occasion is a pretense that masks its dark reality—the hecklers kill, as Brian does, because they have to. But if they, unlike Brian, are blind to their motives, equally imperceptive is "the American lady" who tells Moodie the story. She sees it as "a disgraceful piece/of business," yet distances herself from its violence and death by nonchalantly finishing "her tea." Lest we miss the ironic point, Moodie appends a parenthetical "note," addressed to "teadrinkers, and inadvertent/victims and murderers," admonishing them "never" to "pretend" that "this isn't/part of the soil too"; every one of us, she implies, may succumb to the "cracked/drumbeats" of the charivari. The instinct is within us all. If we recognize that fact, says Moodie, we may be able to "resist" the impulse to kill or be killed by its savage force. The point is elaborated by the third dream, "Night Bear Which Frightened Cattle" (38–39), in which Moodie and her children, gathered in "the lighted cabin" that ostensibly protects them from the approaching bear outside, become, in effect, the terrified bride and bridegroom awaiting their tragic destiny.

This destiny is captured particularly for Moodie in the two poems that frame the social comments and the dreams and provide the essential development of Moodie's character in "Journal II." The journal begins with "Death of a Young Son by Drowning" (30–31). Here, Moodie sees her son's death as part of life's journey, "a voyage of discovery/into the land I floated on/but could not touch to claim." His is a voyage that we may all undergo, suggests Moodie, if we are able, for it is in fact a return to "distant regions," to "a landscape stranger than Uranus/we have all been to and some remember." Moodie herself, however, cannot retrieve the memory, cannot join her son, as the poem shifts to a recapitulation of lost hopes and details of rescue, "the swamped body" picked from the water "with poles and hooks/from among the nudging logs." For Moodie, "the dreamed sails" of her son's voyage "collapsed, ragged." Her own foot hits "rock," as the earth's deceptive solidity captures her once more. Yet the poem ends ambiguously. For, despite the tragedy of the son's death and Moodie's own imprisonment in life, "it was spring, the sun kept shining, the new grass/lept to solidity"—and thus life's cycle continues in other forms. The tone, more celebrative than ironic, presents a romantic vision of the unity of all living beings in nature's mysterious design. The final lines, for all their seeming bitterness, are curiously prophetic: "I planted him in this country," says Moodie, "like a flag." Her son thus becomes a token of the country's meaning, an emblem of the land itself.

The connection of the self and the land is further developed in the second poem about Moodie's losses, "The Deaths of the Other Children" (41). Here Moodie acknowledges the relationship between decaying flesh and flourishing vegetation, between her own body and the bodies of her children as they contribute to the detritus that constitutes the land: "The body dies / little by little / the body buries itself / joins itself / . . . to the black- / berries and thistles." Moodie laments this process, regretting the years spent in creating her public, her "composite / self, this crumbling hovel." Yet, for all her anguish, she is coming more fully to accept the land of which she is inextricably a part. Although she is yet not fully merged with it, the land beckons her to join:

> My arms, my eyes, my grieving
> words, my disintegrated children
>
> Everywhere I walk, along
> the overgrowing paths, my skirt
> tugged at by the spreading briers
>
> they catch at my heels with their fingers
> [41]

Atwood's deliberate syntactic ambiguity—we are not certain whether it is "my disintegrated children" or "the spreading briers" that "catch at" Moodie's "heels with their fingers"—enhances the idea that the children share an identity with the briers, that they have united fully with the land. No longer merely emblems of the country, they are concretely a part of it.

To accept that physical reality and its spiritual implications may provide some comfort for the loss of loved ones. But gross decay is a reality also; and the pain-boggled mind, as Moodie realizes in "The Double Voice" (42), must often paint over the darker side of nature with rose-tinted fictions. In this final poem of "Journal II" Atwood powerfully reiterates the controlling concept of her poetry: that there are alternate realities in our experience, one the ritualized creation of the artistic imagination, the other a more concrete actuality that expresses the dynamic savagery of life. It is the same point she makes in "The Animals in That Country." But, while the duality is objectified in the earlier poem, here Atwood captures Susanna Moodie's individual and subjective torment. As Moodie tries to cope with her existence in the Canadian wilderness, she expresses what Atwood, in the afterword, refers to as the "paranoid schizophrenia" that is Canada's "national mental illness" (62). One of the voices that "took turns using my eyes," says Moodie, "had manners,/painted in watercolours," and perceived "the rituals of seasons and rivers." The opposing voice recognizes "that men sweat," and "that there is nothing to be done/about mosquitoes." Atwood ends the poem with this voice speaking of death and decay, as it finds "a dead dog/jubilant with maggots/half-buried among the sweet peas." It is no accident that Atwood shapes these final details so that they are simultaneously two-voiced, foreboding in the image of a corpse hidden in the vegetation, yet also mysteriously "jubilant." Neither one voice nor the other tells the entire truth.

"Journal III." The first five poems of "Journal III," which Atwood dates "1871–1969," find Susanna Moodie in old age—alienated, reflecting upon her life, and finally dying. In the first, "Later in Belleville: Career" (47), the Susanna Moodie who "once . . . wrote/verses about love and sleighbells" and "painted butterflies" on mushrooms for "the tourists," in exchange "for potatoes" and her children's shoes, now sits "every day/. . . on a stuffed sofa" in her orderly "fringed parlour" doing little. "There is," she says with ambiguous irony, "no use for art." The photograph of Moodie, in "Daguerreotype Taken in Old Age," depicts her face as a lunar surface, "vapid . . ./pitted and vast." Moodie acknowledges that she has "changed" during her years in Canada, but she is uncertain who this alien creature, decayed by time, "eaten away by light," really is (48). She wishes, in the next poem, "Wish: Metamorphosis to Heraldic Emblem," a symbolic permanence that will stave off decay, or at least substitute for physical disintegration some spiritual significance. But the vision of herself, underground, transformed into a mythic reptilian creature, "with new/formed plumage/uncorroded," is an uncertain one at best. "My grandchildren," she observes, "little guess how/maybe" she "will prowl and slink/in crystal darkness/among the stalactite roots" (49).

As Moodie approaches death, she goes on a "Visit to Toronto, With Companions" (50–51). Here she sees the city, with its new streets and harbor; but her main interest is the lunatic asylum. Entering the first floor, she sees demented women calmly "sitting, sewing." The second floor contains the more violent inmates, "crouching, thrashing, / tearing off their clothes." The third floor, apparently a metaphorical one (it does not appear in the real Susanna Moodie's discussion in *Life in the Clearings*), takes Atwood's Moodie to a transcendent realm, a higher insanity perhaps, "a different kind of room." This place, opposed to the urban reality outside, "where there were streets and / the Toronto harbour" manufactured by the land developers and technocrats, is "a hill, with boulders, trees, no houses." As her companions ask her to return to the outer world, she resists, for "the air / was about to tell me / all kinds of answers." In the next poem, "Solipsism While Dying" (52–53), Moodie succumbs, believing that with her death the world will cease to exist: "What will they do now / that I, that all / depending on me disappears?"

The world continues, of course; and, above her, the technocrats build as she, in "Thoughts from Underground" (54–55) and "Alternate Thoughts from Underground" (57), contemplates her own ambivalent attitude toward municipal growth and supposed progress. In the first poem Moodie recalls her initial and growing hatred for "this country"—its summer heat, weeds ("the green things fiercely / shoving themselves upwards"), and insects, and its winter cold and scarcity of food. "Then we were made successful," she says, "and I felt I ought to love / this country." Her love came, however, not from the land itself, but from its exploitation. Still out of harmony with the land, Moodie's mind boggled: "I said I loved it / and my mind saw double." She appealed to language in a desperate attempt to construct "paragraphs of praise" for the country. But these paragraphs, placed "at intervals" like "highway billboards," were sustained by the language—"look how / fast Belleville is growing"—of technological progress. "We will all be rich and powerful," Moodie remembers this language saying, but somehow it did not alter the reality it denied.

Moodie perceives this disharmony more clearly in "Alternate Thoughts from Underground." Here, her spirit listens to "the shrill of glass and steel," as the invading "inheritors" of the land raise their "glib superstructures," replacing the primitive wooden shelters of earlier settlers. Those wooden structures, subject to destruction by terrible and "sacred" fire, were in their vulnerability part of nature's cycle. Moodie prays to her "wooden fossil God" to "topple this glass pride, fireless / rivetted babylon"; but she sees that its builders "prevail," and she feels that her own vision is "extinct." She feels "scorn" for the interlopers, "but also pity," the same emotion she believes was felt by the dinosaurs who were "done under by the thing . . . outside the circle/they drew by their closed senses/of what was right." Just as the dinosaurs were defeated by their own limited knowledge, pushed out "by the velvet immoral/uncalloused and armourless mammals," so too will modern man be defeated by his tunnel vision.

Moodie's view is wider; and, in the cryptic language of "Resurrection" (58–59), she surges upward from the earth with a prophetic vision—articulated by "those who have become the stone/voices of the land"—that "at the last/judgement we will all be trees." This idea is pursued in the final poem of the collection, "A Bus Along St. Clair: December" (60–61). Moodie, "the old woman/sitting across from you on the bus," proclaims that she cannot be banished from the city, that "this is my kingdom still." She has become the land itself, or at least its avenging angel "destroying/the walls, the ceiling," and reducing to rubble the bulldozer-built "silver paradise" of the city planners. The city has become "an unexplored/wilderness of wires," defeated by the perceptual flaws of its creators. The land, thus transformed into a metaphoric wilderness, regresses to its former state. "Turn, look down," Moodie commands, "there is no city;/this is the centre of a forest." And in place of man, who has in his turn succumbed to the fate of the dinosaurs, there is an absence: look, Moodie says to her companion on the bus, "your place is empty."

"A shameless desecration." *The Journals of Susanna Moodie* embodies Atwood's most concentrated use of the Canadian past to comment on the Canadian present. By tracing out Moodie's transformation from a fear-ridden woman, disgusted with the wilderness and isolated from it, to an individual who accepts the land for what it is and seeks to protect it from the technological exploitation of other humans, Atwood captures the experience of the Canadian pioneer and settler in a potentially savage land. But she expresses also, by implication, an emerging Canadian rebellion—evident during the late 1960s when the poems were being written—against American domination over the Canadian economy. This domination, seen as typical of the historic American pursuit of manifest destiny, seemed to be leading to a transformation of Canadian culture, an "Americanization" of Canadian sensibility. George Grant, a philosopher who has significantly influenced Atwood, saw this sensibility as one that values restraint and the achievement of communal goals and opposes the liberal, Calvinist ideology and rampant individualism of the American, who in suppressing his own passions and in controlling his surroundings has achieved a sanitized, deodorized, death-denying (and therefore life-denying) technological civilization. For Grant, as for Atwood, the American has conquered the heathen wilderness but lost his soul. Atwood suggests in her second novel, *Surfacing,* where the evil "Americans" turn out in fact to be Canadians, that the disease may be spreading north. And even Susanna Moodie, in *Life in the Clearings,* laments the American plan to transform its side of Niagara Falls into a tool "for turning machinery." "Ye gods!" she cries out, "what next will the love of gain suggest to these gold-worshippers? The whole earth should enter into a protest against such an act of sacrilege—such a shameless desecration of one of the noblest works of God."[15]

In thus demonstrating Atwood's ability to transform historic documents and a modern sensibility into an intensely coherent poetic sequence and a compelling philosophic statement, the Moodie collection represents a major achievement in her growth as a writer of poems. But the volume cannot be judged an unqualified success. *The Journals of Susanna Moodie* is a clarion call for community; it asks that we transcend our differences and return to the common source of all creation. Yet it is a cold community, indeed, that Atwood presents—void of love and compassion, determined only by its own logical necessity, presented (except in "Resurrection") in the abstract, formalized language of reason rather than in the emotionally compelling language of faith. The land, personified as a crouching old hag in the closing lines of the book, chooses to claim its own, destructively reducing mere man and his artifacts to rubble. One may have to acknowledge that vision; but one can hardly wish to embrace it. The sense of communion that one may wish from a transcendent philosophy is paradoxically absent. It is not until Atwood enlarges her emotional boundaries—in *You Are Happy* (1974) and, much more completely, in *Two-Headed Poems* (1978)—that her poems evoke in a comprehensive way the emotions of love and compassion, of simple and realistic human warmth. This development is hinted at in *The Animals in That Country,* and it is refined in *Procedures for Underground.* But it is missing almost entirely from *The Journals of Susanna Moodie.*

Procedures for Underground

Published the same year as *The Journals of Susanna Moodie,* Atwood's fourth collection of poems reveals no significant shifts in her poetic style. It does, however, extend her major themes and refine those techniques designed to evoke emotional responses from the reader. The volume contains some of Atwood's most pleasurable poems. In *Procedures for Underground,* according to one reviewer, Atwood returns to the voice of *The Circle Game,* but more triumphantly—its author having "broken the circle, shaken off the persona of Susanna Moodie which . . . was a restriction on her own personality as a poet."[16]

"Wisdom and great power." "Procedures for Underground," the book's title poem, is obviously linked to the final portion of *The Journals of Susanna Moodie,* and it defines Atwood's continuing involvement with the underground or submerged side of our lives. Concluding the first of three divisions in the collection, the poem stands as Atwood's most explicit statement of a central theme in her poetry, the shamanistic role of the artist in a world that refuses to recognize the magic around and within us. It is, Atwood has observed, "one of the few poems I've written about the creative process . . . and I do see it as a descent to the underworld." But if the artist must descend to the underworld, or to the inner recesses of the mind, he must also come back. Atwood had originally called the poem "Underground and Later," a title that expresses more accurately, if less dramatically, the poem's important emphasis on the seer's safe return to commonplace reality.[17]

The underground itself depicts a landscape filled with anomalous details that collide with our normal expectations, or that seem slightly out of focus; it is a country that "has a green sun/and the rivers flow backwards," where "the trees and the rocks are the same/as they are here, but shifted." Having traveled to the underworld and returned, the speaker of Atwood's poem warns us of its dangers and its rewards if we dare pursue the same journey. "For this gift, as for all gifts," she says, "you must/suffer"—haunted forever by the spirits of the underworld, feared by those who walk above and "seek your help." But the "wisdom and great power" that one learns in the underworld—the power of the artist to transform reality—may be worth the effort.[18]

On the surface, however, the artist's wisdom and power may become an intrusion, may disrupt the innocence of our daily lives. To
intensify this collision of two worlds, Atwood builds ordinary scenes,
shifting with acute and surreal suddenness into something grotesque
or other-worldly. In "Game After Supper" (7), for example, she
transports us into a seemingly peaceful past era, where children play
in the fields after supper. The speaker's soothing voice evokes a nos-
talgic world "before electricity, . . . when there were porches" and
where "the living room . . . smells of/smoke and mildew." Though
the speaker employs the present tense, we realize that the scene is an
act of memory, not a literal place in which the speaker resides but a
moment in the now-distant past. It is reflected upon, objectively,
after many other events have intervened. The scene appears idyllic. It
seems to be describing a game of hide-and-seek the children are playing. The speaker, apparently hiding, cannot be seen. But Atwood's
words suggest, alternately, that the speaker is in fact no longer present at all, and that the scene is itself a buried relic of her mind:
"There is a barn but I am not in the barn;/there is an orchard too,
gone bad, . . . but I am not there either."

Thus begins a subtle transformation of mood. Entering the scene,
yet standing outside it as well, the speaker brings to bear upon the
children's game her underground knowledge of past, present, and future, knowledge that is the timeless gift of the visionary. She is able
both to play as child and simultaneously to record the future, our
present: "I am hiding in the long grass/with my two dead cousins,/
the membrane grown already/across their throats." The past cannot
be preserved. The cousins cannot remain children forever. They must
grow old and die. Even in childhood, they intuitively grasp that fact:
"We hear crickets and our own hearts/close to our ears;/though we
giggle, we are afraid." The "tall man . . . coming to find us," they
say, "will be an uncle,/if we are lucky." There is only a hint of terror
here, unformed and tentative, less the result of a threat than of a
childish fear of the bogey-man coming as the shadows of evening
lengthen. But it remains a token of what, in fact, time and mortality
will bring to them.

The reality that death will eventually claim us is part of the underground vision brought by the traveler to the surface; yet paradoxically the artist's power is often employed in what may be a
misguided attempt to escape that vision. In the opening poem,
"Eden Is a Zoo" (6), the adult speaker is looking at a childhood cray-

on drawing of her parents. The title itself suggests the ironic notion that the myth of a perfect paradise is really a spiritual cage. For the speaker, the drawing preserves her parents, yet even she questions the power she has exerted over them. She asks whether her parents, dressed permanently "in the clothes of thirty years/ago," are "bewildered" when they encounter relics of the past; and she wonders whether it bothers "them to perform/the same actions over and over" in empty ritual reenactments of some lost but cherished event. In the poem's final lines Atwood suggests that the speaker, in the very act of keeping her parents for herself, has pushed them away, put them on one side of a fence while she stands, isolated, on the other: "Are they content?/Do they want to get out?/Do they see me looking at them/from across the hedge of spikes . . . ?" Atwood does not deny our need for some fictions to sustain pleasurable illusions; but the questions of this poem clearly suggest that something is missing, that some procedures are inadequate or deny too thoroughly the chaos they are intended to supplant.

"**A dialogue.**" "The Creatures of the Zodiak," which begins the second section of the volume, concludes by defining the wisdom and the power that the traveler to the underground has brought back with her to the surface. It is the poet, says Atwood, the individual human initiated into the mysteries of life, who controls things. The constellations—those gargoyle-like mythical figures representing dark, primitive impulses—have come to life because "I breathed on them, named them:/now they are predictions" (29). But predictions alone, as we have seen, are not necessarily a pathway to happiness or wholeness. The clash between surface illusions and insight may be inexplicably frightening; and the techniques we develop to control fear and transform reality may be inadequate.

Such seems to be Atwood's predominant concern in "A Dialogue" (12–13), a poem earlier in the volume that offers a complex study of the netherworld evoked by dreams. Atwood opposes this dreamworld to a domestic kitchen scene where two sisters converse, the one attempting to contain her fears, the other drawing rigid geometric figures in what appears to be a futile attempt to recapture and control, through art, the visionary experience encountered in the dream. This attempt at artistic control is reflected in the poem's symmetrical structure: the outer world of waking reality—seven lines each at the beginning and the conclusion—surrounds four indented four-line stanzas that relate the two sisters' dreams. The dark revelations of the dreams are thus contained by the daylight world of rational discourse and commonplace events.

Atwood begins the poem by establishing biographical and psychological connections between the two sisters, providing a context that justifies their mutual exploration of the shared landscape they inhabit in their distinct yet somehow interdependent "recurring dreams." The mundane foreground of the poem is the space around the kitchen table where the two sisters speak to each other; the background is the isolated lake and island of their dreams; the middle distance, where foreground and background collide and a resolution of the conflicting sides of the dialogue is attempted, is the poem itself.

For the sister, the wilderness area that envelops her dream is a swampland, the time is night, and thus the vision is shadowy and frightful; it contains "things that live under the water," inherent dangers for the civilized mind nurtured on indoor plumbing and plastic rubber plants. By contrast, the speaker of the poem begins her dream in daylight, with clear skies intensifying the piercing bright greenness of living things. The danger here comes from without, from the machines of civilization ("a motor, a chain-/saw") that will invade the wilderness and destroy it to construct demonic and outwardly ordered yet essentially chaotic cities. The sister's dream emphasizes the fearful imaginings of the neophyte, as she sees only the dark side of the wilderness, its seeming danger enhanced by a feeling of entrapment: despite her desire to get away, she finds that "her feet won't move." For the seasoned traveler to the netherworld, however, the same scene presents a vital arena for life. She fully identifies with it and allows herself to be engulfed by it—both later in the dream when she sinks into the lake, and earlier when she describes with pleasure the implicitly painful, piercing green brightness that surrounds her.

An uncanny interpenetration of the two dreams occurs in the third indented stanza, as the sister's sleep-running body becomes part of the speaker's vision ("I passed her at evening"). There is an attempt at communication, a combining of the two dreams into some kind of resolution, as the speaker attempts to wake the sister but fails. Their perspectives differ too much, represent two ways of seeing that may touch but never yield to each other. For the speaker, submergence into "the dark lake" is a triumphant conclusion to a dream that has been marked by constant, energetic movement, both in time—from daylight to evening—and space. There is vitality in this movement, contrasted to the unmoving feet or the blind, circular, catatonic "running" of the sleeping sister, who fears the darkness and the swamp and who alternately hides her eyes or watches, passively and perhaps analytically, as the speaker—one of the fearful "things that live under the water"—sinks below its surface and merges with it.

The impression that the two sisters react in fundamentally different ways to the subterranean vision contained in the dream is intensified by Atwood's word choice. The analytic, examining mind of the sister causes her to have "watched" as the speaker descends, to see that event as a fact to be cataloged rather than to be engaged in herself. The speaker, on the other hand, "didn't notice/as the dark lake slipped over my head." The rationalizing faculty has disappeared as the speaker melts into the lake, joining "the reeds and lily-pads," a smile on her face indicating her total, unquestioning surrender to her fate. And that fate is not even something she thinks about not thinking about; so closely aligned with nature is she that she and the lake are one—it slips over her as an eyelid, unconsciously, might slip over an eye. The speaker's submergence becomes a mere circumstance of her existence. What she does not notice, "as" the lake slips over her head, is anything. Her not noticing, not examining, thus defines a condition of mind that reveals her total harmony with nature.

As we move back into the poem's outer frame, into the world of kitchen tables and mundane conversations, the speaker observes that relative calmness prevails. Some remnants of the dreamworld carry over into waking life: the sister still is characterized as rational, examining her separate fingers, trying perhaps, without success, to alleviate her fear. Her bitten hands reveal her anxiety. The connection between the speaker's waking world and her dream vision is more problematic. Atwood ends the poem with the speaker's drawing cryptic images, an attempt at control that seems somehow uncertain and unsatisfying: "I draw with a pencil,/covering the page with triangles/and grey geometrical flowers." The pencil is an ambiguous image. It suggests either a desire to erase what may well be unsatisfactory art or it is a medium that in fact allows erasure, permits therefore a more fluid, protean, unconstricting art. Even so, the speaker's images—geometric straight lines enclosing triangles and gray, colorless flowers—suggest a kind of art that is in fact restrictive and deadening. It is the difference, in Coleridge's poem, between Kubla Khan's stately measured pleasure dome and the dome built in air by the speaker's imagination: one enclosed, earthbound, and artificial; the other floating, amorphous, and free.

The ascent from the underground has not fully succeeded. The speaker can draw, but only artificially, creating images that resemble the geometric shapes contrived by land developers and their motors and chainsaws. As the speaker and her sister discuss their respective dreams around the kitchen table, the calm conversation reveals that the speaker is merely another human being, not a shaman "wrapped in an invisible/cloak" (25) bringing messages from below or within.

Of man and nature.   The relationship in "A Dialogue" between objects of art and the less esoteric structures of technocrats and engineers is not accidental. All man's inventive abilities derive from the same source, for Atwood, and all are attempts both to understand the mysteries of existence and to control them. A major portion of *Procedures for Underground* is devoted to the more mundane controls that humans exert over their environment. Like the aesthetic illusions of "Eden Is a Zoo," which constrict human experience rather than release its vital powers, the inventions of technology and of civilization reveal a gap between inner knowledge and the ability to apply that knowledge wisely. Fearing nature, we attempt to subvert its design and substitute our own. If we succeed, we destroy part of that design, the very source of our creative power; if we fail, we perceive our insignificance in the presence of a power infinitely larger than our own.

Both possibilities appear in "Two Gardens" (16–17), where the triangle-drawing artist of "A Dialogue" becomes the weed-pulling gardener attempting to control nature's fecundity. And, in her own way, she succeeds: "What stands in this garden/is there because I measured, placed, reached/down into the soil." Like the insane pioneer of *The Animals in That Country,* who attempted to impose abstract patterns of order on nature's organic design, the speaker here asserts her rational abilities to measure out space and cleanse it of weeds. What she has produced is lovely, but false, as Atwood's metaphors suggest: the "textured zinnias" feel like "fabric," the asters seem printed like "chintz," the marigolds resemble containers shaped by the potter's hand, and the sunflowers, "brilliant as/imitations," are too bright to be real. Nature's own garden, however, is real and overpoweringly lush. Its source is not merely the mundane summer soil. Always there, "outside the string borders" enclosing the carefully constructed human garden, this wilder growth offers strange things that emerge "without sunlight . . . their roots/in another land." They are composed of "mist" that quickly dissipates under the cold, objective scrutiny of merely human vision: "if you touch them, your/eyes go through them." Remove the human eye and, as in an epigraph to *The Journals of Susanna Moodie*, "every-/thing appears" ([7]).

Such an overwhelming vision is something we avoid, facing it when we must only with a fear that blinds us into multiplying the barriers and lashing out at the imagined enemy. In "Cyclops" (42–43) Atwood employs the image of the mythical one-eyed monster to suggest that man, in his fear of nature's dark revelations, may become a more frightful thing to nature's inhabitants than they could ever be to him. What transforms the camper in the poem into Cyclops is his flashlight, which paradoxically limits rather than extends his vision—"the flashlight/a single orange eye/unable to see what is beyond/the capsule of your dim/sight." The speaker, questioning the camper's motives in being in the forest—"Is it true you do not wish to hurt" the animals you fear?—challenges him to submerge himself completely in the darkness. If "you have no fear," she says, "take off your shoes then,/let your eyes go bare,/swim in their darkness as in a river/do not disguise/yourself in armour." To the animals, the camper—with his fragile barriers of flashlight, mosquito repellent, and shoes—is "giant and indefinable," an unnatural "chemical/smell" in the darkness. "In their monstrous night" he is "the hugest monster."

What the animals fear is developed in "Dreams of the Animals" (40–41) in which the barriers become veritable cages enclosing the foxes, armadillos, and iguanas that man has imprisoned. Removed from their natural habitat, these animals have lost their ability to "dream/of other animals   each/according to its kind." Such dreams, containing "meaningful/patterns," have given way to the silver fox's dreams of escape, to the armadillo's nondreams and waking madness, as it "runs/all day in figure eights," and to the iguana's "dreams of sawdust." Even the uncaged animals are affected by man's intervention, their dreams revealing "evil/in the form of soap and metal"—the soap that both cleanses and pollutes, the metal that both cages and kills.

Of man's material barriers to nature, none is more complete than that complex of structures we call "the city." Though it becomes a

wilderness of another sort, filled with its own special monsters hiding
in shadows, the city is our most deliberate attempt to build a fence
against the natural wildness that surrounds us. The speaker in "6
A.M., Boston, Summer Sublet" (33) rises "too early" from sleep one
day and sees through her cagelike "screened window/. . . the leaves
and roofs/of August in the gleaming pause/before dust." Atwood's
play on words—"dust" substituted for the evening's "dusk"—suggests a negative attitude about the daytime city. The shimmering
"rain . . ./in someone else's outdoor grill" shows that nature has asserted itself during the night and cleansed the city of its accumulated
dust and dirt, pollution that the new day, with its "faint smells/of
burning, motors beginning, broken glass," has already started to re-
deposit. Nevertheless, the city provides security for the speaker, who
sees the "windowsill" as a protective "border" between her apartment
and the "dawn mirage of/water" produced by the rain and the haze
of early morning hours. Before she reenters the city, her "mind" tests
"the outside like a foot/withdrawn," waiting to see whether nature
has receded and the water is safe.

Our alternate impulse is to escape this safety that is the city's trap.
In "Hypotheses: City" (36–37) the speaker wishes to leave "this fear
enclosing/me like rubber," wishes to "swim the city freely," and (in
imagery that recalls Emerson's "transparent eyeball") contemplates
total immersion: "What then/to be/the water/itself, the water all/
float in and none notice, to/be everywhere and nothing." A similar
idea of personal annihilation as an escape to nature is worked out in
"Fragments: Beach" (74–76), in which Atwood presents us with a
parable of city-building and its futility. The speaker acknowledges
that "we intrude"; nevertheless, "we arrange the beach, build/a drift-
wood hut out of the empty/huts . . . pack/barricades of sand." What
we have is a crypto-city, the beginnings of civilization, if you will,
in a grain of sand, the hut on the beach an embryonic structure of a
city landscape. But the sand refuses to be shaped. Blowing in the
wind, it "arranges us" instead. We become absorbed into nature's
particular cadences, enter the sea, and "are abolished," returning to
the shore as "washed/shells on the morning beach."

The idea that annihilation may be our final remedy, our only way
back to nature, is offered, too, in "The End of the World: Weekend,
Near Toronto" (32). Here city dwellers are on the highway heading
north out of Toronto in a massive weekend retreat. But Atwood
transforms this commonplace event into a more essential escape: "it

is the city moving,/the drivers intent on getting out, getting/away from something/they carry always with them." This something may be our human fears, our need to dominate and exert power, our self-destructive urges and aggressive drives, which Atwood notes in the image of "two cars which have collided/at a turn-off, and rest/quietly on their sides."

The problem with what we are, with what we have made ourselves into, is that we cannot escape; retreating from the city, we bring our civilization to the wilderness with us. We may return to a more harmonious relationship with nature, but again only in our quiet personal deaths or, as Atwood suggests at the conclusion of this poem, in a general cataclysm that calmly ends the world: "out of the blue sky and the white clouds/something is falling   falling/gently on them like invisible rain, or a blessing." Although Atwood presents the image of a cleansing rain here, it is rain of a different kind from that in "6 A.M., Boston, Summer Sublet." With its suggestion of radioactive fallout, the "invisible rain" offers the possibility that our very attempts to dominate nature will bring us back to it; our destructive technologies will have become a "blessing" in disguise.

A "miracle."   The end of the world is not finally, for Atwood, an appropriate solution. To be swallowed up, in death, by nature, is a surrender too complete. We cannot deny our mortality; but we can view it without despair. Recognizing the frailty of our necessary fictions, we can still build them. Such is the persona's realization as Atwood concludes the second section of the volume. In "84th Street, Edmonton" (52–53) the speaker carries two cans of paint through the sterile cityscape of Alberta's capital and contemplates the emptiness of her life. "The pain in my fingers," she says, "is/the only thing that's real." The other images she encounters are only "a tight surface covering/panic." Considering defeat, she says that "I could stop" and "disappear." Reconsidering, she sees hope, invokes "courage," and asserts that she "will build a history/in the backyard from solid/rocks." Thus she chooses to endure.

The book's final section continues this more optimistic tone. Here the "Chrysanthemums" that earlier (in "We Don't Like Reminders," 22) were emblems of decay become "a gift" of love, revealing not the sadness of death but those redemptive, "brilliant images the eyes/are said to see/the instant before drowning" (61). That frightening twilight edge between life and death, day and night, complacency and revelation remains a part of our existence, but now it is to be accepted and even celebrated for the fine intensity it provides. For the speaker of "Highest Altitude," "impermanence/makes the edges of things burn/brighter." We survive if we maintain our balance, "hold our eyes tight/to the line; the reference point/not the mountains but the moving/car, and each other" (56). Anchoring our lives in love provides, at least tentatively, a way of reconciling death and life's darker visions with the more immediate realities of everyday existence. It provides us with a home. In "Habitation" (60) Atwood comments on "marriage." It "is not/a house or even a tent," she says, not an enclosure at all. Rather it is "the edge of the forest, the edge/ of the desert . . . the edge of the receding glacier/where painfully and with wonder/at having survived even/this far/we are learning to make fire." And in making fire we both acknowledge and survive the cold.

To do both, preserve the things we love and recognize that preservation is futile, seems finally to be the essential role of the artist who has traveled to the underground. She becomes someone who denies nothing and affirms all. In "Woman Skating" (64–65) the cage-like paradise of "Eden Is a Zoo" becomes a poignant vision that complements rather than denies the mortality of the speaker's mother and her world. The poem opens with pleasing images of a woman "moving/in perfect circles" on a frozen "lake sunken among/cedar and black spruce hills." It is "late afternoon," and the diffused sun is nearing the horizon, bringing the day to its close and hinting at the scene's transience even as the poem's images sustain its beauty. The speaker acknowledges that this scene is at best a memory, perhaps an illusion: there is no lake, there are no hills, only an "outdoor skating rink/near the cemetery," surrounded by "streets of brown/brick houses" and "the park building." The woman moving with perfection in the pristine beauty of the countryside is "actually . . . my mother"; and "the snow banked around the rink/is grey with soot." This is reality; it cannot be denied. Yet the other vision is also true; it resides in the speaker's mind alongside the gray and immediate city. Memory or illusion—or merely a toy before the speaker's eyes, a "miniature human/figure balanced on steel/needles"—the skating woman is borne up by time, living through it, yet "circling" transcendently "above" it as well. For the speaker, who sees "the ice/as what it is, water," and "the months/as they are, the years/in sequence occurring/underfoot," the contradictory yet tensely sustained realities of a decaying city and a bucolic country scene become, in their ability to reside side by side, a "miracle": "Over all," she says, "I place/a glass bell." Though the bell may be an image of art enclosing life and denying the passage of time, Atwood's tone is affirmative here: her speaker acknowledges the passage of time and sees it as an integral part of the complete vision covered by the bell, which becomes less an enclosure and more a window to see the world. In place of the troubled questions of "Camera" and "Eden Is a Zoo" there is, at the end of this poem, a breathless and exhilarating sense of composure.

The final poem in the book, "Dancing Practice" (77–79), enhances this impression. The speaker and her friends, "feeling superior and younger," watch their parents awkwardly "practise their country dances." Soon "the record/will be over," the party will end, and "the clock hands" will whip around, speeding the memory of the dance into oblivion: "The dancers/will recede from us, be lost/among the thousands of things that once happened." The imperfect dance becomes a symbol for life, which eventually ends in death. The speaker acknowledges that fact, sees her own smug youth passing by as inexorably as the needle plays over the grooves of the record. Yet, she asserts, there is another realm, where "the dance itself, the way/it should have been, goes/on in a different/time." And it goes on, the speaker says, "because/I say it" does. The artist's wisdom and power to create, re-create, and transform reality reach an affirmative climax as Atwood concludes the poem and the volume in a rush of ever-shifting images tied to the rhythms of nature. No longer offering the discordant dance of the children in "The Circle Game," she describes a precise and perfect movement on "a green lawn," with music emerging—cosmically—"from everywhere." And though it is an ideal, transcendent vision, it is not an aesthetic cage. The green lawn may be a beach, with the sea ponderously ebbing and flowing onto the shore. It may be evening, or the sun may be rising. The vision may be permanent, but time is fluid. And there is constant alteration: "new feet," "changed hands," circles "breaking" and "forming" anew, "the whole/rhythm . . . transformed/for this moment/ always." Seen here in a new light, the cagelike circles of "The Circle Game" have become a device for transformation and renewal.

Chapter Three
The Bus to Alliston, Ontario

A More Public Voice

Atwood's first four major collections of poetry defined her essential vision during the first decade of her career; they dwelt on the private interior journey, the source of her poetic power. With the 1970s came both continuity and shifting emphasis, as Atwood asserted a tone both more sharply political and, alternately, more compassionate, humane, and affirmative. Having staked out her territory, she continued to exploit its key images, but in ways that coincided with changes in her personal relationships, with her role as public advocate of Canadian cultural nationalism, with her taking up residence on a farm near Alliston, Ontario, with her giving birth to her first child, and with her increasingly vital interest in political terrorism and torture, manifested by her affiliation with the worldwide human rights organization, Amnesty International. This varied and disharmonious mixture—of the joys of parenthood and the torments of political horror—may be a clue to the radical shifts in tone in her work during the 1970s and early 1980s: a reflection of an ever more compelling need to counter human brutality with a vision of hope and endurance, to see in the otherwise harsh milieu of *Power Politics,* for example, a "tenacity" in the human spirit that goes "beyond" futile assertions of "truth" that often serve merely as one more weapon of the hostile surrounding world.[1]

Power Politics

Procedures for Underground ends with a celebration of the artist's power to transform reality. Atwood—never content with simple or permanent solutions—investigates in her fifth collection of poems the more insidious implications of such manipulative skill. Published in 1971, *Power Politics* carries the reader through the agonies of two lovers caught in a drama of mutual exploitation and misunderstanding. Thus focusing on the decay of a romantic relationship, the volume has been seen, narrowly, as an autobiographical retelling of circumstances surrounding the eventual dissolution, in 1973, of Atwood's marriage to James Polk, an American writer she met at Harvard in 1962 and married in 1967.[2] Such interpretation, however, severely strains the book, whose rich texturing and varied themes extend well beyond its surface drama.

Despite its welcome reception by women, it is also more than a document of the women's movement. Atwood has observed that neither *Power Politics* nor her first novel, *The Edible Woman,* "was a product of what is commonly termed the Women's Movement. . . . I see both books as amplifications of themes that have been present in my work since I first started writing and publishing. To say this is not to disparage anyone's politics. It is merely to indicate that . . . being adopted is not, finally, the same as being born." Despite such disclaimers, *Power Politics* thrust upon its author the onus of being a general in the war between the sexes, "women greeting the book with recognition, men with fear," perceiving "it either as a display of perversity on my part or as an attack, a conspiracy, a war or an inhumane vivisection of Love, nasty and unfair as cutting up a puppy."[3]

Even read on the level of sexual politics, the collection defies easy categorization. Although its female persona certainly appears to be the victim of her lover's manipulation, it is also her own power to impose meaning on her relationship that preoccupies Atwood. In *Power Politics* Atwood asks the question she posed in a 1971 review of A. W. Purdy's *Love in a Burning Building:* whether it is "possible for men and women"—both—"to stop mythologizing, manipulating and attacking one another."[4]

"Please die . . . so I can write about it." The first section begins with the startling yet whimsical hook-and-eye epigram in which Atwood, through clever wordplay, transforms an innocent image of domestic activity into an act of violence. The epigram also establishes the sexual nature of the relationship between "you" and "I" (eye)—"you fit into me" (1)—and thus comments pungently on the violent nature of sexual love. The initial victim of this violence is the speaker, who attempts in the next poem ("He Reappears," 2) to engage the returning hero in friendly discourse: "Can't we/be friends I said." He chooses not to answer, however, and in the following poem merely takes her hand as they descend into an affair that transforms love into pollution or sickness: "I have to/peel you off me/in the form of smoke and melted/celluloid/Have to face it I'm/finally an addict." She feels that she is "suddenly in a bad movie," where "the smell of popcorn and worn plush/lingers for weeks" (3). In "He Is a Strange Biological Phenomenon" (8) the male lover becomes a "scavenger," who feeds "only on dead meat." He is "widespread/and bad for the garden,/hard to eradicate," moving "from place to place like a disease." Later (13) he leaves; and "nothing/remembers" him "but the bruises/on my thighs and the inside of my skull."

Atwood thus establishes the female as victim. But if the speaker is indeed the character whose "eye" is painfully "hooked," the metaphor is her own creation. Whatever power her lover holds is subordinate to the power of words and images that she as speaker controls. In "He Reappears" (2), for example, it is she who imagines him as mythic monster, shivering "cunningly," as he rises "from a snowbank/with three heads," his "six eyes" glowing "red." And her initial greeting, a hackneyed ploy designed to "hook" him into a relationship ("I said, haven't/I seen you somewhere before"), shows her as aggressor. Atwood thus reverses the traditional roles of male seducer and female victim, creating a female character who chooses to employ for her seduction the manipulative power of insipid clichés. In this context, the silence of the male may be a positive trait after all.

The speaker's powers of imagination (and manipulation) extend throughout the first section. When they argue about the mundane issue of "which of us will pay for your funeral" ("They Eat Out," 5), she asserts that "the real question is/whether or not I will make you immortal." Raising her "magic fork," she plunges it into his heart, producing a grotesque "pop" and "sizzle." He, in turn, rises up through his "own split head," glowingly transfigured into a Superman image ("blue tights and a red cape"), his "eyes flashing in unison" as "the ceiling opens" and "a voice sings Love Is A Many/Splendoured Thing." Through such grotesque and surreal special effects Atwood condemns the social and commercial myths we succumb to in our attempts to give intensity and meaning to our lives. Somehow these myths invoked by the speaker—these images of perfect, many-splendored love and of Kryptonian superheroes—are all empty. They fail to relieve the essential weariness of our lives: "The other diners regard you/some with awe, some only with boredom:/they cannot decide if you are a new weapon/or only a new advertisement." And, as Atwood's tone suggests, they hardly care. As for the speaker, she continues eating. Her powers exercised, she indifferently observes that "I liked you better the way you were."

More insidious than the physical control and transformative power she exerts over her lover is the speaker's detached, scientific viewpoint, which shrinks the male figure to mere object. "I approach this love," she says, "like a biologist/pulling on my rubber/gloves & white labcoat." She understands his fleeing her scrutiny, "like an escaped political/prisoner," yet she persists: "You held out your hand/ I took your fingerprints/You asked for love/I gave you only descriptions." He becomes, too, a device for the journalist, ghoulishly searching for stories: "Please die I said/so I can write about it" (10).

"This is the way it is." For all her power, real or imagined, the speaker is caught in circumstances that make both her and her lover victims of the same traps of history, biology, and culture that appear throughout Atwood's writings. She really cannot help seeing her lover as an object; he cannot help envisioning himself as a conquering hero; neither can avoid manipulating the other. In "You Want to Go Back" (9) the speaker reflects upon that time, long past, when "the sky was inside us/animals ran through us, our hands/ blessed and killed according to our/wisdom, death/made real blood come out." Evolution, she sardonically observes, has "improved" us, made "our heads float/several inches above our necks" and filled "our bodies/. . . with billions/of soft pink numbers/multiplying and analyzing/themselves."

Love, under such circumstances, has become a matter of grids and efficiency: "I love you," she says, "by/sections and when you work" (9). And life generally has become a sequence of standard roles and futile gestures. Her "beautiful wooden leader" (7), with his "heartful of medals," sits "magnificent" on his "wooden horse," heroic. Deflating that heroism, the speaker observes that, as he points with his "fringed hand," his troops "all/ride off in the other direction." Caught in his self-conceived heroic stance, part of his "struggle to become real," he neglects the utter unreality of his posture. The speaker, earlier, experiences much the same problem, with similar results. She asks, of the "bad movie" that has become her life, "why am I fascinated." Here, too, "other people are leaving"; yet, caught in her own fantasy, she always stays "till the end." Having paid her money, she wants "to see what happens" (3).

What happens is her recognition that the self-inflicted cruelties of such a life may be all we can hope to achieve. "This is the way it is," she says, "get used to it" (9). The violence implicit in these words is less a threat than a cynical recognition of our inability to prevail, our

inability to do much more than merely survive. In our private relationships, which endure without vitality or purpose, we sit apart
from one another, or we engage in sex that has become "the agony in
the guest/bedroom" (6). In the final poem of the section the speaker
acknowledges this failure as she describes herself and her lover warily
staring at each other in bewilderment or distrust. "We will never
know/each other," she insists, "any better/than we do now" (14).

   "Power games, power struggles." The uncertainties of section 1 continue in the middle portion of the volume. Here Atwood
expands the implications of our private wars, relating them directly
to the overt violence of the public world. "So many of the things we
do" privately, she has observed, "are simply duplications of the external world of power games, power struggles."⁵ The surreal violence
of the speaker's mental scenarios becomes all too real in these public
struggles, in the tactics of tree-killing enemies of the environment,
freedom-suppressing, tyrannical leaders, and button-pressing, world-
weary fanatics whose fingers determine whether we live or die in nu-
clear holocaust. The speaker, in this realm of external power plays, is
more feeble. In the section's introductory epigram (15) she says to her
lover, "Imperialist, keep off/the trees," but she finds her mere words
to be of "no use: you walk backwards,/admiring your own footprints." His footprints, supposed marks of immortality and significance, blind him to the destruction he has caused, blind him as well
to the futility of his striving for immortality. The speaker, nevertheless, feels conquered. "Let's go back please," she says in "Small Tactics," back "to the games, they were/more fun and less painful" (17).

   As her lover is transformed, in the speaker's mind, to a tyrant, his
silences become more pervasive, more dangerous: "We hear nothing
these days," she observes, "from the ones in power." Sheer force,
when it is employed, destroys even the ability of language to create
alternate and perhaps more pleasant realities: "Why talk when you
are/helmeted with numbers," why talk when you are a fist? "A fist
knows what it can do/without the nuisance of speaking," she says,
"it grabs and smashes," proclaiming that "language . . . is for the
weak only" (31).

   The speaker recognizes that she cannot help her lover very much,
sees that her powers are limited ("you'll outlive/even my distortions
of you," she says to him). Far from being a three-headed monster or
a Superman, he is "after all . . . quite/ordinary" (16). Yet, spurning
his commonplace, ordinary self, he willingly takes on the identities,

defined by others, that give him power. "You refuse to own/your-self," the speaker tells him, "you permit/others to do it for you." Denying his essential self, dividing himself against himself, accepting clothes that measure (as Thoreau would have it) not his depths but his surfaces, the lover becomes "slowly more public," less clearly defined. "In a year," the speaker observes, "there will be nothing left/ of you but a megaphone." And he dissolves into the gray mass of the bureaucratic, aggressive, power-hungry, corporate elite. No longer attaining even the colorful status of comic-book hero rising gloriously to the rafters, he now descends back "through the roof/with the spurious authority of a/government official." In more private terms, his kiss is "no longer literature/but . . . a set of instructions." He can choose an alternative scenario, he can "deny these uniforms" and "repossess" himself. But in a world where "it is no longer possible/to be both human and alive," his "death will be sooner" (30).

Even these "uniforms," of course, cannot guarantee immortality. They do provide a spurious dignity, and they do shield us from pain by allowing us to "cauterize" our "senses"; but they also bring us into confrontations with a reality whose effects we cannot escape. "You did it," the speaker says to her lover: "it was you who started the countdown." And "it was you," she adds, "whose skin/fell off bubbling/all at once when the fence/accidentally touched you." The destruction that Atwood here invokes thus envelops both the creator of the holocaust and the other victims over whom he wishes to exert his power. Not only for others, but also for himself, he attempts "merely power" and accomplishes "merely suffering" (32).

"Allow me to touch you."   Playing out his traditional role of silent hero involves more than self-destructive assertions of power over others. Atwood sees the traditional myth of the crusading warrior as a major obstacle toward becoming human, in the private as well as public arena. It forces the man into physical and spiritual journeys that both isolate him from the speaker and contribute to his death; and it keeps the woman in her traditional supporting role of patient wife, passive sufferer, waiting at home for her warrior to return.

In a parable (28–29) of these respective roles as manifested in distant past, present, and not-so-distant future, Atwood shows how our technological accomplishments have accelerated the inevitable moment of death, changed it from a temporally and spatially distant happening to an immediate event. "At first," the speaker says "I was

given centuries/to wait in caves, in leather/tents, knowing you
would never come back." As the ages pass, and the devices of human
destruction become more efficient, "it speeded up: only/several years
between/the day you jangled off/. . . and the day . . . I rose . . . at
the messenger's entrance." From several years ("that happened twice,
or was it/more"), to only "a good eight months," to "at least three
weeks before/I got the telegram and could start regretting"—Atwood
contracts the time between departure and death to intensify the shock
of the human march toward better machines of war. The final two
stanzas bring the poem to its climax. Now, "there are only seconds
. . . and I can scarcely kiss you goodbye/before you run out into the
street and they shoot." What is interesting about this final stanza is
that, ever so subtly, it suggests the speaker's complicity—not only in
her blasé acceptance of the inevitable (a tone, undercutting the violence, produced by Atwood's restrained language), but also in the
Judas-kiss she wishes to place on her doomed lover. Having accepted
her passive role, having consented to the myth, she automatically involves him too. If women and men are to be released from their ancient roles, Atwood suggests, then men and women—both—must
break the chains.

The section ends with a plea for openness and understanding. The
public gestures of power that have defined the lover's actions toward
the speaker—and hers toward him—are portrayed, in one poem, as
a shield covering and constricting his emotions. "Believe me," the
speaker says, "allow/me to touch you/gently, it may be the last/
time." He still pulls away, however, his silence an affliction as much
as an act of will: "there is something in your throat that wants/to get
out and you won't let it" (34). Earlier, in "Small Tactics," the
speaker has asked to be like him, "closed and useful" (19). Here she
recognizes the life-denying suffocation of such a posture.

In the section's final poem, "They Are Hostile Nations" (37–38),
the speaker sees nature's being obliterated by man's domination and
foretells the possible end of the world. Animals are disappearing,
"the sea" is "clogging," and "the air" is "nearing extinction." An ice
age seems to be approaching: "It is cold and getting colder." We
must, the speaker says, gather ourselves together to face a world
emptied of all the supposed truths that call for strategies of power
politics. Alone in a barren world, we have only each other. And so
"we should be kind, we should/take warning, we should forgive each
other." Old habits die slowly, however, and the speaker finds that

she and her lover still "touch as though attacking," still bring "gifts" that "warp in our hands to/implements, to manoeuvres." She observes that, in the snow-swept "dormant field" where they stand alone, "there are no armies" to command; and "surviving/is the only war/we can afford." Peace may come, she says, "if we can only/make it as far as/the (possibly) last summer." The peaceable kingdom she is appealing for is a questionable one; there is no clear indication that her lover will join her in kindness and in trust; and it may be that survival will last only a short time, as the earth and all on it succumb after a glorious final summer. But, like the tenacious cactus of the previous poem (36), she seems to be saying, we ought, in the face of such danger and possibly because of it, do the best we can.

"**Returning from the dead.**" The third section of *Power Politics* returns to Atwood's typically ambivalent consideration of death, of submergence into nature, of the journey into the underground side of the human soul. An epigram (39) states the problem succinctly:

> Returning from the dead
> used to be something I did well
>
> I began asking why
> I began forgetting how

We have gone beyond the battle between the speaker and her lover. He seems no longer present as an antagonist. And she seems no longer present as an individual undergoing the torments of a torturous love affair. The supposed "last summer" has come and gone, winter has effaced life on the earth, and spring has miraculously returned. Yet the speaker, now all humanity, questions her rebirth, hesitates, appears unwilling to accept the natural cycle of seasonal birth, growth, dissolution, death, and regeneration. In the next poem (40) it is "spring again," yet the speaker wonders whether she can "stand it/shooting its needles into/the earth, my head, both/used to darkness." "Darkness" implies death, but also it implies a freedom from the pain of life and subsequent death that rebirth will inevitably bring with it.

Opposed to such deathly darkness is light and life-giving water, which the speaker believes her lover can offer her. Like the speaker, he has been transformed in this third section. He appears to be an emissary—an imperfect one to be sure—tentatively guiding her back to a proper relationship with the earth, transporting her through

what we have come to know in Atwood's world as an underground
realm filled with supernatural wisdom. Yet even as she craves his gift
of "moonlight smooth as/wind, long hairs of water," and even as she
appeals for his help, she holds "back/Not ready" (40).

In "Hesitations Outside the Door" (48–51) Atwood scrutinizes the
speaker's motives for her erratic behavior and her shifting evasions of
reality. "I'm telling the wrong lies," she says, "they are not even useful." As creator of the games that constitute *Power Politics,* she could
invent "lies" that "would at least/be keys" to "open the door" which
is now "closed." But the speaker wishes not to relinquish her power
or the identity that her fictions provide her: she says, "If I wait outside" the door, "I can salvage/this house . . . I can keep/my candles,
my dead uncles/my restrictions." These material tokens of a life un-
burdened by explorations into the depths of the spirit comfort the
speaker, who is able to fabricate ever more complex strategies of
avoidance. In the poem's second part she observes of the closed door
facing her that "I could go in if I wanted to,/that's not the point, I
don't have time."

Time, however, is exactly what she fears, as she attempts to subvert its inexorable movement by inventing "alternate versions" of her
relationship with her beloved, who is at one time a Christlike figure
sporting on his "head a crown/of shining blood," beckoning her to
join him beyond the door, and at another time a destroying angel
who advances "through the grey streets of this house," annihilating
the walls of resistance she constructs. She realizes his attacks on her
are projections of her own entrapment of him. "Don't let me do this
to you," she says, "you are not those other people,/you are yourself."
Offering him his freedom, she tells him to forsake "this love/which
does not fit you," to leave this house "while you still can." Her seeming compassion, her relinquishment of her power over him, is, of
course, also an evasion, a tactic for avoiding a confrontation with
whatever sits beyond the closed door. Summing up the strategy, she
notes that "if we make stories for each other/about what is in the
room/we will never have to go in."

The book's movement accelerates in the next two poems as the
speaker again momentarily succumbs and, though resisting, enters a
fantastic realm in which the beloved has again taken on the role of
guide to an ecstatic inner reality. Pushing him away as he lies beside
her, she proclaims that "this is not something I/wanted," yet she
perceives also the spiritual invigoration of the sphere to which she is

being transported—"so far/up, the sky incredible and dark/blue, each breath/a gift in the steep air." The beloved is no longer clearly human; he has left behind the restrictions, excuses, and fears of humanity to accept a freedom which she, still fearful, does not "know how to accept." As he lies asleep, seeing "what there is" beyond consciousness, she decides to "bend and enter" (52). What she discovers, in the next poem (53), is the corridor that connects her with the earth's past: "you smell of tunnels," she says, "you smell of too much time." The beloved, having himself been absorbed by the earth, now rises above the speaker to absorb her as well: "you descend on me like age/you descend on me like earth."

Though she regrets the state she is in ("I should have used leaves/ and silver to prevent you"), the speaker knows that the journey she has embarked upon is one that she has "summoned" upon herself. She understands her position more clearly now. Though she refuses, finally, to relinquish her powers, she realizes they are limited. "The sea," she says to her no-longer-listening lover in the next poem, "is on your side/You have the earth's nets/I have only a pair of scissors." Hers are the destructively analytic powers of separation and exclusion; his are the fluid powers of transcendent unity, of synthesis, of "water or moving shadow" (54).

In the penultimate poem of the collection Atwood summarizes the weaknesses of her persona's position. The speaker sees that all the disguises she foisted upon her lover were "inaccurate." These are now "peeling away from" him "in scales." She observes that he both "helped" her create these fictions and "enjoyed it," but that she was primarily to blame. Now, however, "neither of us will enjoy/the rest." He will follow her "down streets" and "hallways," yet he will melt when she touches him, "avoiding the sleeves of the bargains/I hold out for you,/your face corroded by truth." He wishes her to join him in a free, ecstatic relationship, asking her "like the wind, again and again and/wordlessly, for the one forbidden thing:/love without mirrors and not for/my reasons but your own" (55). She, however, cannot assent, cannot yield her own reasons, her own fictions, her words and distortions that safely encircle the chaotic freedoms he offers.

The final poem, "He Is Last Seen" (56), poignantly expresses the ultimate futility of the speaker's refusal. She is able, for the moment, to hold her lover off; even so, he walks toward her "carrying a new death/which is mine and no-one else's." Whatever her fictions, nature will eventually claim and enfold her in a death that "is curved, . . . the shape/of doorknobs, moons/glass paperweights." The angular rhythms of human reason cannot conquer the curved cadences of nature that, like doorknobs, open the way to endless vision and, like moons over a barren landscape, brighten the darkness. As he walks inexorably toward her, she realizes that her powers are gone: "Nothing I can do will slow you/down, nothing/will make you arrive any sooner." He is "serious, a gift-bearer," setting his "one foot/ in front of the other," traveling through torments of time and space toward eventual achievement, "towards firm ground and safety."

Power Politics thus ends, as do Atwood's other collections, on a note of ambiguous triumph and potential harmony between nature and humanity. The possibility of our creating new relationships, free from the stifling mythologies we carry with us, is clearly evoked. But it is only a possibility, and one singularly ambiguous image in this final poem suggests either the difficulty of the journey or Atwood's failure to control the metaphors by which she offers her vision. The glass paperweight—with its "snow and lethal/flakes of gold . . . endlessly" falling "over an ornamental scene,/a man and woman, hands joined and running"—is ostensibly an emblem of the gift of death offered by the speaker's lover. It presents an image of ecstatic union: man and woman, hands together, running with joyous affirmation through nature's "lethal," death-bearing flakes of snow. Yet the paperweight, for all its curved shape, is also an emblem of conventional love, defined by those confining roles and power strategies that one must escape. It is a glass-enclosed, artificial environment; and it differs, for example, from a more vital image of joined hands that Atwood offers in her 1978 volume, *Two-Headed Poems*.

Poetry or polemic? For all the emotional power of the final poem, then, and for all the aphoristic cleverness that pops sharply up from pages throughout the volume, Atwood's achievement in *Power Politics* may be a limited one, both technically and emotionally. At the time of its publication its evocation of women's movement ideology helped it achieve a notoriety that contributed to Atwood's stature as a recognized literary figure. But some of its readers were dubious about its artistic quality and its emotional range. One reviewer, doubtless oversimplifying Atwood's philosophic position, saw the book as merely a cruel and "self-defeating" attack on men and questioned whether what Atwood had written was poetry or "polemic." Another writer, giving Atwood more credit, still felt that "we are left with a desolating sense of futility, or at best, the nagging hope that the whole thing is a deliberate exercise in poetic control [that] leaves us with a very lopsided vision. . . . What about compassion, humour, kindness?"[6] It may well be true that Atwood's particularly tight-lipped, cold-blooded scrutiny of a hostile world in this volume excludes an entire universe of emotions. Patterned after *The Journals of Susanna Moodie* in its presentation of a coherent drama, *Power Politics* also parallels that earlier volume in the intensity of its underlying pessimism.

You Are Happy and *Selected Poems*

The first poem in *You Are Happy* continues both the tone and the subject matter of *Power Politics*. Presented with a "Newsreel: Man and Firing Squad," we see once again the results of our public and private power struggles: the "botched job," the "serpents of blood jerked from the wrists," the "shattered faces."[7] Yet, arriving on the scene three years after *Power Politics,* this 1974 volume both builds upon the more affirmative features of Atwood's earlier work and carries her poetic art in significantly new directions. More fully than the previous volume, *You Are Happy* attempts to put to rest the myth-making powers and the stereotyped predictions that create such human havoc; and it reveals those more vital responses to life that may indeed make us happy and whole. Atwood's title poem may be deceptive, since it speaks of happiness as the consequence of concentrated pain or of numbness; but even this potentially bitter interpretation, coming early in the volume, is by the end of the book transformed into an unquestionably affirmative vision that accepts pain as a necessary component of being alive.

The volume includes, for the first time in Atwood's repertoire, several prose poems that seem to allow her to comment, with more precision, on the conflicting truths offered by reality and myth. Structurally, the volume conforms to her earlier collections, providing what is essentially a three-part organization: "You Are Happy," the first section, presents the political struggles, public and private, that degrade our lives; two middle segments, "Songs of the Transformed" and "Circe/Mud Poems," derive from Homer's *Odyssey* and comment on the mythical substructure underlying our political and personal behavior; and "There is Only One of Everything" offers a formula for renouncing this mythology and becoming mortal.

"**We might be happy.**"   The first section contends with the
fictions we employ to order our lives and the failures we encounter in
that pursuit. Ostensibly an affirmation of the happiness we may
achieve, the final poem of this section, "You Are Happy" (28), offers
instead a picture of alienation, of distinct individuals walking "sepa-
rately/along the hill to the open/beach." It is a wintry scene that the
speaker describes, one that both numbs the mind and pierces the
flesh, producing a happiness that is built, apparently, on an emotional void:

> When you are this
> cold you can think about
> nothing but the cold, the images
>
> hitting into your eyes
> like needles, crystals, you are happy.

The needle-like pain evoked by these lines may be an essential part
of a truly vital life. But surrounded as it is by images of mind-numb-
ing cold, separateness, and grotesque mutilation ("in the ditch a
deer/carcass, no head"), the assertion of happiness seems insincere.
The words proclaim that emotion, but they are words only, detached
from reality, and subject to the same misinterpretation that appears
in the first poem, where the characters' agonized bodies and "shattered faces retreat." "We might be/happy," says the persona, "from
a distance we could be dancing" (9). It is this distance and subsequent distortion—created by all our evasions—that the poems of *You
Are Happy* attempt to dispel.

The problem is broached in "Chaos Poem" (12–14), in which the
speaker returns to an empty house, her lover having left her. Wishing
not to confront pain, she lies "on the mattress," rehearsing "the polite and terrible slogans/by which we live"; and she washes her hair,
playing out a ritual that gives her "the illusion of safety." Atwood
carries this metaphor-building, life-deadening process to an extreme
in "Tricks With Mirrors" (24–27), a witty, pun-filled poem that
evokes the myth of Narcissus and warns of the dangers of love turned
inward upon the self. Here the speaker of "Chaos Poem" becomes the
inanimate mirror of the self, evading the torments of exposure to another person: "You are suspended in me," says the speaker to her
lover, "beautiful and frozen, I/preserve you, in me you are safe."

This poem thus returns to one more metaphor for the "hard marble" and "carven word" of *Double Persephone*. Frozen permanence may be fine and "flawless," the speaker notes, but it is also "reversed," also a distortion. Surrounding the mirror, she observes, there is a "frame" that "does not reflect you," but has "reflections"—contemplations—"of its own." "Think about the frame," she warns, "it is important." It contains the emotions that she has suppressed in transforming herself into a mirror: "Don't assume it is passive/or easy, this clarity/with which I give you yourself," she says to her lover; "consider what restraint it/takes: breath withheld, no anger/or joy disturbing the surface." And, transforming the metaphor once more, the speaker confesses, "this is not a mirror,/it is a door/I am trapped behind." She calls on her lover to "say the releasing word," the one that will "open the wall." But he, not responding, merely continues to stare into the mirror and comb his hair. In a final, darkly humorous attack on the lover's blindness the speaker-mirror justifies her earlier assertion that "mirrors are crafty":

> You don't like these metaphors.
> All right:
>
> Perhaps I am not a mirror.
> Perhaps I am a pool.
>
> Think about pools.
> [27]

The poem thus ends, alluding to the fate of Narcissus, who, peering obsessively into the pool that reflected his mirror-like yet insubstantial image, pined away with self-love and died.

"Within range of my words." Narcissus was transformed into the flower that bears his name. In the second section of *You Are Happy*, "Songs of the Transformed," we hear from others whose identities have been altered, either by the goddess Circe—who, in Homer's *Odyssey*, transformed half of Ulysses' crew into pigs—or by some other force. These are songs of victims—victims of others and of themselves. The speaker of "Bull Song," for example, asks "who brought me here"; but he also acknowledges that his fate was self-imposed, "a mistake, to have shut myself/in this cask skin" (31). They are songs, moreover, of creatures able to educate or entrap those who listen to them.

"Siren Song" (38–39), in particular, suggests the power of words to create a compelling and dangerous distortion of reality, through a chronically repeated story that in a perversely humorous way "is irresistible." The poem proceeds in three sections that deviously enmesh the reader in its trap, ironically revealing its trickery even as it obscures its intent. In so doing, the poem becomes a paradigm for our inability to break free of the patterns that control and deaden our existence; it becomes a description of the process that impels us to fulfill a fate we had no intention of pursuing, even as we see where the process is leading us.

At its beginning, the poem seems an objective description of the duplicitous nature of the siren's song, one "that forces men/to leap overboard in squadrons/even though they see the beached skulls." These "skulls," the warning words of the song itself, continue as the speaker notes it is a "song nobody knows/because anyone who has heard it/is dead." Playing upon the egocentric sense of self-importance that we all individually feel, the siren next appeals to her newest victim's altruism and his belief that he is somehow different. She complains that she does not enjoy her sorcery, and promises to tell the secret of her song, if he will free her:

> I will tell the secret to you,
> to you, only to you.
> Come closer. This song
>
> is a cry for help: Help me!
> Only you, only you can,
> you are unique
> [39]

The lulling repetitions of the song serve their purpose: abruptly and with a comic twist reminiscent of the hook-and-eye epigram in *Power Politics,* the poem dissolves into a scene containing a siren who is, "at last," once more alone. "Alas," she says, "it is a boring song/but it works every time." And it works not simply because of the witty confidence with which the siren lures her prey. Equally significant is her victim's inability to perceive the truth of the words she is speaking. To be warned and yet to persist: thus does Atwood reveal the grim absurdity of the traps into which we allow ourselves to fall.

If language is thus a weapon, it is also a necessity for human growth, a medium for change, a way of articulating a reality that transcends the predictable archetypes that constrain our lives. In "Corpse Song" (43–44) the speaker enters "your night/like a darkened boat" to "bring you something/you do not want." This unwelcome "something" is "news of the country/I am trapped in,/news of your future." The corpse-speaker observes that "soon you will have no voice," and he admonishes the listener to "sing now/while you have the choice . . . or you will drift as I do . . . swollen with words you never said,/swollen with hoarded love." Dangerous though words may be, without them we are bereft of life and love. As the boat which is both the corpse and ourselves glides across the pages into the first of the "Circe/Mud Poems," Atwood begins to explore most fully this major theme of the volume. *"You move within range of my words,"* says Circe to the listener, *"you land on the dry shore/You find what there is"* (46). What there is may be the distortions of myth, the words becoming a weapon and we their target. Or what there is may be a more vital reality.

Circe and Ulysses. The "Circe/Mud Poems" continue as Circe initiates a discussion of the grotesque distortions created by myth and of her responsibility for these transformations. "Men with the heads of eagles," she says, "no longer interest me/or pig-men, or"—in an allusion to Icarus—"those who can fly/with the aid of wax and feathers." Concluding the list of creatures she is renouncing, she observes that they are "common as flies," clumsy, and boring, as well as useless: "on hot days you can watch them/as they melt, come apart,/fall into the ocean." It is those who have not succumbed to "these/mythologies" that Circe is now searching for, "the others,/the ones left over," who "have real faces and hands" (47).

But who is responsible for those who have been grotesquely transformed? Not I, says Circe in the next poem (48); "it was not my fault, these animals/who once were lovers." She does have the power to effect these transformations, but here it is more an act of omission that is at fault. These transformations, she says, simply "happened": "I did not say anything, I sat/and watched, they happened/because I did not say anything." Having withheld the words that would save these men from their predictable fate, Circe protests perhaps insincerely that it was not her fault. Yet she regrets "these drying skeletons/that . . . litter the ground," these bodies that, like the "beached skulls" of "Siren Song," have become "these/wrecked words."

To clarify her position, Circe explains in the first prose poem (49)

that her role as a keeper of language is a difficult one. She speaks of
the visitors to her island, those who come with their grotesquely dis-
jointed bodies and spirits to be healed by her power. "They offer me
their pain," she says, "hoping in return for a word, a word, any word
from those they have assaulted daily, with shovels, axes, electric
saws, the silent ones, the ones they accused of being silent because
they would not speak in the received language." Having renounced
all but the "received" and predictable words of myth and technology,
the words they have used as weapons, and having suffered for the pain
they caused others, the "suppliants" now wish to hear the words of
those they refused to listen to before, the words of healing and for-
giveness. But those words are few: "I spend my days," Circe says,
"with my head pressed to the earth, to stones, to shrubs, collecting
the few muted syllables left over; in the evenings I dispense them, a
letter at a time, trying to be fair."

Into this context of two languages, of two ways of viewing reality,
and of Circe's somewhat limited powers as seer and sorceress, comes
Ulysses. Then begins a retelling of *The Odyssey* from Circe's point of
view. Circe questions both Ulysses' motives and the predictable scenario in which the words of *The Odyssey* and his own heroic gestures
have trapped him. In the first poem of this sequence (50) Circe insists
that Ulysses take responsibility for his own fate. "I made no choice,"
she says, "I decided nothing"; and, in words that both mock Ulysses'
pretensions and scorn the banality of his journey, she asserts:

> One day you simply appeared in your stupid boat,
> your killer's hands, your disjointed body, jagged
>   as a shipwreck,
> skinny-ribbed, blue-eyed, scorched, thirsty, the usual,
> pretending to be—what? a survivor?

In the next poem (51) Circe questions Ulysses' inability to break free
of the preordained journey which he passively accepts: "There must
be more for you to do/than permit yourself to be shoved/. . . from
coast/to coast to coast." She invites him to ask at her "temples" for
news of a different fate, "a future you won't believe in." And she debunks the ritual behavior he is locked into:

> Don't you get tired of killing
> those whose deaths have been predicted
> and are therefore dead already?

> Don't you get tired of wanting
> to live forever?
>
> Don't you get tired of saying Onward?

In the prose poem that follows (52) Circe attempts to draw Ulysses out of the patterns of the past that control the events of the future. Explaining why she is "not describing the landscape for" him, she points out the obvious: "You live here, don't you? Right now I mean. See for yourself." Admonishing him to rely upon his own resources, to perceive things firsthand rather than through the distortions of myth, she is also insisting that he become alive, that he live "right now" in the present, freed of the constraints of both past and future and of the language that imposes those constraints upon him.

In the next eight poems Circe tries to make Ulysses human, that both may escape the fate that traps her on her island, sends him off on ritual journeys, and alienates them from each other. Wanting his love, she is willing to relinquish her powers—of artist, manipulator of reality, and word-maker—to achieve it. Accepting his greed ("you know how to take"), she gives him everything of hers that he desires, pronouncing for him the words that make them real ("This is mine, this/tree, I give you its name," 54). She yields herself to his violent "extortion," as he forces her "body to confess/too fast and/incompletely, its words/tongueless and broken" (55). The love they achieve thus regresses once more to the narcissistic circle games of Atwood's earlier mirror images: "Look at me," Circe says to Ulysses, "and see your reflection" (56).

Having become the passive object of Ulysses' desires, Circe ironically can no longer transform him from the mythic pasteboard figure he is. "The fist," her amulet of power, "withered and strung/on a chain around my neck," decrees Ulysses' transformation; but "the dead fingers mutter/against each other," striving inconsequentially against Ulysses, who is somehow "protected." "The first stutters"—loses its power to give words to its decree—and "gives up." Ulysses is now in control, unbuckling "the fingers of the fist" and ordering Circe "to trust" him (57). Their love, however, has become a grotesque, because one-dimensional, affair. Ulysses achieves his physical desires and hers as well, but in a way that excludes the more complete relationship Circe wishes. As she ambiguously says of Ulysses' "flawed body" in the last of these several poems, "this is not what I want/but I want this also" (60).

The prose poem that follows (61) elaborates on the passive mud woman that Ulysses is forcing Circe to become. Circe tells a story of a traveler who "constructed a woman out of mud," to whom he and another boy made love "when the sun had warmed her . . . , sinking with ecstacy into her soft moist belly." It was a "perfect" love, he said, and "no woman since then has equalled her." Scorning this vision of perfect, passive, uncomplicated, narcissistic love, Circe asks, "Is this what you would like me to be, this mud woman? Is this what I would like to be? It would be so simple." It would also be an evasion of human complexity; and it is not enough. Two poems later, Circe rebels: "I don't have to take/anything you throw into me. . . . Get out of here" (63).

With this rejection by Circe, and the failure of a more natural, unmythic existence that it implies, Ulysses is thrust back into the predictable fate of *The Odyssey*. "It is not finished, that saga," Circe tries to warn him; but she knows he "will not listen" (64). She notes (68) that "it's the story that counts. No use telling me this isn't a story." Still wishing for alternatives, she worries "about the future" and about her own fate: in *The Odyssey*, the given story with its words of prediction, "the boat disappears one day over the horizon, just disappears, and it doesn't say what happens then. On the island that is." She wonders whether she is "really immortal," and she asks whether, when he leaves, he will return to her the magical words she has yielded to him. "Don't evade," she insists, "don't pretend you won't leave after all: you leave in the story and the story is ruthless."

The concluding poem (69–70) of "Circe/Mud Poems" comments on the two ways of looking at the world, recalling images of islands that extend throughout *You Are Happy* and that appear as early as *The Circle Game*. But here, the *"two islands"*—two visions of reality, two individuals isolated from each other, two kinds of love or immortality—*"do not exclude each other."* The first island is the locale of received myth—the "ruthless" story—where *"the events run themselves through/ almost without us."* It is predictable and boring, repeating itself endlessly like a silent film, a Chaplinesque comedy—*"jerkier this time and faster, . . . it goes and goes,/I could recite it backwards."* The second island is unknown, *"because it has never happened."* Nothing is *"finished,"* nothing carved in icy permanence for all time. Recasting the images of "You Are Happy," Circe imagines two lovers, this time walking truly together, licking *"the melted snow/from each other's mouths,"* and seeing a season not yet in the icy grip of an intractable winter. Instead of a solid stream and a deer's mutilated carcass, they see *"a stream, not frozen yet, in the mud/beside it the track of a deer."* Thus ends the "Circe/Mud Poems" section of the volume, with the image of a predictable and ruthless story transformed into something not yet formed, something capable of metamorphosis into anything one may happily imagine.

"**To take that risk.**" "There is Only One of Everything," the volume's final section, elaborates on this freer, unformed vision, beginning in "First Prayer" (72–73) with an invocation that we "not forget our bodies . . . in favour of word games or jigsaw puzzles." The speaker is here admonishing us not to continue the spirit/body dichotomy that has split us into grotesque and mutilated beings. In a theme she asserts yet more fully in her next volume, *Two-Headed Poems,* Atwood thus proposes a Whitmanesque synthesis necessary for a happy and whole life—neither the body nor the soul alone, but both together. Calling not upon the muse for inspiration, the speaker invokes rather her "body," asking it to "descend/from the wall where I have nailed you," and pleading that it "let me inhabit you, have compassion on me/once more, give me this day." What she wishes is not that this god-body give her this day her daily bread, but indeed that it provide her with her daily life, "this day" itself. As she says in "Is/Not" (74–76), addressing herself now to her lover, "permit me the present tense." Renouncing "predictions," acknowledging the commonplace and unheroic stature of their lives ("we're stuck here . . . where there is nothing spectacular/to see and the weather is ordinary"), she sees yet (in "Head Against White," 87–91) the difficulty of escaping completely the rituals by which we define our lives. *"Break it,"* she pleads with her lover, *"Break/it.* Geology wins. The layer/of trite histories presses you down,/monotony of stone. Oval frame." The need is "to move beyond the mirror's edge," and "to pronounce" one's "own flesh," to float "up through/the softening white rock/like a carved long-buried god," to cease being the received word of myth and become instead a "revealed word," the precursor of a new order, a more vital reality.

The final three poems of the volume shift from questions to answers, uncertain as always, but emotionally compelling nevertheless. The title poem (92) of this section begins with a belief that there is indeed "only one of everything," a world in which "the tree/we saw . . . will never exist . . . like that again," a world in which "there will/have to be other words," a world in which the received "lan-

guage vanishes" when the speaker's "eyes close." The speaker has
moved from being "unable to say how much I want you/unable even
to say/I am unable" ("Four Evasions," 77). Now, looking at her lover
as he dances quietly by himself in the commonplace "winter
kitchen," "delighted" with life, waving a "spoon . . . in one
hand"—an image of simple joy, however fragile, achieved—now, she
"can even say it,/though only once and it won't/last: I want this, I
want/this."

"Late August" (93) plunges us into a Keatsian reverie, as Atwood
recaptures the luscious imagery and sensuous tone of "I Was Reading
a Scientific Article" from *The Animals in That Country:* "This is the
plum season, the nights/blue and distended, . . . the season of
peaches/with their lush lobed bulbs." In this ripening season, regeneration already achieved, love has taken on a pleasurable calmness:
"No more the shrill voices/that cried *Need Need.*" In this season "the
air is still/warm, flesh moves over/flesh," and "there is no/hurry."

In the final poem, "Book of Ancestors" (94–96), the season has
moved to midwinter, a time of contemplation and a time of acknowledgment and affirmation. The poem begins with a renunciation of
"the gods," with "their static demands" and ritual sacrifices. "His-
tory/is over," says the speaker, "we take place/in a season, an undi-
vided/space," without those words and patterns that "distort/us."
Love, always a risk, always a replication of ancient sacrifice and
blood, always an acknowledgment of mortality, must be attempted.
And now, perhaps, it can be, as "you turn/towards me," vulnerable,
and "open/yourself to me gently," hoping it can be done "without
blood," but accepting the possibility it might not be: "to take/that
risk, to offer life and remain/alive, open yourself like this and become
whole"—at least for the moment.

An expression of joyous celebration, undeniably, this final emotional appeal remains typically ambiguous, the thrust of its words
working wonders of imagination upon us, yet working with the
power of poetic manipulation that may well spell its own defeat. Atwood evokes more intensely here than in much of her earlier poetry
the world of possibilities she wishes to imagine, but there is still the
inescapable paradox that the "revealed word," here spoken, may yet
become the "received word" of a future time, a new myth, a new
trap, a new "Siren's Song" that "works every time." Atwood's problem, of course, is every poet's dilemma. And what is remarkable
about *You Are Happy* is that its attempt to transcend, through its own

necessarily duplicitous language, the static demands of frozen word and ancient myth, succeeds so well. It is as though her poetry had reached a discernible plateau. The 1976 publication of Atwood's *Selected Poems,* containing all of *The Journals of Susanna Moodie* and major segments of her other five volumes, may in part have been a business decision, a response by her publisher to her growing fame, a way of capitalizing on her career. But it was read, too, by some observers, as evidence that her poetic art had completed a journey and was now ready to strike off in new directions. For one reviewer, the final poems of *You Are Happy* (chosen by Atwood to conclude *Selected Poems* also) represented a new voice, "a soft rather than a brittle vitality . . . vulnerable but . . . tenacious. It is very unlikely," wrote this critic, "that the poet can go back now with any success to the old images and the old voice. . . . What follows *You Are Happy* . . . must be different."[8]

Two-Headed Poems

When we read Atwood's *Two-Headed Poems,* however, published in 1978, we may in fact be impressed initially with its sameness. The title of one poem, "Nothing New Here," may (with unintentional irony) seem to suggest that Atwood has hit a dead end. "What defeats us, as always," she says, "is/the repetition: weather/we can't help, habits we don't break." The almost-stale images in the volume—of "savage flowers/reclaiming their lost territory," of "untold stories" and "a fresh beginning," of "words" that "knot/and harden, grow sideways, devious as grass," of "this ragged place, an order/ gone to seed"—may remind us too much of earlier work.[9] But, as we move into *Two-Headed Poems,* these disconcerting echoes become rare and serve as a touchstone to Atwood's vigorous development of fresh details that underpin both a new philosophic strength and a continued mellowing of her habitually caustic tone.

"All waves are one." Both familiar and newly etched is Atwood's prevailing belief in the compelling need for some unity to emerge out of the divisions that characterize the world in which we live. Our self-motivated isolation from our fellow humans, for example, the "thickened skin" we fashion to make ourselves "impervious to the wiry screams/and toy pain of the others," is the object of Atwood's scrutiny in "April, Radio, Planting, Easter" (96–97), the final section of two groups entitled "Daybooks." The poet acknowledges that "there's a limit to how much/you can take of this battering," but she also sees that our ability to separate ourselves from the commotion is falsely perceived: "there is one rift, one flaw:/ that vulnerable bud, knot,/hole in the belly where you were nailed/ to the earth forever." If this sounds all too familiar and contrived an image, we are not alone in recognizing its inadequacy. Atwood herself comments poignantly on the weakness of such abstract metaphor and shapes it into a more concrete and compelling statement: "I do not mean *the earth*, I mean the/earth that is here and browns your/ feet, thickens your fingers,/unfurls in your brain and in/these onion seedlings/I set in flats lovingly under/a spare window." With this image of the umbilicus that is our birthright, Atwood asserts that all things are connected and worthy. We are, she says, not separate: "all waves are one/wave; there is no *other*."

Because we do not always perceive this unity, we often—like "The Trappers" of an earlier volume—act cruelly and (out of guilt or fear) conduct ritual slaughter as a means of redemption and a means of control. In *Two-Headed Poems* Atwood expands upon this notion that, in our dualistic world, there exist many warring factions: political (as in her not-so-guarded allusions to the Anglo-French separation quandary), or personal (as in the ages-old separation of mind and heart, soul and body), or interpersonal (as in our emotional alienation from others), or transcendental (as in our isolation from the earth and nature and some universal force or spirit). But a major dynamic of the collection, in both its imagery and its structure, is the hope that these warring factions will come together finally in harmony and love. Or, if we cannot quite manage that, at least in acquiescence, toleration, and peace.

It may seem no great leap from the unbreachable chasm between art and life in *Double Persephone* to *Two-Headed Poems*, where Atwood continues to scrutinize the troubling and awkward doubleness of our existence on this planet. But in 1977, when she was composing *Two-Headed Poems*, she read and was influenced by Julian Jaynes's *The Origin of Consciousness in the Breakdown of the Bicameral Mind*. In his book Jaynes speaks of a time in civilization before man became conscious of himself as an individual being apart from his community. Hearing the voices of the communal gods that unconsciously ordered society, he was completely absorbed into the social fabric. His body and soul were truly one and in harmony; and his society was, relatively speaking, without chaos, and free of the disorder that arises when individual desires assert themselves against communal truths.

Working from clinical evidence and speculation, Jaynes contends that, in such pre-conscious times, the right hemisphere of man's brain controlled man's volition through the gods—hallucinatory voices that told the outwardly dominant left side of the brain what to tell the body to do—and provided a controlling collective social vision of correct behavior. Society was whole and cohesive. It was the golden age of myth and legend. The left side of the brain became fully dominant, and the right side became quiescent, when the demands of civilization grew too complex and required the formation of an introspective awareness of self that could contemplate the past and project itself into the future. The individual, no longer an automaton doing the will of the introjected gods, thus became separated from the community; and the conscious mind, having lost the certitude of divine guidance, felt a separation from something within, prayed for the return of the lost gods, and thus formed the authorizing rituals of what we know as modern religion—something which Gershom G. Scholem, in his study of Jewish mysticism, sees as signifying "the creation of a vast abyss . . . between God . . . and Man." The attempt to journey back, to bridge the gap, to dissolve the false duality that has been imposed upon us, is, of course, a major theme of our literary heritage; and poetry, emanating from the brain's right hemisphere, according to Jaynes, is one of several contemporary vestiges of the gods still within us, shouting out, as it were, for an audience that, by and large, no longer listens. [10]

"After Jaynes." Atwood's familiarity with Jaynes's book is most directly expressed in a poem whose title may seem, to the uninitiated, rather cryptic. The sixth of Atwood's "Daybooks," "After Jaynes" (31), refers not so much to an idea the poet acquired after reading Jaynes as to the fact that the poem's imagery is in imitation of Jaynes, a variation on material he presents in his chapter on "Gods, Graves, and Idols," where he describes Cocom idols prepared from the cooked, flayed, and decorated heads of their decapitated dead. Atwood begins her poem with a similar description of "the old queen's head cut off/at the neck" and adorned "with plaster," dye, and "bright stones." To the Cocoms, such heads contained divine voices; and Atwood adds that, "after this transformation," the queen's head "can sing,/can tell us what we think/we need to hear."

Idols, of course, may not work too well. An old stuffed head may tell us only what we "think" may be the truth. And what it says may be no more useful than what the poet, in "Five Poems for Grandmothers," creates to ward off fear and mortality: "I make this charm," she says, "from nothing but paper; which is good/for exactly nothing" (39). In "After Jaynes" Atwood suggests that the "song" of the idol is nothing more than "the wind across teeth"; and in a rhyming and rhythmic pattern rare in her poetry she emphasizes that "what we think/we need to hear" is only the uncommunicated and mutilated "message from the flayed tongue/to the flayed ear" of the idol itself. With quotation marks that assert her doubt, she observes only ironically that "this is 'poetry.' "

What may give authenticity to our lives are the concrete realities that we may touch, literally, with our hands, thus rediscovering the miraculous in the mundane—the truth present here and now, not in some unattainable transcendent realm. As Atwood says at the end of the volume, "this is what you will/come back to, this is your hand" (111). Such imagery has been a staple of her writing (*The Circle Game* ends with the children of "The Settlers" running "across/the fields of our open hands"; the gods that the protagonist of her novel *Surfacing* encounters "give only one kind of truth, one hand").[11] But in *Two-Headed Poems* it evolves into a pervasive system of images that serves to enhance the implications of dualism suggested by the title. One hand is not enough. In the thematically crucial poem, "The Right Hand Fights the Left" (56–57), Atwood makes abundantly clear why this is so.

Appearing about halfway through the collection and ending the first of three major divisions in the book, this pivotal poem retells the story of the ancient battle between the two hands of human awareness. It is almost a summary of Jaynes's thesis. "Why should there be a war?" asks the speaker; "once there was none./The left hand sang the rituals,/the right hand answered." But this harmony has disintegrated and the active right hand, controlled by the dominant left hemisphere of the brain, "makes lists/of its enemies," turning the world and the body it inhabits into a barren, sterile, mechanical wasteland. The right hand "swivels/on the wrist like a spy, a radar,/a tentacled silver eye"; and when "dawn comes," it "blasts/another tree from its burrow." The weaker "left hand, you will observe,/is soft and smaller." It awakens at night, calling us at sunset, inhabiting our dreams with primal life. In the conscious world of our waking life, where technological reshaping and order prevail, "the right hand holds the knife,/the left hand dances."

"Siamese twins." The eleven-part second division of the book (59–75), from which the volume's title is taken, investigates the battle at length and in images that evoke both the internecine conflict between English Canada and Quebec and the cultural collision of Canada and the United States. An epigraph refers to Siamese twins who, in the words of an advertisement, are "Joined Head to Head, and still alive." Yet, "like all Siamese twins," says Atwood, "they dream of separation." It is the question of separation and survival that these poems debate.

Allusions to the struggles of French and English Canada emerge strongly in the eighth part of the sequence. "If I were a foreigner, as you say," one of the several voices of "Two-Headed Poems" observes, "instead of your second head,/you would be more polite" (the Americans, "those south of us," the voice remarks in the second poem of the sequence, benefit from our apparent good manners: "we're still/ polite, god knows, to the tourists"). But, living in the same country, inhabiting the same landscape, "we are the pressure/on the inside of the skull, the struggle/among the rocks for more room,/. . . the grudging love,/the old hatreds." The separation toward which these two sides are moving, notes the speaker, may be more dangerous than they can readily imagine: "Why fear the knife/that could sever us," she asks, "unless/it would cut not skin but brain?" As the narrator of *Surfacing* observes of her own fragmentation, her aborted child, "it was taken away from me, exported, deported. A section of my own life, sliced off from me like a Siamese twin, my own flesh cancelled" (48).

Throughout "Two-Headed Poems" its various speakers invoke unity but express anxiety that peace may not be achieved. The first poem adopts a colloquial tone, appropriate for friendly enemies or potential friends—one may be reminded of the embraces of Egypt's Anwar Sadat and Israel's Menachem Begin as they moved toward peace in the Middle East: "Well, we felt/we were almost getting somewhere/ though how that place would differ/from where we've always been, we/couldn't tell you." But something has happened, "this joke or major quake"—perhaps an allusion to the election in Quebec of separatist Premier René Lévesque—"a rift/in the earth, now everything/ in the place is falling south." Typically, Atwood goes beyond politics to voice a more fundamental rift, not between Anglophone and Francophone, but between the "coarse" words, "spreading themselves everywhere," and an earlier, more primal tongue, a lost language of the innermost self, "a language so precise/and secret it was not even/ a code." She is speaking about the language of the Jaynesian gods that has been crowded out in our attainment of consciousness. In poem 7, the object of attack seems to be Pierre Trudeau, "our leader," who "has two voices,/therefore two heads, four eyes,/two sets of genitals, eight/arms and legs and forty/toes and fingers." With these attributes, the speaker asks, "who does our leader speak for?/How can you use two languages/and mean what you say in both?" Alluding to Eliot's Prufrock, she observes that "our leader scuttles/sideways," irresolute. Yet since he is only a token of ourselves, she adds, we have no right to complain.

"Moving together." In the final segment of "Two-Headed Poems" Atwood comments on the distinctive languages of the two hemispheres of the bicameral brain. One "is a language for ordering/ the slaughter and gutting of hogs, for/counting stacks of cans." It consists of the stolid verbiage of nouns, forced upon us "till our tongues are sullen and rubbery." The other language sings and gives us "our dreams . . . of freedom." We cannot count on such dreams, however, and must somehow resolve the conflict, somehow accept— even if we cannot fully reconcile—the two poles of our existence. "This is not a debate," Atwood finally says, "but a duet/with two deaf singers." There is, as Jaynes himself contends, no conflict, only misunderstanding.

There is always danger of succumbing to our two-sided nature, Atwood suggests in "The Bus to Alliston, Ontario" (76–78); but to travel the bus is essential. In this poem, which begins the third division of the book, Atwood shifts extensively from images of irresolution, fear, defiance, and conflict, to images of acceptance, compassion, and love. The bus becomes a microcosm of humanity on its "ordinary voyage" through life, filled with "those who hear voices and those/who do not." But Atwood invokes a momentary lull in the potential battle and dramatizes the notion that the conflict is in fact a duet rather than a debate. In the midst of talk about disasters, disease, and death, through the dark snow-ridden road filled with imminent destruction, the singers and the uncomprehending sung-to wend their way, "moving together, warm/and for the moment safe,/ along the invisible road towards home."

The treacheries of time, of history (expressed, for example, in

"Footnote to the Amnesty Report on Torture" and "Four Small Elegies"), of death, and of darkness, are primary in the first half of the collection. Everything is questionable, as the speaker sails "downhill/ from one day to the next" ("Daybooks I," 27) and as she sees the danger of duplicitous nature beckoning her daughter to the pond's edge ("Today," 22–23). Doubt persists in the second half of the book, but the speaker has a firmer grip on reality. We see the shift in paired poems such as the early "The Woman Who Could Not Live With Her Faulty Heart" (14–15) and the late "The Woman Makes Peace With Her Faulty Heart" (86–87). It is only "an uneasy truce," she says, but it at least ensures survival. A similar accommodation is hinted at earlier, in "Marrying the Hangman" (48–51), a prose poem based on an actual incident in which a woman condemned to hang saved herself by marrying the hangman, a fellow prisoner whom she convinced to take the job. The two have little in common: he is the realist, she the mystic; his language is of "foot, boot, order, city, fist, roads, time, knife"; hers is of "water, night, willow, rope hair, earth belly, cave, meat, shroud, open, blood." But, putting differences aside, "they both kept their promises." It is another "uneasy truce" and a less than fully optimistic story; but, says the narrator, "the fact is there are no stories I can tell my friends that will make them feel better. History cannot be erased, although we can soothe ourselves by speculating about it." For all its blood and turmoil, history is necessary; as the speaker in poem 9 of "Two-Headed Poems" says, "history/breeds death but if you kill/it you kill yourself" (71).

Further reconciliation with time and its ravages becomes the subject of the third poem of "Daybooks II" (92). Here Atwood traces the growing cycle of apples as they move through the seasons, condensing "out of nothing" in the summer, ripening and being eaten in the fall, the few that remain withered and decaying in the winter being unremembered in the spring, a season in which "the word *apple*" is said "but . . . means nothing." Yet, in its focus on the continuity of the seasons, this poem conveys a sense of ever-returning life and provides at least a tentative hope for our accommodation with the mysteries of decay and death: "the apples condense again/out of nothing on their stems/like the tree bleeding; something/has this compassion." Like Robert Frost's "Secret" that "sits in the middle and knows," it is only "something," an inscrutable truth that we no longer hear, that holds the key. But it is at least something; and, in giving us apples, it gives us purpose. In the following "Daybook" poem (93), entitled

"Apple Jelly," the speaker observes that there is "no sense in all this picking,/peeling & simmering/if sheer food is all/you want; you can buy it cheaper." But the act of making apple jelly becomes a sacrament that connects us to the earth that has spawned the apples; it is "what we keep/the taste of the act, taste/of this day."

A sacrament, indeed, is what Atwood moves toward as the book approaches its conclusion. In "All Bread" (108–9) she reworks the sacrament of Holy Communion; the wafer becomes the bread, formed of "wood,/cow dung, packed brown moss,/the bodies of dead animals," the "dirt" that "flows through the stems into the grain." This bread "smells/of . . . death," but in eating it we are reaffirming our communion with the earth and with our fellow mortals: "Lift these ashes/into your mouth . . ./to know what you devour/is to consecrate it,/almost. All bread must be broken/so it can be shared. Together/we eat this earth." It is, of course, only "almost" a consecration; but it sounds very much like an answer to the question—"What can be shared?"—that is voiced by the speaker of "Return Trips West" in *Procedures for Underground*.[12]

"There is never any death." It is in the innocence of the child, however, that creature who may (in the words of *Surfacing*, 191) be "the first true human," that Atwood seems finally to transcend the tensions of a life filled with blood, pain, and conflict. To the child, only the present instant is essential; the mythic and historic fears of the adult world simply dissolve when faced with infantile delight. So it is in "A Red Shirt (For Ruth)" (102–6), where the speaker and her sister are sewing a garment for the speaker's daughter. Atwood catalogs all the traditional implications of the color red—it is, she says, the color of "death," of "passion," of "war," of "anger," of "sacrifice," and of spilled blood. But when the shirt is completely sewn and "my daughter puts it on," for her the color has no meaning "except that it is warm/and bright." As "she runs across the floor, . . . waving her red arms/in delight," the poem comes to a merely joyful conclusion "and the air/explodes with banners."

The magic of a child's delight again conquers adult fears in "The Puppet of the Wolf" (100–101). The wolf is a figure formed by the right hand of the speaker as a bath-time entertainment for her daughter, who "laughs at its comic/dance, at its roars/and piglet murders." The wolf kills the pigs, "the bones of my left hand," but the wolf too succumbs—to the scalding hot water being adjusted by the mother's right hand, "which now, restored to normal,/slides like an ordinary/hand past the seahorse/and orange boat of the bath." Yet in this private childhood world, where anything is possible, a "miracle" occurs: "there is never/any death:/the wolf comes back whenever/he is called." And resurrection extends to the mother's adult, "dying right/hand, which knots and shrinks/drier and more cynical/each year," yet now "is immortal,/briefly, and innocent" again. The Jaynesian conflict between right and left is momentarily suspended in the last stanza, as the two hands, wolf and piglets, join in harmonious pursuit: "my . . . right/hand," says the speaker, "together with my left hand, its/enemy and prey, . . . chases/my daughter through the warm air,/and muted with soapsuds, lifts her/into the water." Atwood, it appears, has come a long way from the stark and driven, submerged world of *The Circle Game*. The lake, that appalling pathway to potential knowledge in so many of those early poems, has become a joyful, suds-filled bathtub; the invisible, drowned speaker of "This Is a Photograph of Me," dangerously questing for an uncertain truth, has been transformed into a giggling child, her trusting body lifted into the now carefully adjusted water by a pair of joined and peaceful, loving hands.

At the end of *Surfacing* the narrator, reborn childlike into the world, faces the ancient conflicts and observes as she tenses forward yet hesitates to move, "we will have to begin" (192). And a beginning may be all that we have a right to expect. The utopian vision of Isaiah's prophecy, with its little child leading a wolf and a lamb into a peaceable kingdom where they dwell in harmony together, is always somewhere just out of reach. If the narrator of *Surfacing* sees the need to begin again, she also says "we will probably fail" (192). And, in *Two-Headed Poems,* if Atwood delights us with the vision of a happy child, we know the moment cannot last.

Yet the power of this volume lies precisely in Atwood's acceptance of that fact. In "You Begin" (110–11), appropriately enough the final piece in the collection, a mother instructs her child in the ways of the world. "This is the world," she says, "which is fuller/and more difficult to learn than I have said." In these words of acceptance Atwood achieves with clarity a tone of compassion and of love that surpasses all her prior attempts to engage her readers in such emotions. The poem is a triumph in evoking the bittersweet joys of an imperfect existence—joys that can be brought about, perhaps, only by a little child looking us in the eyes, and holding our hands, and reminding us of all those things we can no longer truly possess.

True Stories

Early in the 1970s Atwood observed that "books don't save the world," thus renouncing Shelley's idea that poets are the world's un-acknowledged legislators. "If you are going to save souls or save the world," she said, asserting a view she would repeat in many inter-views during the decade, "you should be a preacher or a politician." By late 1979, commenting on her involvement with Amnesty Inter-national, the worldwide human rights organization, she modified her position, noting that in some countries, where speech and action are controlled and thought is manipulated, "writing a poem *can* be [a political] act of enormous courage because the penalty for doing so could be death." But she reiterated her belief that in Canada, at least, "one doesn't get killed for writing poetry. . . . Essentially, the gov-ernment doesn't care what you write."[13] In *True Stories,* published in 1981, as in her novel *Bodily Harm,* published the same year, these dual perceptions are taken up with a vengeance.

The central sequence of *True Stories* is entitled "Notes Towards a Poem That Can Never Be Written." The explicit subject of these poems is political torture. Atwood here picks up on themes developed as a minor motif in *Two-Headed Poems,* elaborating on images that depict the details of physical abuse. "He's a maker of machines/for pulling out toenails,/sending electric shocks/through brains or geni-tals," the speaker notes, with apparent nonchalance, in "A Conver-sation." She adds, sardonically, "He doesn't test or witness,/he only sells."[14] These words counterpoint the more essential assertion and yet more painful image she presents later, in the title poem of the sequence: "The razor across the eyeball/is a detail from an old film./ It is also a truth./Witness is what you must bear" (69).

It is the very question of truth, however, and witness-bearing, and the validity of the poet's role in the process, that the volume, by and large, examines—from the initial title-sequence of "True Stories," whose truths are suspect, through the fourteen-part "Small Poems for the Winter Solstice," where the poet/speaker is "of course . . . a teller/of mundane lies" (35), through the five prose poems entitled, with continuing irony, "True Romances." Once again the question of vital reality versus art confronts Atwood in these poems, as it has throughout her career, but in this volume it appears with more bluntness, perhaps, than ever before. "Screw poetry," the speaker says early in the book, "it's you I want,/your taste, rain/on you, mouth on your skin" (20). And it appears, too, with searingly graphic details of torture—inflicted in war, imposed in peace, designed to gratify sexually manifested violence—that insist on Atwood's thesis: "There is no poem you can write," she asserts, that will effectively contain the terrible realities of human malice. These wretched pain-scarred bodies that "we turn . . . into statistics & litanies/and into poems like this one," says the speaker, these bodies are real, they exist; and the kind of event that produced them, now as always, really "happens" (66). Of the "exhibits" in the ambiguously titled "A Women's Issue," she says, "this is no museum," no artifact. It is a woman with "a four-inch/wooden peg jammed up/between her legs"; it is a "young girl" whose scraped thighs have healed together, to be cut open and then re-sewn for every childbirth (54–55).

Atwood has not abandoned the point that words do have power. Such power, for example, as can turn the speaker's innocent daughter into a sorceress: "learning how to spell," she also learns "how to make spells" (63). Or power to destroy, as in the case of the woman who "is dying because she said./ . . . dying for the sake of the word" (67). But Atwood is questioning again the extent of that power and the legitimacy of its use ("How can I justify/this gentle poem then in the face of sheer/horror?"—34). She is also questioning its ability to confer extraordinary stature upon those who dabble in wordplay. In the eighth of her "Winter Solstice" poems, as if in response to those who would transform her into a mystical cult figure, Atwood asserts the very ordinariness of the poet. Through a catalog of commonplace details—"crumbs & greasy knives," "dogsmells" that "filter through the door"—she debunks the idea that "I live in a glass tower." "What I want you to see," she insists, "is the banality of all this." At the poem's end, defying conventional wisdom about creative art, she asserts, "There's no mystery . . . none at all." Yet we may have some doubts. For, if the poet's job has "no mystery . . . no more/ than in anything else," we may well wonder what "anything else" entails. "What I do," says the speaker, "is ordinary, no/surprise, . . ./no trickier than sunrise" (33). Only from a myopic viewpoint, however, is a sunrise—the miracle of the world continuing each successive day—an unsurprising event.

It is, finally, with this most ordinary of miracles, embodied in words that evoke its power, that Atwood synthesizes the conflicting strains of the book into a coherent and affirmative vision. These strains appear in "Damside" (98–99), a few pages before the end of the volume, where the speaker notes that "if this were a poem you'd live forever." But the life she is describing is less ideal: "As it is," she says, "I can offer you/only this poor weather," with its "east wind which includes/both of us, and the stained river,/a prayer, a sewer, a prayer." Thus, for Atwood, are the facts of life. They offer no frozen immortality; but, in the image of a unifying "east wind" and in the promise of "a prayer," they do reveal the possibility of hope.

The final poem, its rising-run image an allusion to Ecclesiastes, is the prayer itself. Ironically entitled "Last Day" and suggesting precisely that very apt conclusion to a text built on images of political terror, torture, and death, the poem provides instead a recognition that all will endure, as each "last day" gives way, miraculously, to the ever-forming next one: "the sky/turns orange again and the sun rises/again and this is the last day again" (103). Earlier, in "Last Poem," Atwood speaks of poetry in much the same way, the parallel title and the similar idea clearly suggesting that she associates the writing of a poem with the coming of a sunrise. "Each poem," she says, "is my last and so is this one" (75). Predictions are futile: the next poem and the next day may never come. But, as she observes in *Power Politics,* "beyond truth," there is "tenacity." Here, in the demanding repetition of "again and . . . again and . . . again," that belief, that creed, is reasserted with firmness and with passion. And, too, with a glimmering, finally, that there is in this sewer-like, torture-ridden world a place for poetry—that ever-renewing, light-giving (though possibly powerless) miracle of words.

Chapter Four

Home Ground, Foreign Territory

"The Two Roads Joining"

Atwood first achieved fame as a poet, with the publication in 1966 of the award-winning *Circle Game*. Her fiction did not receive wide recognition until the 1969 publication of *The Edible Woman*. But her prose craft, like that of her poetry, had an early apprenticeship. She wrote her first, unpublished novel, "Up in the Air So Blue," in 1962–63, while studying at Harvard. Her published short stories (some collected in *Dancing Girls,* 1977) date from the beginning of her career. Even *The Edible Woman* was composed well before its publication date: completed in October 1965, while Atwood was teaching at the University of British Columbia in Vancouver, the manuscript was misplaced by its eventual publisher; resurrected, and revised somewhat in 1967, it did not appear in print until two years later.

Atwood's novels and short stories show her to be a skilled and versatile stylist capable of working with success in a variety of genres. Some early reviewers, stressing her poetic style, thought differently. They seemed indignant that this poet had dared enter the world of prose fiction, had dared map out a literary journey for which she had not been intended. One critic noted that *The Edible Woman* contained "a clutter of inessentials through which the reader must dig"; another observed that "the poetry-ridden prose" of *Surfacing* (1972) "is a shame, for we can hardly hear through it what Miss Atwood is genuinely trying to say." And yet one more, who felt he could hear what Atwood was saying but preferred to hear it in her poems, asserted that her novels were "auxilliary to the poetry," merely a reduction of its themes "for the wider fiction audience."[1]

Those critics who appreciated Atwood's fiction found her poetic craft and her venture into prose to be a happy combination. "Its poet-

author," one writer said of *The Edible Woman*, has created a novel
"exceptional for its finely textured prose and . . . cuttingly ironic
perception"; "Margaret Atwood," observed a reviewer of *Surfacing*,
"is a Canadian poet, one of the best, and this is a poet's novel."[2] It
could be argued that even these positive reactions to Atwood's fiction
suggest ambivalence, pointing as they do to her known strengths as
a poet. Yet, with the subsequent publication of *Lady Oracle* in 1976,
Life Before Man in 1979, and *Bodily Harm* in 1981, Atwood's prose
writing became a literary presence that critics would have to reckon
with on its own merits.

The Edible Woman

Like much of Atwood's work, *The Edible Woman* is essentially realistic in its theme and in its acute attention to detail—detail enhanced, in part, by her reliance on patterns of experience closely
derived from her own life. She has often denied any significant autobiographical substance in her work; and she has pointed out, specifi-
cally, that *The Edible Woman* "is about someone who does not know
what to do with her life and that has never been my predicament."[3]
Yet surely Atwood's position, in 1963–64, as a writer for a Toronto
market research firm, has found its way effectively into the character-
ization of her protagonist, Marian MacAlpin, whose job with Seymour Surveys provides an apt backdrop to a consumer society that
Atwood satirically attacks.

"**Taking aim.**"   In part 1, which comprises the first twelve
chapters and covers four days of Marian's adventure, from Friday to
Labor Day Monday, the reader meets Marian, speaking in her own
voice. Also present is a dubious cast of secondary characters who reflect various facets of Marian's personality or provoke the conflicts
that move the plot: Ainsley Tewce, Marian's grasping roommate,
who envisions herself as an earth-mother of sorts, a fertile being who
hopes to cajole some unknowing super-male into fathering her child,
yet has no intention of either marrying him or letting him know of
his parenthood; fecund Clara, an old friend and true earth-mother,
who has all the children she needs, with more on the way, and a too-
diligent house-husband who, though obliging, is oblivious to Clara's
spiritual needs (he, at least initially, is what Ainsley hopes to avoid—
"The thing that ruins families these days is the husbands");[4] Leonard
Slank, a candidate for Ainsley's machinations and their eventual vic-

tim; the three office virgins, Marian's colleagues, all husband-hunt-
ing, sex-fearing, artificial blondes, substituting travel as a doubtful
remedy for their frustrations; the landlady, repeatedly referred to,
with mythic overtones, as "the lady down below" (13), whose puritan
ethic reflects that side of Marian which is, or wishes to be, proper;
Peter, the egocentric, pre-packaged, *Playboy*-defined pseudo-man
whom Marian intends to marry; and, finally, Peter's apparent opposite, slovenly graduate student Duncan, an alter ego for Marian, and
possibly her salvation. Duncan, who is subtly and namelessly introduced in the first section of the novel, emerges in part 2, with gothic
inevitability, as the most interesting character in Atwood's menagerie—a seemingly omniscient, omnipresent demi-god or gremlin,
frog-prince, or even fairy godfather, who eventually (in part 3) puts
what may be the most accurate interpretation on the events of the
novel.

In this first section of the book Atwood caricatures the pretensions
of our consumer society and the machinery that both supports and
engenders its absurdities, from Marian's canvassing a neighborhood
on the subject of beer consumption, to Ainsley's deceptively packag-
ing herself as a youthful, innocent seductee out to catch her semen-
bearing impregnator. Marian, as an agent of this machinery, is in a
unique position—both a victim of her society's obsessive consumer-
ism and its unwitting advocate, not always aware of the mundane evil
of her activities. The connection between her two roles is dynamically
exploited through a series of interrelated image patterns and seemingly unrelated circumstances that eventually become highly textured, baroque elaborations of each other. These patterns suggest
that, even as Marian pursues her job to increase public consumption
of the product she is surveying, her decision to wed Peter will make
her, as one of the married, into one of the consumed. Her identity as
a consumable item—one that plays out its role by being assimilated
into the body that consumes it—is established early. She is describing her position at Seymour Surveys, commenting on the fact that
the job has little future: "The company," she observes, "is layered
like an ice-cream sandwich, with three floors: the upper crust, the
lower crust, and our department, the gooey layer in the middle" (19).

Marian is that delicious gooey layer, comfortably sandwiched in,
even protected, but ultimately a victim of someone's appetite. When
she agrees, in her search for normality, to become sandwiched into
Peter's life as his obliging wife, it is the idea that she is going to be

consumed and assimilated that Atwood stresses. Peter is treated as
"a rescuer from chaos, a provider of stability," but that stability has
its price, a loss of self that involves becoming, in effect, a product
picked from the shelf or the showroom floor by a voracious consumer:
"you're such a sensible girl," Peter says to her, "I've always thought
that's the first thing to look for when it comes to choosing a wife"
(89). Earlier, when Marian, sitting in Peter's car, has accepted his
proposal of marriage, Atwood plays upon a typical metaphysical conceit to suggest the virtual horror of Marian's position: "A tremendous
electric blue flash, very near, illuminated the inside of the car. As we
stared at each other in that brief light I could see myself, small and
oval, mirrored in his eyes" (83). In John Donne's "The Good-
Morrow," two lovers stare at each other and, each reflected in the
other's eye, become united in mutual love. Not so here, where Marian is captured and frozen within Peter's eye, its target and its victim
rather than its beloved and vital partner defying the intrusions of the
world. A few paragraphs earlier Peter's eyes have been characterized
as the tools of the hunter capturing his prey: "He glanced quickly
over at me, his eyes narrowed as though he was taking aim" (81).

"Bridal nerves." The terrifying implications of this image are
elaborated upon in two climactic scenes, connected by the author's
subtle transformation in each of a comic tone to one of gothic horror.
The first has occurred just prior to Peter's marriage proposal, in the
bar atop the Park Plaza Hotel, where Peter is talking with Len, relating to him a particularly gory hunting story, filled with images of
"blood and guts all over the place." As the image sinks into Marian's
mind, unconsciously triggering an empathy between herself and the
stricken rabbit, whose "guts" in Peter's story are "dangling from the
trees," her alcohol-influenced perceptions become increasingly dis-
torted, voices sound distant, and "in dithering mazes of panic" she
begins to cry. Momentarily, as Atwood builds suspense, Marian regains control. But then "the panic swept back over me. . . . I had to
get out." The chapter ends as she breaks away from Peter's grip and
runs down the street (69–71).

Although this episode culminates in Marian's succumbing to Peter's marriage proposal, it sets the pattern for the later gathering in
part 2: their engagement party at Peter's apartment. The soiree is
ending and, even viewed through Marian's increasingly intoxicated
vision, it seems typical enough—the disoriented figures bidding fare-
well, the montage of details rushing past. But Marian, imagining an

all-too-normal future as a mere fixture in the life of a middle-class, balding Peter, enters a spiritual labyrinth that retraces "through time the corridors and rooms" that make up her "long search" for "the real Peter," whom she herself has "evoked." At first, time seems "to be slowing down" for Marian as she considers such an image to be "reassuring." But soon the figures around her move "faster and faster," and she sees herself distant and detached, a "tiny two-dimensional small figure . . . posed like a paper woman in a mail-order catalogue," a consumable item "fluttering in the white empty space." The scene is transformed into a surreal nightmare, as Marian once again loses control, sees herself as a target, seeks escape, and (searching for the door to freedom) runs into Peter's camera with its "blinding flash of light" that counterpoints the earlier lightning in Peter's car. Avoiding both the camera and the bedroom mirror that would similarly fix her image—trap her "indissolubly in that gesture, that single stance, unable to move or change"—Marian runs from the apartment, down through the streets, and over to the laundromat where she knows her savior Duncan will be (242–45): Duncan, whose desire to be an amoeba ("they're . . . sort of shapeless and flexible," 201) reflects her own underlying wish to escape the stasis and frozen images of a "normal" life.

It is still in part 1, however, immediately after Marian has agreed to marry Peter and accept such normality, that her body begins to react—most perversely—to her future role as Peter's consumable private property. As she goes to her refrigerator for breakfast, the morning after her engagement, she wonders whether she can "face an egg" (83). Before very long, this mild ambivalence becomes a full-fledged case of something resembling anorexia nervosa, the neurotic syndrome that compels a young woman to avoid food as a means of reconciling unconscious conflict: between asserting her particular identity and relinquishing control over her body to become thin, thus fitting into the image prescribed by her society. It is the perfect disorder to capture at least one element of Marian's problem—her desire to be attractive to Peter and to others, her wish, more profoundly, not to become old and dumpy like certain other characters in the novel, her need to avoid physical corruption and mortality.

For Atwood, Marian's neurosis is more than a misplaced desire for achieving thinness, for competing with the other women in their quests for male companionship. It seems also to reflect her feeling that she ought not victimize other living things. Marian identifies with the objects she needs for sustenance, forgetting that her own survival rests with her consumption of these things; and, soon, one food item after another becomes repugnant to her.

Realization dawns on her, in part 2, when she perceives with horror "that this thing, this refusal of her mouth to eat, was malignant; that it would spread; that slowly the circle now dividing the non-devourable from the devourable would become smaller and smaller, that the objects available to her would be excluded one by one" (153). The second section of the novel, until the climactic engagement party scene, recounts two opposing, yet causally related movements in Marian's odyssey through life. The first, more obvious movement is her conscious, growing acceptance of her bourgeois fate and her subordination to Peter's whims. The other is this seemingly inexplicable inability to eat, this rebellion, which grows ever more intense as she—in a variety of ways—succumbs to her role as a consumable product. As her problem with food worsens, Marian confides in Clara, who observes, with more accuracy than she realizes, "I expect it's bridal nerves" (206).

"An endurance of time."   That something important has happened to Marian is signaled by Atwood's narrative technique, a shift in perspective that both fosters and explains Marian's disease. The shift is initiated in part 1, whose final chapter ends with Marian's preparations for marrying Peter. "So here I am," says Marian (101), suddenly speaking in the present tense, at the conclusion of the four-day holiday weekend that comprises the time-scheme of part 1. It is as though Marian has reached a plateau in her life, has—in effect—completed her development. Her life is now arrested, as she later realizes, in "a period of waiting, drifting with the current, an endurance of time marked by no real event; waiting for an event in the future that had been determined by an event in the past" (184). Her status now defined and confirmed, she can simply drift, relinquish her personal identity, and (as she earlier says to Peter) "leave the big decisions up to" him (90).

Marian's stability, however, is problematic. For, having entered a timeless world "marked by no real event," having become in effect the static spatial image on Keats's urn, Marian can no longer be a vital, acting human being. Captured and frozen by the camera's eye—in this prose version of an image that pervades Atwood's poems—Marian is simply no longer herself. And, in the lengthy second part of the novel, as if to reflect this new state, she no longer refers to herself in the first person. Rather than an "I" telling the story, there appears a narrator at the beginning of part 2 who refers to "Marian" in the third person. That it is still Marian speaking, but deliberately seeing herself as an object of study rather than a subjective human being, becomes clear at the beginning of part 3. Then, having broken free of her engagement, Marian regains her identity, reenters the world, and begins "thinking of myself in the first person singular again" (278).

It is toward Marian's reentry into time that the second part of the novel moves. Allusions to time become more pervasive as she increasingly rejects Peter's exploitation of her: at her engagement party, she observes that "she had no idea what time it was" (244); later, at Toronto's ravines with Duncan, she wonders "what time it is" (262); and, guided by Duncan's revelation that it was he who had seduced her the previous night rather than she ministering to his sexual inhibitions, she observes that "now I've got to decide what I'm going to do." Duncan adds, advisedly, "it does look as though you ought to do something. . . . But it's your own personal cul-de-sac, . . . you'll have to think of your own way out" (264). To make her decisions, she realizes in the next chapter, "she needed time" (266).

Circles and spirals. Part 2 ends with Marian's baking the woman-shaped cake referred to in the book's title. Peter, earlier invited by Marian, arrives at her apartment and is offered the cake as a symbolic surrogate for Marian herself: "You've been trying to destroy me," she says, "to assimilate me. But I've made you a substitute" (271). Horrified, Peter leaves. And Marian, "suddenly . . . hungry" and apparently cured, eats part of the cake herself.

The experiences Marian has undergone suggest the possibility of a positive transformation in her life. Yet, at the conclusion, it appears she has changed very little. Debunking the symbolic potential of Marian's cake and tossing her fantasies about Peter into the hopper with all the other discarded scenarios that have pervaded the novel, Duncan observes that "Peter wasn't trying to destroy you. That's just something you made up. Actually you were trying to destroy him." Or, alternate version (after Marian—her delusions exposed—experiences "a sinking feeling"): "But the real truth is that it wasn't Peter at all. It was me. I was trying to destroy you." Or again: "Maybe Peter was trying to destroy me, or maybe I was trying to destroy him, or we were both trying to destroy each other, how's that? What does it matter, you're back to so-called reality, you're a consumer" (280–81).

Earlier in the novel, as she sits in Duncan's apartment listening to his two roommates—Fischer (Fish), the bearded and extravagant scholar, and Trevor, the homosexual whose vocal inflections Atwood stereotypes with precision—Marian is presented with what amounts to a self-mocking précis of *The Edible Woman,* a commentary by Fish on his work with *Alice in Wonderland.* A parody of the dubious intellectual pursuits undertaken by graduate students in English literature, it is also a comment both on the stylistic pretensions of Atwood's novel ("These patterns emerge," says Fish, wisely. "Patterns emerge") and on Marian's (Alice's) "sexual-identity-crisis," her attempt to define "her role as a Woman": "One sexual role after another is presented to her but she seems unable to accept any of them. . . . And of course there's the obsession with time . . . but she refuses to commit herself, you can't say that by the end of the book she has reached anything that can be definitely called maturity" (193–94).

Marian has come full circle. Certain things have changed, of course: Ainsley is pregnant by Len and married—to Duncan's roommate Fish; Duncan's household arrangements are thus destroyed; and Peter is no longer Marian's husband-to-be—but he wasn't that, we recall, at the beginning either. Like Alice undergoing her adventures in wonderland, Marian has awakened from an interesting, at times fantastic and implausible, interlude, merely to reenter her previously "stolid" (11) existence. She has regained time, but only—as in the two-day renovation of her neglected apartment—to put herself back into order. Having broken off her engagement to Peter, she finds her anorexia cured; and we come to understand that her gastronomic distress was—as much as anything else—a response to her fear of growing up. No longer having to face the sexual and social commitment of marriage, her "bridal nerves" thus eliminated, she can eat once more; maturity can be postponed for another day.

And so Marian returns to reality—as in Atwood's world she must—without having resolved any of the ethical burdens her experiences have forced upon her. However fantastic, stylistically, the events of *The Edible Woman* may be and however much they may be analogous to Alice's fairy-tale descent through the rabbit hole and into the underground, what prevails in this novel is Atwood's realistic perception that some of us may be unable to bring anything of worth back from those underground journeys, may be unable to extricate ourselves from the societal circle games that entrap us. But *The Edible Woman* is not Atwood's final word on the matter. As she observed in a 1976 interview, suggesting a more positive vision in her second novel, "the tone of *The Edible Woman* is lighthearted, but in the end it's more pessimistic than *Surfacing*. The difference between them is that *Edible Woman* is a circle and *Surfacing* is a spiral . . . the heroine of *Surfacing* does not end where she began."[5]

Surfacing

On the front cover of an early paperback edition of Atwood's second novel a blurb describes *Surfacing* (1972) as "the most shattering novel a woman ever wrote." Other comments refer to the work as "a woman's novel" and a "novel of a woman's self-discovery." Given the time and place—the 1970s in North America—it is understandable that a novel written by a woman about an unnamed woman protagonist who rediscovers herself during a mythic journey to the northern Quebec woods would evoke such remarks; understandable, too, that the novel would be considered, by some, to be a document of women's liberation. But readers of *Surfacing* should be cautious. As has been observed of another novel often treated as a feminist tract (Kate Chopin's *The Awakening*), the protagonist "interests us not because she is 'a woman,' [but] because she is human—because she fails in ways which beckon seductively to all of us. Conrad might say that, woman *or* man, she is 'one of us.' "[6]

Certainly the reference to Joseph Conrad applies to Atwood's novel. For, as in *Heart of Darkness,* where Marlow edges his way ever more deeply into the jungle to realize the darkest secrets of the human spirit, so too does Atwood's protagonist wend her way to discoveries of a reality she had forgotten existed. The novel surveys human foibles—questions of power, guilt, innocence, expiation for a variety of sins—rather than solely female ones. And it is not surprising that, speaking in San Francisco in 1975, Atwood noted that the best article she had read about *Surfacing* was one that comments on the protagonist's coming to understand "the nature of human limitation."[7]

"On this road again." *Surfacing* relates the story of a young woman who travels north with her companion, Joe, and two friends, a married couple, David and Anna. The woman has been informed that her father has disappeared from his lakeside cabin in northern Quebec, where he has lived for many years. Though geographically detached and emotionally estranged from her father—her mother has already died some time before of brain cancer—she feels compelled to return to this outpost of her childhood to search for him. After settling into her father's cabin, and during what has already become for her a psychological and not merely geographical journey, she dives beneath the surface of the water and sees what appear to be the remains of her father. Surfacing (both physically and spiritually—an indication of the complex meaning inherent in the title), she finds that discovering her father's corpse has triggered yet more intriguing discoveries about herself. It also leads to a climactic episode—part paranoid fantasy, part quasi-mystic quest, part hallucination—in which, shedding all trappings of civilization, she attempts to return to the primitive, to merge with the surrounding wilderness, to escape humanity and unite with her parents' spirits and her ancestral past.

During this passage she realizes that her latent hostility toward her parents has resulted from her inability to accept their mortality, their deaths seeming to her a repudiation of her desire to keep them, in memory, eternally young. When she comes to grips with the reality of her parents' deaths, when she accepts that particular human limitation, she surfaces from the nonrational state she has entered, bringing with her the wisdom—the gifts—her parents have provided for her. She understands, however, that their gifts, the "gods" they have revealed to her, "give only one kind of truth, one hand"; and she finds herself, as the novel ends, almost ready to return to the world she has attempted to escape—the real world of time, of decay, and of imperfection. "Withdrawing," she says, "is no longer possible and the alternative is death."[8]

The first chapter establishes, if tentatively, the major themes of the novel, its first sentence suggesting the multiple significance of the narrator-protagonist's journey: "I can't believe I'm on this road again, twisting along past the lake where the white birches are dying, the disease is spreading up from the south, and I notice they now have sea-planes for hire" (7). This juxtaposition of personal emotion, of disease and death, and of progress in modes of travel is more than a sign of the speaker's incoherence. It serves also to imply the relatedness of what may seem initially to be disparate images. Here, the reference to the dying of the cancerous birches extends metaphorically to another disease, that implied by the presence of sea-planes: the technological malaise (apparently transmitted by that country to the south, the United States) that would transform the virgin wilderness into condominiums (later in the story, indeed, an American arrives to bid on the land).

This initial reference to disease is part of a mosaic of guilt and un-redeemed evil that pervade the action and the imagery of *Surfacing*. A dead heron, fatally mutilated and hung grotesquely from a tree, becomes a recurring symbol, evoking in the narrator's mind, and in ours, connections with other evils. The fact that the "Americans" who have apparently killed the heron turn out to be Canadians sug-gests that the novel's overt anti-American sentiment is less a specifi-cally nationalistic attack, more a metaphorical one, a comment on the pervasive modern mentality that has no coherent ethical basis for be-havior, that controls, captures, and destroys only to assert power for its own sake and without remorse. The protagonist, relating this mentality to a "virus," notes that they "killed the heron anyway. It doesn't matter what country they're from . . . they're still Ameri-cans, they're what's in store for us, what we are turning into." Not yet comprehending fully her own sins and her own (though unac-knowledged) assertions of power, the protagonist nevertheless feels "a sickening complicity" in the transgressions of others: "The trouble some people have being German," she says in reference to the Nazi atrocities, "I have being human" (129–30).

Not until the book's conclusion, however, does her understanding of her capacity for evil become complete. To renounce power, to re-main a passive victim of others, she sees, is an exercise in futility: if she wishes to survive in the historical, struggle-ridden world into which we are all born, she must "join in the war, or . . . be de-stroyed." She wishes there were "other choices" but sees there are not. What is morally essential, however, is for her to acknowledge her power, accept her imperfection, take responsibility for her ac-tions, and "give up the old belief that I am powerless and because of it nothing I can do will ever hurt anyone" (189, 191).

The controlling metaphor of the book, that which carries her to this understanding, is the journey itself. But, as certain phrases in chapter 1 suggest, the way toward redemption and renewal will not be easy. Crossing over the border into French-speaking Quebec, the narrator observes that she is now "on my home ground, foreign ter-ritory" (11). It is foreign, of course, because of the language barrier and its resulting conflicts: the mutually incomprehensible conversations between the narrator's mother and the area's other residents, her own difficulties with the proprietors of the village store. But it is foreign, too, because of the woman's nine-year absence and her immersion into what has become, with powerful psychological barriers to the past, another life. As Anna, reading the narrator's palm, observes, "some of your lines are double. . . . You had a good childhood but then there's this funny break" (8).

As the geographical journey proceeds, the narrator's inability to identify with this "home territory" intensifies: dissociating herself from her surroundings, she peers through the car window "as though it's a T.V. screen." And the road, the one that "ought to be here," has (like the protagonist's severed connection with her past) "been closed for years." Seeing the difficulties of the journey, the narrator wishes to turn back, to remember her father as he was, to avoid recapturing the absent years and the changes they have brought about. The journey, however, continues and, as the chapter draws to its conclusion, she finds that the old road crosses the new one "at intervals." It is in that limited way still accessible. The line to the past, though broken, may still be retrieved (11–12, 14).

At the end of chapter 1, as she approaches the village that is her destination, the protagonist finds "the two roads joining . . . but widened," and she comments on the shortness of the physical journey: ". . . they've cheated, we're here too soon and I feel deprived of something, as though I can't really get here unless I've suffered; as though the first view of the lake, which we can see now, blue and cool as redemption, should be through tears and a haze of vomit" (15). What the narrator—whom we have already begun to see as unreliable—cannot yet know is that her real journey has only just begun: the symbolic redemption offered by the shining surface of the lake is illusory, the journey back cannot be so easily achieved, and repressed guilt cannot be so easily assuaged.

"To keep myself from telling that story."   In the first chapter, recalling her days as a child, the narrator refers to her parents, herself, and her brother "as if they were somebody else's family." She catches herself, however, and notes that such fabrication "won't work . . . I have to keep myself from telling that story" (14). That the narrator tells stories—multi-layered tales that obscure painful truths and allow her to achieve a comforting selective amnesia—becomes increasingly evident as her fable of discovery progresses. Another relatively early clue to her state of mind occurs in chapter 8 where, having remarked to herself that she has always felt "safe" in the wilderness, she finds her "own voice" speaking aloud, *"That's a lie";* and, thinking "hard about it, considering it," she agrees that "it is a lie." That the narrator has to think so intensely about a simple memory suggests the difficulty she has distinguishing between truth and fabrication. She comments further, moving toward panic, "I have to be more careful about my memories, I have to be sure they're my own" (73).

What the protagonist has been denying most radically—what captures most emphatically her complicity in the elaborated evils of her world—is the abortion she underwent, succumbing to the desire of her lover, a married man who wished not to complicate their relationship. Yet when we first hear of this particular episode in her life, we are told that she had been married, is now divorced, and has a baby who is in the custody of her former husband. We do not perceive these "facts" as deliberate lies; rather, they are related to us as elements of the narrator's most profound belief regarding her past. If we recognize them as falsehoods at all, we realize that they are the protagonist's psychological defense, her means of avoiding yet one more death, one more sign of mortality—but this one a result of her own actions, her own decision to act, her own assertion of power. It is this secret, what she later calls this "death . . . inside me," that she has layered "over, a cyst, a tumour, black pearl" (145). And it is this repressed guilt that she must bring to the surface, must exorcise, before she can become whole.

As the narrative proceeds, we see the details of this singular event in the protagonist's life undergo gradual elaborations and transformations. It is, however, in the climactic chapter 17, after she has seen her father's corpse, that we undergo with her the most crucial part of her psychological renewal. Here all the scenarios—about the marriage, about the child—collapse, separating into the unrelated details that she had forged together into what had become for her an acceptable version of reality. Like *Random Samples,* the similarly piecemeal movie her companions have been making, the protagonist's vision of her past had been a composite of grotesquely isolated images, random samples indeed, that she had "pieced . . . together the best way I could." Her "wedding," for example, previously described as occurring "in a post office," on "a hot day," with pigeons outside near a "fountain," is now seen as the aftermath of her abortion, her

"husband" arriving after the operation "to collect me." He has been
with "his own children, the real ones," who, ironically, "were having
a birthday party. . . . It wasn't a wedding, there were no pigeons,
the post office and the lawn were in another part of the city where I
went for stamps" (87–88, 143–44).

As a torrent of revealed memory rushes upon the narrator in this
chapter, we see with clarity how earlier remarks hinted at truth even
as the metaphors in which they were phrased displaced and obscured
it. The narrator comments here, for example, that, following the
abortion, she felt "emptied, amputated." Yet, as early as the fifth
chapter, she describes her "divorce" as being "like an amputation,
you survive but there's less of you." In retrospect, we know there has
been no marriage, hence no divorce; yet the emotional impact of the
word "amputation" persists. Later in chapter 5, speaking about her
child, the narrator observes that "I have to behave as though it
doesn't exist, . . . it was taken away from me. . . . A section of my
own life, sliced off from me. . . , my own flesh cancelled" (144, 42,
48).

Ostensibly a reference to her having lost custody of the child, this
remark suggests the nature of the narrator's distortion of reality: a
process of sometimes minor linguistic alteration that both affirms and
denies the reality it asserts. Here, the phrase "as though" allows her
to reject her knowledge that indeed there never was a child, even as
it raises the question of why precisely she cannot accept its existence.
The narrator recognizes the problems caused by a language that is
somehow "wrong." She says in chapter 9, in one of many expressions
throughout *Surfacing* of a central theme present in all of Atwood's
work, "I was seeing poorly, translating badly, a dialect problem"
(76). A faulty language, she sees, distorts reality even as it allows us
to conceptualize and organize the facts that constitute our world; such
language "divides us," she says, "into fragments," prevents us from
being "whole" (146); and it causes us to misinterpret what we know
instinctively to be true. This problem in epistemology—in coming to
grips with the process of knowing and with the effect of language on
that process—is at the core of *Surfacing;* and it helps explain some of
the power this novel exerts over its readers, as they involve themselves in the narrator's turmoil, sometimes mistaking reality even
after she has plunged to the depths of her spirit and seen the truth.

Surfacing. Given the clarity with which Atwood reveals the
protagonist's true history—the denial that a marriage ever occurred,
the vivid, if still somewhat fanciful description of the abortion ("they

scraped it into a bucket," 143), and the confession that she is an unreliable narrator—we may well wonder why some readers have left the novel still believing that the protagonist actually gave birth to a child or that, having had an abortion, she nevertheless had been married.[9] It would be easy to consider such misperceptions merely as examples of careless reading. Yet an understanding of Atwood's technique in *Surfacing* may explain some of the confusion. As the narrator, speaking in the present tense, relates her story to us, we become involved with her voice. Certain false details, simply because they are given in an offhand manner, seem truthful enough at the time—for example, her remark concerning David's and Anna's having gotten "married about the same time I did" (40). As such details accumulate, they create a powerful impression of truth that may be difficult to renounce completely when more accurate versions of reality are announced. Thus does Atwood create strong reader empathy for the protagonist: her confusion and struggle are ours; her difficulties with life become our own.

The novel's present-tense narrative compounds our difficulty in sifting fact from fabrication, as it places the action into the realm of spontaneous discourse, unmediated by time, lacking retrospective contemplation that authenticates what is being said.[10] Rather than being a history of the protagonist's discoveries, one that has been evaluated beforehand by a reflective narrator and rendered reliable, *Surfacing*'s narrative is the act of discovery itself—seemingly random, incoherent, and unresolvable—as the narrator engages in a conversation with herself and with the reader. Truth in this novel, rather than being imposed upon the protagonist's ramblings by an objective narrator, emerges out of what is, in effect, extemporaneous discourse. To be evaluated as truth, however, it must first be discerned as such.

In practical terms, the reader of *Surfacing* is beset with the problem of determining whether any of the narrator's tales is true. When a single event in a character's life is obsessively repeated in a narrative, each successive alteration—in this case of the protagonist's marriage-child-abortion story—calls into question the validity of all previous versions. But these alterations also put the latest version into question. Why believe even the final version when the present-tense discourse that constitutes the novel continues, in a sense, beyond the final chapter? Why not simply consider the revelations of chapter 17 as additional falsehoods, intended for subsequent revision as the narrator's life goes on?

What makes Atwood's technique a remarkably executed achieve-

ment and prevents the novel from becoming an act of narrative an-
archy is that, ultimately, the work contains an irrefutable inner logic.
The narrator-protagonist may be confused; some readers may be; but
Atwood is not. The disclosure of the abortion comes only after the
narrator has undergone a gradual peeling away of surface fabrications,
part of a process that relates to the novel's title. We must believe the
narrator's revelations about the abortion, moreover, because that traumatic event is what motivates her amnesia and explains her pervasive
feelings of personal guilt. Her remembering the abortion—an event
consistent with the novel's pattern of images involving remorseless
violation of life—also explains the protagonist's erratic behavior following chapter 17. Armed with the gift of truth that her search for
her father has provided her, she is now able to seek further: "It would
be right," she says, "for my mother to have left something for me
also, a legacy. . . . I was not completed yet; there had to be a gift
from each of them" (149). And so, perhaps with the aid of hallucinatory mushrooms she has apparently consumed, she descends into
the mystical state that climaxes with her seeing a vision of her
mother, whose gift of love complements her father's gift of mind and
thus helps heal the breach between mind and heart that the protagonist shares with the rest of humanity.

Finally, the abortion relates to the protagonist's allowing Joe, in
chapter 20, to have intercourse with her: "He trembles and then I
can feel my lost child surfacing within me, forgiving me" (161–62).
Later, at the very end of the novel, as she decides to return to civilization, she comments with regard to this potential child, "it must be
born, allowed" (191). She thus echoes her earlier words—"I didn't
allow it" (143)—about her aborted child. To deny the fact of the
abortion is to render these words meaningless; to fail to see the possibly conceived child as a replacement for the aborted one—and as
another act of healing—is to miss a major key to understanding this
novel.

"I tense forward." If, however, the protagonist has healed
during the course of the experiences she has related to us, Atwood
makes certain that we see her improvement as necessarily partial. Her
descent into the underground—that part-hallucinatory merger with
the wilderness—has provided her with knowledge, the very kind of
knowledge she refers to when she speaks of her brother's near-drowning: "If it had happened to me, . . . I would have returned with secrets" (74). But it is also clear that what she has learned is tentative,
less an absolute ethical formula from the mystic beyond, more a re-

alization of the strengths and weaknesses of one's humanity. As she awakens from her mystical state, she realizes that, in the real world, there are "no gods to help me now, they're questionable once more" (189).

To attain such partial knowledge, however, is not to fail. If *Surfacing* is a study in the procedures needed to become truly human, then we do have some indication of what these procedures are. They involve a re-commitment to human relationships and to an acceptance of the pain those relationships provoke. As the narrator says of her future with Joe, "we will have to begin." Any more utopian vision would be a disaster for the novel, a romantic excess doomed to failure by its own rigidity. By leaving us in a protean environment—Joe "only half-formed"; the protagonist balanced between retreat (to the animal state and death) and return; the dock "neither land nor water"—Atwood leaves open and possible that more radical vision; and, dramatically, the last scene of the novel (captured in the immediacy of the present tense) becomes, for the protagonist and for Atwood's readers, a decisive moment (192).

A critic has written that "there is a terrifying starkness" to the end of *Surfacing* and that this starkness suggests a world in which there is no mediation from past to present, "where the individual must start again from nothing, essentially alone," unable "to postulate an acceptable definition of . . . community," thus calling "into question the cultural affirmation of the novel."[11] Yet such starkness is appropriate for a moment in which a human being, stripped of all remnants of civilization, returns to the world of time, of order, and of language. The protagonist, at the end, is not alone; Joe is present, and present, the narrator observes, as "a mediator." Language has been restored—"for us it's necessary," the narrator realizes, "the intercession of words." And the past—it too is here, in the figure of the possibly conceived child, "the time-traveller," brought "from the distant past five nights ago . . . , the primaeval one," who "might be the first one, the first true human." It is tentative, this triumph, certainly; but what else could it be? To come to the devastating realization of one's sins, finally to feel emotion (earlier the narrator envies Joe his pain), to lose one's innocence and see oneself as part of corrupt humanity must, of necessity, make one hesitate. It is this hesitation—"I tense forward," the narrator says, "though my feet do not move yet"—that concludes the novel on its appropriate aesthetic, poetic, and dramatic note (191–92).

Given these artistic qualities and the universality of its quest theme, *Surfacing* may well become Margaret Atwood's most enduring masterwork. De-emphasizing the overt comedy of either *The Edible Woman* or her next novel, *Lady Oracle, Surfacing* nevertheless sustains a fablistic quality that is the stuff of myth. In providing—clearly and forcefully—a view into a central enigma of the human condition, it is a contemporary classic.

Lady Oracle

Commenting in 1976 on *Lady Oracle,* published that year, Atwood noted that "the . . . book I set out to write was a kind of antithesis to *Surfacing,* which is very tight and everything in it fits and there's not anything that's out of place and no tangents. . . . In *Lady Oracle* I set out to write a book that was all tangents." Insofar as *Lady Oracle* is a book of many facets, Atwood's intent would seem to have been achieved. A comic tour de force, her third novel is at once a parody of the gothic romance, a spoof of the quest myth developed in *Surfacing,* a satire on activist politics and Canadian nationalism of the 1960s and early 1970s, a poignant anatomy of childhood terror and alienation in the late 1940s and 1950s, a meta-fictional narrative employing the technique of the novel-within-a-novel to dramatize—with chilling effect—the fortunes of Atwood's author-protagonist, and (according to some reviewers, though with Atwood's denial) a roman à clef in which Atwood mocks the manners and mores of the Toronto literary scene and uses "her fiction to pay off old scores."[12]

"To scroll and festoon."   The book opens with Joan Foster, the first-person narrator, telling us about her "death," the choreographed, phony suicide that she hopes will remove her from the complex turmoil that she has made of her existence thus far: "I planned my death carefully," she says, "unlike my life, which meandered along from one thing to another, despite my feeble attempts to control it. My life had a tendency to spread, to get flabby, to scroll and festoon like the frame of a baroque mirror. . . . I wanted my death, by contrast, to be neat and simple, understated, even a little severe. . . . No trumpets, no megaphones, no spangles, no loose ends, this time."[13]

What we learn in the five-part narrative that constitutes *Lady Oracle* is that Joan's life, indeed, has "meandered," and it has done so in large part because of her continuing need to embellish reality and to control—and thus try to escape—a haunting presence from her childhood. That presence and that need to play the artist manipulating the images of life is manifest in the first paragraph of the novel, with its interconnected allusions to flabbiness and baroque mirror frames. For as a child Joan was extremely obese, a horror to her middle-class, social-climbing, Toronto-suburbanite mother and an object of ridicule to her childhood acquaintances. These include her Brownie sidekicks who, when she is eight years old, tie her up on a cold, late afternoon and leave her on a bridge over one of Toronto's ravines, where she is approached and freed by "the daffodil man," the same "bad man" that Joan had earlier seen exposing himself by lifting up from in front of "his open fly" the "bunch of daffodils" he was holding. For Joan, whose relationships with men become increasingly problematic, this is one of the first experiences that cause her to wonder about the complex nature of human personality—in men, by virtue of this particular episode, but by extension in herself as well: "Was the man who untied me a rescuer or a villain? Or, an even more baffling thought: was it possible for a man to be both at once?" (60, 64).

Although Joan realizes that she "can't have been a very exciting sexual object, a fat, snotty-nosed eight-year-old in a Brownie outfit" (62–63), her mother blames her for the near-catastrophe in the ravine, thus further confirming Joan's growing belief that her mother is "a monster" (67). But the far more painful event in Joan's childhood occurs when she is seven and enrolled in Miss Flegg's dancing school, where the girls are rehearsing for " 'The Butterfly Frolic,' a graceful number," according to Joan, "whose delicate flittings were . . . my idea of what dancing should be." As the dress rehearsal proceeds, Miss Flegg and Joan's mother agree that the dance would be "reduced to something laughable and unseemly by the presence of a fat little girl who was more like a giant caterpillar than a butterfly." Joan is manipulated into changing roles, into doing (as Miss Flegg puts it) "something special": she is to become a "mothball." Joan asks, futilely, whether she can still wear her wings, but "it was beginning to seep through to me, the monstrousness of the renunciation she was asking me to make." The performance is a success, and Joan is its star; but for her it is "a dance of rage and destruction, tears {rolling] down my cheeks behind the fur" of the costume (45–50).

Eventually, Joan develops a continuing fantasy in which she envisions herself as "the Fat Lady from the freak show at the Canadian National Exhibition . . . wearing pink tights . . . , a short fluffy pink skirt, satin ballet slippers and, on her head, a sparkling tiara. She carried a diminutive pink umbrella; this was a substitute for the wings which I longed to pin on her." Joan imagines this Fat Lady doing an extravagant high-wire act, but she notes that "I knew perfectly well that after her death-defying feat she had to return to the freak show . . . and be gaped at by the ticket-buyers. That was her real life." It is such a reality that Joan wishes to escape, to leave behind, even as she realizes it would be better to learn to accept herself "for what I was." "Very true, very right, very pious," she adds; "but it's still not so simple. I wanted those things, that fluffy skirt, that glittering tiara. I liked them" (102–3).

The novel is soon thrust into a series of disjunctive locales, relationships, and personalities that reveal other details of Joan's distraught adolescence and her emergence into adulthood, while also serving to explain her current, ambiguous situation. For, as Joan has attempted to accommodate herself to her childhood and subsequent traumas, she has developed a rich capacity for fantasy—the baroque frame around the mirror—that has propelled her into sustaining various identities, all determined by the expectations of those around her. Even her adolescent gluttony—largely an act of rebellion against her mother's psychological abuse—is Joan's way of accommodating her mother's negative attitude toward her. Later, when Joan begins to lose weight as a result of blood-poisoning and her conveniently deceased Aunt Lou's two-thousand-dollar bequest (conditioned on her reducing by one hundred pounds), her mother cannot relinquish the perversely comforting belief that her daughter has been a failure: "She went on baking sprees and left pies and cookies around the kitchen where they would tempt me, and it struck me that in a lesser way she had always done this. While I grew thinner, she herself became distraught and uncertain" (123).

The conflict between mother and daughter reaches a climax when Joan, at age eighteen, reveals she is going to leave home. This revelation provokes an attack—partly physical but mostly psychological—that sends Joan to a Toronto rooming house, where (increasingly thin and attractive) she lives under her aunt's name, Louisa K. Delacourt: "This," she says, "was the formal beginning of my second self" (137). After several months she has reduced sufficiently to obtain her inheritance and is "face to face with the rest of my life. I was now a different person, and . . . I was the right shape, but I had the wrong past. I'd have to get rid of it entirely and construct a different one for myself, a more agreeable one" (141). What Joan discovers, however, as she relinquishes one set of facts for another and refabricates her "life, time after time," in the belief that "the truth was not convincing" (150), is that such fabrications tend to cloy about one's presence, that the baroque mirror frame becomes increasingly a labyrinthine trap. She leaves for London, where she meets Paul, the Polish Count, who deprives her of her virginity because she is too embarrassed to admit that she had interpreted his offer to share his apartment merely as a gesture of friendship. When she meets Arthur, whom she eventually marries, she falsifies her past for him, revealing to him neither her obese childhood nor the facts of her relationship with Paul. She also fails to tell him that she is a writer of costume gothics, pulp for the masses, under her aunt's name. The photograph she has of herself as a child, she tells him when he asks, is of another aunt, Aunt Deirdre, whom she eventually kills off (one more attempt to bury the past), to mask as an inheritance the money she has received for selling one of her gothic romances. Meanwhile, in her role as Joan Foster, she has written a book of quasi-mystic poems called *Lady Oracle,* which catapults her into becoming an overnight literary cult figure. Her fame as one of Toronto's literary elite provokes both an affair with a bizarre avant-garde artist named the Royal Porcupine and a notoriety that compels Fraser Buchanan, a parasite stalking the periphery of Toronto's literary establishment, to seek her out, discover her secrets, and blackmail her. It is this threat, as well as her increasing inability to juggle her separate lives, that sends Joan to her staged suicide and her journey to Italy and yet another life.

"You can't change the past." Even as Joan begins to tell her story, however, we discover that her "death," like her life, is indeed filled with "loose ends": she is hiding in an Italian village, Terremoto, where she and Arthur had spent the previous summer, a place—"the same town, the same house" (11)—where she can be recognized; she is wearing the "waist-length red hair" that has become her "trademark" as a celebrated author (13–14); and she still has her "wet clothes, in a green plastic Glad Bag," the clothes she was wearing when she "drowned" in Lake Ontario. Although Joan notes that she was "quickly practical again"—burying her clothes, cutting and burning her hair—these remnants of her past become emblematic of her inability to leave that past behind, to renounce it, or to alter it (19). "You can't change the past," Joan's "Aunt Lou used to say" (10); and, later—as the clothes resurface from the ground and as Joan laments, "I wanted to forget the past, but it refused to forget me" (214)—we see the truth of Aunt Lou's folksy wisdom.

Like Atwood's two earlier protagonists—Marian MacAlpin and the unnamed adventurer of *Surfacing*—Joan Foster's difficulty can be seen as resembling a particular clinical syndrome, a special psychological quirk. For Marian, it is anorexia nervosa; for the woman in *Surfacing,* it is amnesia; for Joan, it is suggestive of something like multiple personality disorder, in which traumatic episodes, initiated in early childhood, trigger the formation of separate personalities which constitute distinct parts of the victim's psyche and exist side by side. As Joan says at one point, referring to her "double life," actually "I was more than double, I was triple, multiple" (246). And, commenting on Arthur's various guises, she notes that "the difference was that I was simultaneous, whereas Arthur was a sequence" (211). Clinically, of course, Joan is not precisely a multiple personality, even despite her troubled childhood (including the physical absence of her father during the first five years of her life and his psychological detachment afterwards). But to some degree Joan's conscious, artistic creation and manipulation of her many identities is similar to the mind's clever adaptability in responding to unacceptably cruel psychological or physical violation. The effects, too, are similar: "It was true I had two lives, but on off days I felt that neither of them was completely real. . . . I got a reputation for being absentminded" (216–17).

The problem is that the separate, incomplete identities thus formed cannot be ignored or discarded; rather they have to be reintegrated into the total self. To achieve this remedy, in the context of *Lady Oracle,* Joan must accept reality, must come to see that the baroque frame around the mirror of her life surrounds a looking glass whose distortions must be shattered, must realize that the way to shatter the glass is to plunge through its center as one would journey to the center of a maze to unravel its secret. As the novel draws to its climax, Joan sees the latest of several spectral visitations of her mother's image. Recognizing at last the significance of the haunting love-hate relationship between herself and her mother—that her mother, too, is part of her being, an element of her personality that cannot be renounced—Joan asks whether her mother can "see I loved her? I loved her but the glass was between us, I would have to go through it" (329).

"**Through that door.**" From the beginning of *Lady Oracle* Joan has been composing her current gothic romance, *Stalked by Love*, segments of which have been interspersed throughout Atwood's novel as a vague, romantic mirror of Joan's own experiences. As Joan begins to realize that *"I must collect myself"* (339), these intrusions begin to impinge with eerie and unerring accuracy on her life in Terremoto. She notes about one of her characters, with whom she has been identifying, "Charlotte would have to go into the maze, there was no way out of it. . . . But her feelings were ambiguous: did the maze mean certain death, or did it contain the answer to a riddle, an answer she must learn in order to live?" (331).

Earlier, commenting on the escapism her romances provide for her readers, Joan notes "the pure quintessential need of my readers for escape, a thing I myself understood only too well" (34). But romantic escape—Joan's life imitating the art of her romances—will simply not do. And, as *Lady Oracle* moves toward its conclusion, it is art that begins intensely to imitate life; the interspersed segments of *Stalked by Love* converge ever more radically with Joan's life and become less a comic parallel to that life, more a chilling response to Joan's dilemma. Having just imagined a formulaic conclusion to her story, in which Charlotte is rescued from chaos and lives happily ever after, Joan comments that "that was the way it was supposed to go, that was the way it had always gone before, but somehow it no longer felt right. I'd taken a wrong turn somewhere" (333). The problem, as Joan realizes even earlier, is that Charlotte is a bore, unlike her adversary, Felicia: "Sympathy for Felicia," says Joan, "was out of the question, it was against the rules, it would foul up the plot completely . . . she had to die. . . . But what had she ever done to deserve it? How could I sacrifice her for the sake of Charlotte? I was getting tired of Charlotte, with her intact virtue and her tidy ways. . . . I wanted her to fall into a mud puddle, have menstrual cramps, sweat, burp, fart" (319).

By escaping to Terremoto, Joan has effected the sharpest parallel yet to Charlotte's life-denying existence. Joan's "death," her escape, her happy ending, she finds, is not only impossible, but it is indeed a bore. It is the culmination of all her prior efforts to find safety in being exempt from life, in preferring "the sidelines" (217). But, she asks herself at the beginning of part 5, "what price safety?" Having escaped to "the Other Side" (both the European shore of the Atlantic and the other side of the veil separating life from death), she notes that "the Other Side was no paradise, it was only a limbo. Now I knew why the dead came back to watch over the living: the Other Side was boring" (309). To reenter life, Joan must bring "the separate parts of my life together": tidy art and messy reality, Joan Foster and Louisa K. Delacourt, Fat Lady and ravishing red-haired beauty, gothic novelist and mystic poet. She fears that doing so will result in "an explosion," but she realizes that it is a hazard that must be faced (217).

In the penultimate chapter of Lady Oracle Joan tempts that explosion as she offers up a revised version of the concluding chapter of Stalked by Love, one that defies the romantic conventions of the genre. It is now Felicia who enters the maze, plunges to its center, and there (as Joan) sees gathered the various personalities that constitute collectively the whole woman we have come to know under so many guises. Though the garden maze in which Felicia finds herself is in fact a trap—an artistic contrivance as suffocating as the conventions of romance—it is also the key to discovery: for only by entering it completely can one see truly the need to get out and regain life. Felicia is told that "the only way out . . . is through that door," the one that reflects the barricade Joan has set between herself and others all her life. Opening the door, Felicia finds a man who offers both love and, in an instant transformation—as the flesh falls "away from his face, revealing the skull behind it"—death as well (342–43).

The connection is apt. For, throughout Lady Oracle, in continuing allusions to Tennyson's Lady of Shalott (the woman who ends by escaping her mirror-imaged fantasy world and being carried away a corpse in the bottom of a boat), Atwood has reflected on the premise that a truly vital life—including a potentially rewarding love—can be obtained only by accepting the dangers of life, including death. As Joan observes, late in the book, "maybe they were right, you could stay in the tower for years, weaving away, looking in the mirror, but one glance out the window at real life and that was that. The curse, the doom" (313). Earlier, and in a way more directly related to Joan's urgent need for love, she wishes "to have someone, anyone, say that I had a lovely face, even if I had to turn into a corpse in a barge-bottom first" (143). And so, as the appropriately titled Stalked by Love reaches its climactic moment in Joan's meditation, she opens her eyes and hears footsteps approaching her own door. Determining finally not to hide behind the barricade, and unwilling merely to pause at the threshold (as the protagonist in *Surfacing* does), Joan opens the door and steels herself "to face the man who stood waiting for me, for my life" (343).

"Something about a man in a bandage." In the final chapter, Atwood undercuts the terror she has wrought for Joan, and the chills she has created for her reader, by plunging us abruptly back into the ordinary world. The threatening man behind the door, this gothic fiend reaching out for Joan's life, is only a curious, story-hunting reporter; and the Cinzano bottle Joan hits him over the head with is hardly a magically protective dagger with an elaborately carved baroque handle. As she concludes her recitation of events, Joan notes that "I keep thinking I should learn some lesson from all this." And, it would seem, she has. No longer seeking escape, no longer avoiding responsibility, she says of her wounding the reporter, "I suppose I could still have gotten out of it. . . . Or I could have escaped. . . . But somehow I couldn't just run off and leave him all alone." Knowing, too, that Sam and Marlene, the friends who aided her in her "suicide," have been arrested and accused of her murder, she intends to return to Toronto and explain what has occurred, thus revealing to all who may care (but especially to herself) the secret of the various lives she has tried so hard to maintain separately. And, in a further act that symbolizes the merging of her various identities, she tells the reporter her story, thus putting him, at once, in possession of her total personality. As she says, "I've begun to feel he's the only person who knows anything about me." The reporter is going to write up Joan's story; and in that story, "once he's written it," the complete and true Joan Delacourt Foster will emerge (344–45).

Or at least as true as reality permits. For, as Atwood has noted in a 1976 interview, "we all have our scenarios. . . . It's realistic to describe people as having fantasies because everybody does." Certainly that is true of Joan, who is capable still of altering the facts of the story she has told the reporter ("the odd thing is that I didn't tell any lies. Well, not very many," 344), and of viewing the reporter himself as a potential romantic hero ("he doesn't have a very interesting nose, but . . . there is something about a man in a bandage," 345). Though she "won't write any more Costume Gothics," Joan thus suggests she has not forsaken completely her tendency to embellish reality. But that may be all right. Difficulties arise, says Atwood, "only when you get so completely wrapped up in your fantasies that you cannot untangle your fantasy projections from the real person."[14] For Joan, such confusion now seems less likely. In her final words she acknowledges her worst flaw, noting that her hitting the reporter with the bottle "did make a mess"; and, although she adds the potentially threatening observation, "I don't think I'll ever be a very tidy person," she seems now to be accepting herself with more honesty than she has previously managed (345). It may not be an enormous advance, Atwood seems to be suggesting, but it is at least, for Joan, a refreshing possibility.

Dancing Girls and Other Stories

Published in 1977, the Canadian edition of *Dancing Girls and Other Stories* contains three original tales and eleven others that had appeared as early as 1964, in magazines as diverse as *Alphabet, Harper's, Ms., Saturday Night,* and *The Malahat Review.* Together, the stories offer a full range of Atwood's fictional moods and strategies, a variety of tone and subject that illustrates her versatility as an artist. Within this mixture certain typically Atwoodian themes emerge, providing a coherent link between the several stories in the collection.

The first piece, "The War in the Bathroom," concentrates on the polarities that exist within each human being and on the almost paranoid suspicion an individual may feel for fellow dwellers in an urban apartment building. The title refers to the tactics the narrator employs to gain territorial control over the communal bathroom which she believes has been monopolized by the other tenants. It refers also to the "war" between two people whom the narrator hears beyond the wall of her flat, which backs against the lavatory. Only hearing the voices of an old and helpless woman and her nurse, the narrator believes at first that there is in fact only one individual, battling herself in alternating "voices, one high and querulous, the other an urgent whisper."[15] The narrator's suspicion is linked to her own divided character. She is the passive, verbal, thinking aspect of a complete human being—the mind; and she controls the other side, the body, who acts on the narrator's orders and whom the narrator—"I"—refers to as "she." Atwood exaggerates the separation by applying action verbs to the physical portion of the self, and thought or emotion verbs to the mental perambulations of the narrative voice ("as she walked I thought" is a typical construction, 16).

Like the two people in the bathroom, the narrator and the body she inhabits conduct a war for control, a war related in the form of a journal. At the story's end, the narrator has her body occupy the bathroom, "my territory," and exclude the old man who is her primary antagonist: "He made a choking noise, an inarticulate sound of rage and despair . . . then there was a crash and a thumping sound and a wail of pain that faded into silence." The narrator's body attempts "to get out of the bathtub," but the narrator—content that "for the time being I have won"—tells "her to stay where she was." The enemy defeated, and "the bathroom door . . . securely locked," she feels safe at last (18).

The surreal fantasy of "The War in the Bathroom" contrasts with the second story, "The Man from Mars," whose essentially realistic portrayal of events and commonplace milieu belie the science-fiction implications of its title. Here again, though, Atwood presents us with a tale of urban fear, allied this time—as in the title story—with a suspicion of alien cultures, whose inhabitants may well seem like visitors from foreign planets. The story involves a college student, Christine, who meets another student, from an unnamed Third-World country. She becomes increasingly an object of his attempts to involve himself with her; his shadowing of her becomes increasingly alarming; and her actions to extricate herself from his attentions become increasingly warlike, as Atwood once again develops images of battle (when the foreign student holds Christine's tennis racquet which he has retrieved for her from the ground, she feels "deprived . . . weaponless," 23).

At first, Christine is only mildly frightened, her own unattractiveness suggesting to her that she could hardly be a target of someone's malign intentions. But as the months pass, and his pursuit becomes at once both comic and pathetic ("she was aware of the ridiculous spectacle they must make, galloping across campus, . . . a lumbering elephant stampeded by a smiling, emaciated mouse," 33–34), she finds herself confronting both his intransigence and her own liberal ideology: "Was he deranged, was he a sex maniac? He seemed so harmless, yet it was that kind who often went berserk in the end" (36–37). Eventually—as a result of other womens' complaints and the involvement of the police—the foreigner is deported to his home country, and Christine settles down to her now once-again-mediocre life. Years pass, an unnamed Far Eastern war begins, and Christine realizes that the country involved is the home of her foreign visitor.

Despite her own warlike relations with him and the significance she gave to his absurd and misguided attempts to relate to a culture that was as foreign to him as he was to those he pursued, she sees that he was too insignificant to be in mortal danger: rather than being in the army of his country—North or South—"he would be something non-descript, something in the background, like herself; perhaps he had become an interpreter" (42). Thus ends the story, on a calm note that points to the absurdity of our daily fictions.

The collection's third story, "Polarities," is less calm, as it plays out the increasingly evident madness of Louise, a graduate teaching assistant at what seems to be the University of Alberta in Edmonton (though Atwood, typically, provides no place names), and the attempts by Morrison, an American instructor who has a developing relationship with Louise, to understand her. Like the protagonist of *Surfacing*, Louise begins to question technology (in the form of the telephone) and to develop a notion that structures can be entered only from a certain direction ("I can't go through this door any more. It's wrong," 57). She gathers up a small cabal of individuals, who she believes somehow constitute a unifying force, part of a "private system, in aphorisms and short poems which were thoroughly sane in themselves but which taken together were not" (63). They, in turn, bring her to the hospital for treatment.

For all her madness, Morrison realizes that "the only difference is that she's taken as real what the rest of us pretend is only metaphorical." And he sees that her perception of himself, contained in her notebook that he and the others spy through, is, for all its exaggeration, accurate: "Morrison is not a complete person. He needs to be completed, he refuses to admit his body is part of his mind. He can be in the circle possibly, but only if he will surrender his role as a fragment and show himself willing to merge with the greater whole." By the end of the story, Louise remains in the psychiatric ward of the hospital, her mad vision shattered; and Morrison, realizing he loves her, seeing the futility of his life, stares out into the frozen tundra that suggests the coldness of his existence. Between the warm madness of Louise's vision of unity and the "chill interior" of Morrison's isolation, Atwood seems to suggest, there is no connection possible; the polarities remain (63).

Set off against the paranoid fantasies of "The War in the Bathroom" and the mad visionary fantasies of "Polarities" are the more mundane quirks of the mind as it sometimes seriously, often humorously, creates and examines scenarios of abuse and destruction that characterize the modern world. In "Rape Fantasies," especially, Atwood's narrator speaks in a curiously benevolent voice as she reflects on the fictions she and her friends have developed about being raped. Chrissy, for example—alluding to a setting that links this story to several others in the volume—imagines herself "being in the bathtub," her rapist somehow getting into the room and crawling into the tub with her (104). Although the narrator pours some mild sarcasm upon these stories (she notes that Chrissy might get bubbles up her nose), she ends lunch with her friends thinking about her own fantasies. These, to the end of the narrative, she plays out for us, providing humor in such images as the bungling rapist's getting his zipper stuck. By the end of the story, however, Atwood has carefully modulated the tone into a poignant recognition of human frailty that bonds the narrator and her imagined assailants, with whom she imagines having long conversations: "Like, how could a fellow do that to a person he's just had a long conversation with," she asks; "that's the part I really don't understand" (110).

More terrifying fantasies occur in "When It Happens" and "A Travel Piece." In the first we meet middle-aged Mrs. Burridge, who while tending her rural ways, putting up her yearly pickles, contemplates the beginnings of World War III and prepares, in her mind, images of herself, gun in hand, protecting her territory. Atwood ends the story benignly, however, as Mrs. Burridge is transported out of her fantasy and back into the daylight world of her mundane kitchen. In "A Travel Piece" Annette, a free-lance journalist, undergoes a plane crash on the water: bewilderment over whether the crash has really happened or exists only in Annette's drug-and-liquor-muddled imagination is part of Atwood's strategy, as she examines a character—much like the protagonist in *Bodily Harm* (1981)—to whom "real events" never "happen" and whose articles tell similarly of places "where all was well, where unpleasant things" do not occur (148, 150). For her, the crash may be at last a real event. And, though at first she still feels "it is as safe in this lifeboat as everywhere else" (155), the story moves inexorably to a horrifying conclusion, as Annette must decide whether she will participate in an act of cannibalism which seems to define "what it means to be alive," an act that for all its evil is also a "mundane" reality, "bathed . . . in the ordinary sunlight she has walked in all her life" (159–60).

Several stories—"Under Glass," "The Grave of the Famous Poet,"

"Hair Jewellery," "The Resplendant Quetzal," "Lives of the Poets"—
concentrate on the conflicts between men and women, the attempts
to carve out a life that is both sane and human. In "The Grave of the
Famous Poet," for example, the narrator analytically surveys the bat-
tleground that is her relationship with her lover, notes that "we've
had our quarrel, . . . the one we were counting on," and observes
their isolation from each other: "If there were separate buses we'd
take them. As it is we wait together, standing a little apart" (97).
"Under Glass," in tones reminiscent of *Power Politics* ("I steer my
course so he will have to go through all the puddles. If I can't win,
I tell him, neither can you," 78), tells of the ambiguous, sordid affair
between the quasi-mad narrator and her promiscuous partner, who
has, on the eve of her moving into an apartment with him, made love
to yet another woman. Reconciling herself, the narrator thinks about
the plants under the glass of a greenhouse she has visited, "the plants
that have taught themselves to look like stones"; and she wonders
how long it will take to transform herself into stone also (83).

A similar theme is evoked in "Training." Rob, the protagonist,
has been sent by his family to work at a crippled children's camp
where "for the first week" he "had nightmares" about "bodies, pieces
of bodies, arms and legs and torsos, detached and floating in mid-air"
(189). Of the reality behind such grotesque visions, one of the other
characters notes that "you have to laugh or go crazy" (192). At the
story's conclusion, as he watches a dance performance put on by the
crippled children, Rob recognizes in their grotesque movements a
parallel to his own crippled soul. And he ends, not in a stone-like
silence, but in a saving hysterical laughter.

The final story, "Giving Birth," offers a more compelling salvation, as Atwood examines the physical process of "giving birth," the
spiritual implications of creating a new life, and the phenomenological significance of the term itself. "But who gives it," the story begins, "and to whom is it given? Certainly it doesn't feel like giving.
. . . Thus language, muttering in its archaic tongues of something,
yet one more thing, that needs to be re-named" (239).

In this story Atwood creates an extraordinary interplay of fiction
and reality to allow the narrator (in some respects clearly Atwood herself, writing out of the emotions following the 1976 birth of her
daughter) to recapture through the words of the narrative the experience of birth that is rapidly escaping into the irrecoverable past. As
the narrator speaks of her own commonplace existence and the solid

reality of her own baby—"now she's having her nap and I am writing this story" (241)—it becomes increasingly evident that the story's protagonist, a pregnant woman named Jeannie, is the narrator as she was before giving birth. The story itself is the narrator's attempt to remember, through the uncertain medium of words, "what it was like" (252). "You may be thinking," she says, "that I've invented Jeannie in order to distance myself from these experiences. Nothing could be further from the truth. I am, in fact, trying to bring myself closer to something that time has already made distant. As for Jeannie, my intention is simple: I am bringing her back to life" (243).

By bringing Jeannie "back to life," Atwood is able to resurrect the experience whereby the narrator was transformed into her present self, to describe Jeannie's becoming "drifted over with new words," ceasing "to be what she was," being "replaced, gradually, by someone else" (254). The narrator observes that "it was to me, after all, that the birth was given, Jeannie gave it, I am the result" (253). Finally defining the terms we use to describe the experience of birth, explaining the process whereby she achieved her new identity, the narrator thereby defines herself. Moreover, by relating Jeannie's creative act in giving birth and the narrator's creative act in putting that event into words, Atwood is celebrating, in yet one more guise, the artist's power to accomplish miracles. Here, as in *True Stories,* Atwood questions the mystery and miraculousness of the creative act—the birth, she says, brings no "vision . . . no special knowledge" to Jeannie (252). But in the communion between child and mother—as in the communion between narrator and reader—the creative act becomes, nevertheless, an affirmation of life, an event that may change us into something we have never been before. As the narrator says of her baby's attempt to name the objects of her world, "I am waiting for her first word: surely it will be miraculous" (240).

Life Before Man

Atwood's fourth novel, published in 1979, relates the story of several characters caught in an unremittingly banal existence in 1970s Toronto: Elizabeth Schoenhof, a special projects administrator at Toronto's Royal Ontario Museum, who is haunted by a childhood filled with an absent father, a drunken mother who burns to death in a rooming-house fire, an emotionally deranged sister who eventually dies in a mental institution (having drowned in her bath when left unattended), and a rigidly proper aunt (Auntie Muriel) who raises the two daughters after their mother's dissipation becomes unacceptably grim; Elizabeth's husband, Nate, a one-time lawyer now toymaker, who in his cynicism is oppressed by his mother's continuing activist attempts to make the earth a better place to live; Lesje, a museum paleontologist, who dreams of a better life "before man" among the dinosaurs of the Mesozoic era, and who begins an affair with Nate only to find herself in conflict with Elizabeth, whose own most recent extramarital affair, with a museum taxidermist named Chris, has ended in his violent suicide (Elizabeth, in turn, now takes up with William, an environmentalist who ends his affair with Lesje by attempting to rape her). Some other characters, in what may aptly be called an Atwoodian soap opera, include Martha, Nate's previous mistress, who understands that being Nate's lover is tantamount to being Elizabeth's maid—no problem unless the assigned hours for adultery are transgressed; and the Schoenhofs' two daughters, Janet and Nancy, who stand poignantly on the sidelines as not-so-subtle reminders of the need to maintain appearances.

   "They didn't intend to become extinct."   Given this all-too-familiar scenario of urban infidelity—born, as one reviewer put it, of "moral and emotional torpor"—it is perhaps not surprising that the first three sections of Atwood's five-part narrative may seem relatively unexciting; and this despite the witty verbal play of her language, the interweaving of fantasy and realism so typical of her work, and the occasionally brilliant intensity of several scenes. As another reviewer noted, *Life Before Man* "is subtle, beautifully written and shaped, but, oddly enough, not always interesting."[16]

   To understand both the ennui of *Life Before Man* and the narrative strategy Atwood employs to evoke and give significance to that mood, we have to listen in on the thoughts of Lesje as—late in the novel—she contemplates an answer to a letter written by a schoolchild, requesting information for a Grade Six report on dinosaurs and the Mesozoic: "Why is it called the Mesozoic? The correct answer, the one the teacher wants, is on the fact sheet. *Meso,* middle, *zoos,* life. . . . But does the Mesozoic exist? When it did it was called nothing. The dinosaurs didn't know they were in the Mesozoic. They didn't know they were only in the middle. They didn't intend to become extinct; as far as they knew they would live forever."[17] In this passage Atwood offers us the intellectual crux of her novel, caught also in such narrative junctures as the discussion between Nate and

Lesje, in which he affirms that "dinosaurs are dead. . . . But I'm still alive," and Lesje asks him whether he is sure (258). The correlation between the species *Homo sapiens* and the unwary inhabitants of the Mesozoic is clear. Just as Atwood's characters are associated with the Royal Ontario Museum, that home of fossilized relics that provide some clue to prehistoric species, so too is *Life Before Man* Atwood's museum, her showcase, her exhibit of those contemporary fossils that display the natural history of the twentieth-century creatures who call themselves "man" (but, in another twist of the title's meaning, may not yet have achieved that status)—a history revealed by the independent, but in many ways indistinguishable specimens who constitute the museum world that defines their existence.

But it is the uncertainty, in particular, in Nate's and Lesje's discussion that is most crucial: the idea not that our utterly banal lives can offer us a certain, sudden death—neat and complete and discernible, like Chris's—but rather that, in our rootless, lassitudinous wandering from one empty relationship to another, we have consigned ourselves to a spiritual emptiness that costs us entirely our individual identities. In the first of two epigraphs with which Atwood precedes her narrative, taken from *The Age of the Dinosaurs,* Björn Kurtén notes that a fossil, instead of being "a part of the organism itself, . . . may be some kind of record of its presence, such as a fossilized track or burrow"; such fossils "give us our only chance to see the extinct animals in action and to study their behavior"; only "where the animal has dropped dead in its tracks and become fossilized on the spot" can "identification" be more definite ([7]). The record of our lives, suggests Atwood, may be found, possibly, only in the fragmentary tracks or burrows of an insubstantial presence.

Atwood extends this theme through her experimentation with narrative perspective. She offers a kaleidoscopic view of reality—reminiscent of Faulkner's *As I Lay Dying*—whereby given events are filtered through the fragmented, alternating perceptions of Elizabeth, Lesje, and Nate, as they play out their lives in the precisely dated episodes that make up the novel's time scheme: "Friday, October 29, 1976" through "Friday, August 18, 1978" (this nearly two-year period is extended by two flashbacks, the only interruptions of the narrative's straightforward chronology—one for "Thursday, August 28, 1975," when Nate realizes that Elizabeth and Chris have begun an affair; the other for "Thursday, October 7, 1976," just after Elizabeth has told Nate that the affair is over and just before Chris commits suicide).

As at least one critic has observed, this narrative structure—"the discrete, static units," the "series of dated and labelled scenarios"— is an attempt to replicate a scientist's "collection of file cards, or even field notes," an attempt "to sum up the species it purports to describe."[18] Even so, as Atwood weaves these "field notes" into a novel, they coalesce into a vision that transcends the disparate—and mundane—elements out of which it is comprised; and the narrative, in parts 4 and 5, achieves an intellectual intensity that helps counteract the dullness of the lives it is attempting to describe. This vision—if dismal in import—does, nevertheless, make *Life Before Man* more than an inconsequential, contemporary melodrama. We may well agree with Lesje's contemplations early in the novel: "The real question is: Does she care whether the human race survives or not? She doesn't know. The dinosaurs didn't survive and it wasn't the end of the world. . . . Nature will think up something else. Or not, as the case may be" (27).

"So far, it stands." But if Lesje's contemplations, the novel's first epigraph, and Atwood's narrative structure yield this inescapably burdensome theme, the second epigraph seems to balance intellect with emotion, attempts an affirmation of life even at its most dismal: "Look, I'm smiling at you, I'm smiling in you, I'm smiling through you. How can I be dead if I breathe in every quiver of your hand?" ([7]). Certainly the brooding presence of Chris—emphasized by the two narrative segments that disturb the novel's chronology—offers the possibility of this more positive message. But Atwood suggests other potentially redeeming elements in the gray urban landscape of her story. As the novel moves toward its conclusion, she brings her major characters to an understanding of human complexity, of mortality, and of potential regeneration that grants, if only tentatively, some significance to their empty lives.

Lesje, for example, disgusted with Nate's preoccupation with his children, stops taking her birth-control pills and (it appears) becomes pregnant with his child. Although she is ambivalent about the good that can come from a "child conceived in such rage" (293) and wonders whether the museum "will . . . ask her to leave" ("a pregnant paleontologist is surely a contradiction in terms"), she is able to see that this "negligible act of hers can have measurable consequences for other people, . . . the past is the sediment from such acts, billions, trillions of them" (308). A child, obviously representing a regeneration of the species, thus also grants to our actions a larger significance, one that counteracts the mortality that otherwise obliterates the meaning of our lives.

It is an understanding of such mortality and of the complex motivations for human behavior, also, that Atwood brings to her characters before the field notes are filed away. Lesje, at the end, notices Elizabeth, "standing by herself, unconnected with anyone," and sees her as "shorter, worn, ordinary[,] mortal," no longer "permanent, like an icon" (309). Elizabeth, earlier, has shockingly discovered that Auntie Muriel, her lifetime icon and nemesis, now dying of cancer, has not been the wicked, remorseless witch of Elizabeth's illusions: as Muriel begins to cry on her deathbed, Elizabeth sees that "the Auntie Muriel of [her] childhood has melted, leaving in her place this . . . old woman who now drops her blockish embroidery and with eyes closed and weeping gropes with her hands across the hospital covers." Acting out Atwood's typical gesture of reconciliation, Elizabeth grasps "Auntie Muriel's blinded hands" (281–82).

Nate, too, sees his illusions damaged as he discovers that his mother's attempts to help people derived from her own cynicism—much like his own—engendered by her husband's death in World War II. She considered suicide, she tells Nate ("I guess I simply didn't want to live on this kind of an earth"), but thought better of it (287). Initially appalled, Nate is transformed by his mother's revelation; and in his next narrative fragment we find him working on one of her many crusades. As he contemplates leaving, at the end of his shift, he sees himself joining the people on the street, losing "himself among the apathetic, the fatalistic, the uncommitted, the cynical; among whom he would like to feel at home" (306). But Nate, it would seem, can no longer feel completely akin to the uncommitted. In his next segment he is contemplating a role in politics, and his obsessive concern with "his own eventual death" has been put aside (312).

As the novel ends, Elizabeth is examining the Chinese art exhibit she has mounted and comparing its utopian images with the political and social reality of the sordid, actual world: "Underneath the poster-paint colors, . . . there is malice, greed, despair, hatred, death. . . . China is not paradise; paradise does not exist. . . . Like cavemen, they paint not what they see but what they want." To want, however, is in a sense, to have: "China," thinks Elizabeth in the final line of the novel, "does not exist. Nevertheless she longs to be there" (316–17). Earlier, with less idealism but with equally poignant optimism, she thinks about the wreck of her life, about all our lives, and notes of her imperfect, crumbling house that "it's a wonder that she has a house at all, that she's managed to accomplish a house. Despite the wreckage. She's built a dwelling over the abyss, but where else was there to build it? So far, it stands" (302).

Bodily Harm

Bodily Harm (1981) recounts the turmoil of Rennie Wilford, a supposedly innocent journalist, a writer of innocuous "travel and fashion" articles,[19] who has recently had a partial mastectomy, lost her lover through mutual misgivings over whether their affair could survive the amputation, and had a pathetic attempted affair with her surgeon. Coming home one day to find her apartment having been broken into by a potential sadist who may return, she decides to journey from Toronto to the Caribbean and write a travel piece for her magazine.

"Massive involvement." If, as one critic suggests, *Life Before Man* is Atwood's first major thrust into "social and domestic Realism," this fifth novel may well be considered, similarly, a work of political realism.[20] The action takes place on the islands of St. Antoine and Ste. Agathe, where Rennie becomes caught up, inadvertently, in the cancerous intrigues of a corrupt Caribbean island government, CIA agents, and runners of contraband. Eventually, even without having written the courageous political poem Atwood speaks of in *True Stories,* Rennie is placed in a sordid prison cell. There, psychologically tortured, she is forced to witness the physical mistreatment of her companion, Lora, a woman who, less naive than Rennie and more committed to the turmoil of an involved life, once had to stab her stepfather with a can opener to prevent his raping her and who, while imprisoned, offers her body to the guards to obtain the food and favors that will allow herself and Rennie to survive. Through her experiences, Rennie (like the protagonist of *Surfacing*) comes finally to understand that she cannot divorce herself from the rest of humanity, cannot proclaim innocence, and cannot renounce the power she and the words she writes hold over others. As she looks out of her cell into the courtyard where a man is being tortured, she "understands for the first time that" escape from the malignant terror she is experiencing may be impossible; and she realizes that "she is not exempt. Nobody is exempt from anything" (290).

Complementing this surface narrative of events in the Caribbean is a series of flashbacks through which Rennie replays for us both her recent Toronto past and her more distant childhood in Griswold, a puritanical Ontario village, where she "grew up surrounded by old people" and "learned three things well: how to be quiet, what not to say, and how to look at things without touching them" (54). Her grandmother, in particular, pervades her memory, as Rennie recalls a frightening instance in which the old woman wanders vaguely "into the kitchen" searching for her hands—not the ones that Rennie points out are "on the ends of your arms," but "my other hands, the ones I had before, the ones I touch things with" (57).

Through this interplay of past and present—similar to that in her earlier novels—Atwood weaves a fabric of image and event, illusion and memory, that defines Rennie's identity and motivates her behavior. The idea of touching and the imagery of hands, for example, become a central motif, as the plot moves inexorably toward what Rennie considers to be "massive involvement." She notes early in the narrative that such "involvement" has "never been my thing" (34); what she discovers, however, is that it cannot be avoided. In Atwood's novel, indeed, it becomes an inescapable metaphor linking various of the book's images, from the cancerous emblem of involvement in human imperfection and mortality that has scarred Rennie's breast, to her more political (if unintended) participation in the struggles of the island government. The image, though, is also a positive one, as it points to the need for Rennie's joining in communion with her fellow human beings.

"**This is what will happen.**" It is at the end of the novel that this significance is most fully developed. Here, Rennie's memory of her grandmother's hands insinuates itself into the final scene and provides for Atwood a healing image to displace the fabric of personal and social disease imagery that pervades the work. At first, as the two women sit in their cell, Rennie is distant, her puritanical Griswold heritage causing her to judge Lora as somehow beneath her. Lora, hurt, reacts to Rennie's snub and "Rennie is embarrassed. She looks down at her hands, which ought to contain comfort. Compassion." Rennie realizes "she ought to go over to Lora and put her arms around her . . . , but she can't" (286). Soon, however, as the guards beat Lora into unconsciousness, Rennie's attitude begins to change.

To dramatize Rennie's spiritual transformation, Atwood at this point twists into yet one more dimension a narrative perspective that has already been quite complex (the tale is given in part by an omniscient narrator speaking directly to us in the third person, and in part by Rennie in a first-person narrative filtered to us through the implied presence of the omniscient narrator; both narrators speak sometimes in the past tense, for memories, sometimes in the present, for the events on the islands). As Rennie reacts to the brutality she has witnessed and to her own detachment from it, Atwood projects into the future what can best be described as a linguistic wish-fulfillment of Rennie's desires. "This," either Rennie or the omniscient narrator tells us, "is what will happen" (293).

In the first part of this imagined future Rennie undergoes interviews with a Canadian official, who apologizes for having been unable to free her earlier but explains that the situation was too unstable; he implies, also, that it would be best for her not to write about her experiences. To the diplomat's relief, Rennie, in this dream interlude, agrees; and, in the distance, there appears the plane that will take her from the island. After three brief segments—one back in the cell, one a memory of Griswold, and another in the cell—Atwood completes the novel with a continuation of Rennie's imagined release: "Then the plane will take off." As Atwood mixes present and future tense, in an intriguing interplay of reality and imagination, Rennie sees herself now as "a subversive. . . . A reporter. She will pick her time; then she will report." It is not certain whether her future will allow this act of witnessing—"she will never be rescued," says the narrator in reference to Rennie's physical imprisonment. But she has changed—"she has already been rescued," says the narrator about Rennie's chill isolation from her fellow human beings; "she is not exempt" (299–301).

What has effected this change is revealed in those interim segments. In the first Atwood returns us to the cell, where Lora lies motionless on the floor, presenting Rennie with a reality that she must, in fact, report to the world: "I should tell someone," she thinks (297). But it is the memory of her grandmother's searching hands that completes Rennie's newly formed moral landscape. Here Atwood repeats that earlier remembered scene in the kitchen; this time, however, the author elaborates, infusing the scene with a new significance. As Rennie stands "in the kitchen, making herself a peanut butter sandwich," again her grandmother comes into the room, frightening Rennie, moving toward her with "those groping hands." Rennie's mother arrives, in Rennie's memory, and reveals the secret which the now-imprisoned journalist must make her own: "Don't you know what to do by now?" her mother says to both the child and the prisoner; and "she takes hold of the grandmother's dangling hands, clasping them in her own" (297–98). As Rennie holds this image in her mind, we return to the cell, where—looking at Lora's mutilated body—Rennie realizes that she can no longer ignore faceless strangers crying for compassion: "there's no such thing as a faceless stranger," she thinks, "every face is someone's, it has a name." And, as she holds on to Lora's cold hand "with both of her hands," Rennie attempts a miracle: "She holds the hand, perfectly still, with all her strength. Surely, if she can only try hard enough, something will move and live again, something will get born" (298–99).

In this "climactic sequence," wrote one reviewer, "Atwood summons all her best cadences, and although we respond to her powers of incantation, we don't believe in the apotheosis for an instant"; Rennie is "an unlikely healer," too "self-absorbed" and "ungenerous" to become "the hand of God" re-instilling life into Lora's soulless body.[21] And yet it could be argued that this is exactly Atwood's point: humans do not become gods. At the end of the novel we do not know whether Rennie has accomplished a miracle, only that she has tried.

As in *Life Before Man,* Atwood thus concludes with the poignant hope that, bruised and hurting, caught in an imprisoning world that seems to offer no solace, we may possibly—somehow—survive after all. But there is a problem: in the explicitly brutal behavior of this especially dark novel of political realism, Atwood's pessimism seems far more profound than in her earlier work. And, as Rennie Wilford sits in her dark prison cell, rotting away to the bitter end, we may well find it difficult to credit her final affirmation; difficult, indeed, to be convinced that "she is lucky, suddenly, finally, she's overflowing with luck, it's this luck holding her up" (301). A pretty assertion, certainly, contending heroically against reality: but this time the words fail.

Chapter Five
Jail-Breaks and Re-Creations

The Poet as Critic

When *Survival: A Thematic Guide to Canadian Literature* was published by House of Anansi Press in the autumn of 1972, the established poet and soon-to-be-established novelist, Margaret Atwood, was suddenly plunged into an apparently unexpected and undesired notoriety as a literary critic. Viewed—depending upon one's bias—as the messiah of Canadian literature or as a misguided opportunist, she ceased being merely a writer and became, in her own words, "a thing, . . . a culmination of being an icon, that is something that people worship, and being a target, that is something that they shoot at." The publication of this book, more than any other event, marks the point at which Atwood achieved the problematic status of being a personality as well as an artist, "the first [Canadian] writer in our generation," says Dennis Lee, "to have become public property."[1]

Despite the paramount importance of *Survival* in any evaluation of Atwood's significance as a literary critic, her activity as both critic and social commentator extends, like her work in novels and short stories, to her earliest days as a writer. She composed reviews and other prose pieces for the Leaside High School *Clan Call* and Victoria College's *Acta Victoriana* in the late 1950s and early 1960s; and James Reaney's little magazine, *Alphabet,* published her reviews as early as 1962, with a major article on the works of Rider Haggard appearing in *Alphabet* in July 1965. Her academic studies at the University of Toronto and Harvard equipped her with a broad historical knowledge of literature and with techniques of literary criticism, and she has employed this background skillfully in reviews and articles that have appeared in such periodicals as *Canadian Literature, Saturday Night, Maclean's, The Times Literary Supplement,* and *The New York Times Book Review*.

In addition to her literary criticism, Atwood has published informal essays on such diverse topics as Canadian humor, the Toronto

Zoo, Canadian nationalism, and her visit to Australia as a literary emissary to a writers' conference. These articles—like her literary essays—provide additional insights into her vision of her culture and society; and, although echoing similar insights in *Survival,* they have the advantage of not being restrictively and inextricably linked to a controlling and perhaps reductive central thesis.

Survival

The critical reception accorded *Survival* was described by one writer as "the *Survival* shoot-out," the controversy surrounding the book resembling the climax of a Wild West melodrama. It elevated what Atwood "considered to be a rather modest and small scale literary endeavour" into a seminal work at least as important for its effect on the Canadian intellectual community as for what it says about Canadian literature. A catalyst for discussion about Canadian culture and identity, *Survival* (according to Dennis Lee) "made controversy over the nature of 'the Canadian imagination' a legitimate and exciting pastime for a great many people, for a spell at least."[2] Its popular appeal was evident, too, in the fact that it had sold, by 1980, over seventy thousand copies, thus becoming the most visible, widely read critical work on Canadian literature in Canada's history. Despite the fears (or hopes) of some critics, however, it is less clear whether the book directly altered public reading habits, diminished (or enhanced) school curricula, or created a strait jacket of orthodoxy (or a formula of success) for other writers.

The text. Atwood's thesis in *Survival,* explained in an introductory and concluding chapter and elaborated upon in terms of various thematic patterns in ten interim essays, is that every region or country has an overriding mythology or ethos that controls the attitude of writers toward their subject matter and determines their treatment of it. "Every country or culture," she says in the first chapter, "has a single unifying and informing symbol at its core," a symbol which "functions like a system of beliefs . . . which holds the country together and helps the people in it to co-operate for common ends."[3] There is, Atwood admits in her prefatory remarks, nothing new in such an assertion; one need only examine, for example, the controlling metaphors in the titles of critical studies of American literature *(The American Adam, Errand Into the Wilderness, Virgin Land)* to see its application to that country's culture.

And, indeed, to provide a context for her remarks about Canadian literature, Atwood develops her thesis comparatively, observing that the unifying symbol for American culture is "The Frontier, a flexible idea that contains many elements dear to the American heart: it suggests a place that is *new*, where the old order can be discarded . . . ; it holds out a hope, never fulfilled but always promised, of Utopia, the perfect human society" (31–32). Such a view of American culture has had currency certainly since the late eighteenth century, when Crèvecoeur noted that a proper view of America might be had only on the frontier. Even from the very beginnings of American settlement, in the seventeenth century, the Puritans viewed their escape from Europe as an opportunity to enter a new world, to create, as John Winthrop preached on the *Arbella* during the 1630 voyage, "a citty upon a hill," where the Puritans would be viewed as an example of perfection for the entire world.

What the Puritans escaped from, in part at least, was the insular culture of England. And, for Atwood, the English symbol that corresponds to the American frontier is, indeed, "The Island," the "island-as-body, self-contained, a Body Politic, evolving organically, with a hierarchical structure" (32).

Shifting, perhaps inconsistently, from geographical metaphors ("The Frontier," "The Island") to an abstraction evoking a state of existence, Atwood asserts that "the central symbol for Canada . . . is undoubtedly Survival, *la Survivance*," a concept that contains images of "bare survival," such as that faced by "early explorers and settlers," but also suggests "survival of a crisis or disaster, like a hurricane or a wreck, . . . 'grim' survival as opposed to 'bare' survival. For French Canada after the English took over it became cultural survival. . . . And in English Canada now while the Americans are taking over it is acquiring a similar meaning" (32).

But Atwood's focus is on "bare" survival, the tenacious insistence that one endure, hang on, stay alive: "Canadians are forever taking the national pulse like doctors at a sickbed: the aim is not to see whether the patient will live well but simply whether he will live at all" (33). In *Survival* Atwood hopes to be a better physician, to offer a remedy for the dismal, pessimistic view of life that she perceives in Canadian culture. Bare survival, she suggests, has been the necessity, initially in the struggle by Canada's early settlers as they faced the wilderness, more recently in the struggle to sustain Canadian identity in the face of American cultural and economic imperialism; a more enriching kind of survival needs to be the goal. To reach that goal, one must know what the obstacles to it are: "A tradition doesn't necessarily exist to bury you: it can also be used as material for new departures" (246). For Atwood, a close look at more recent authors— whose "exploration consists of making explicit the experience of being a victim in a colonial culture" (238)—will reveal the illness; but it may also show the way to better health.

In chapters 2 through 12 Atwood applies these broad outlines of her thesis to specific works, in a manner typical of a growing tradition of thematic criticism in Canada. Taking her cue from D. G. Jones, in his 1970 study *Butterfly on Rock: A Study of Themes and Images in Canadian Literature,* she treats her material in a way he describes as "cultural and psychological rather than purely aesthetic or literary."[4] We need not here consider the details of these chapters, except to note that Atwood has arranged them into "four groups": the first dealing "with the patterns Canadian literature has made of what white people found when they arrived here: the land, the animals, and the Indians"; the second dealing "with what Canadian literature has made of its 'ancestor' figures"; the third coping "with two representative figures—the Canadian Artist, who is usually male, and the Canadian Woman, who is usually female"; and the last—including the final chapter, "Jail-Breaks and Re-Creations"—providing "some rays of light, in the shape of bonfires and insights" (41).

The critical reception.   Such, then, is the content of *Survival.* Yet, held in the light of the controversy surrounding the book, its substance seems to dwindle in significance, blotted out by the glare of adulation and attack. One reviewer observed that "it is difficult . . . to separate the book itself from the phenomenon surrounding it" and noted that its "greatest merit" lies in its "capacity to provoke such debate in a lively and intelligent manner." Another reviewer, surveying the controversy, observed that the argument of *Survival* was in any event irrelevant, that "the key pattern" of survival "may not be true, but surely this has never been a main criterion in literary criticism." "Why," this reader asks, "should Margaret Atwood's theory excite such hue and cry?"[5] To attempt to answer this question, we must examine some elements of the critical response to *Survival.*

Not all reviewers were unhappy with *Survival.* Some of those who liked the book, or at least appreciated certain of its features, felt that it was "a brisk and brilliant exploration of Canadian literature," and "one of the most *necessary* works ever published" in Canada. Others pointed to specific passages that were "nothing short of brilliant" in their "unassuming economy and incisiveness." Still others, while discounting its general application to Canadian literature, did laud it "as a powerful personal reading of Canadian literature by a strong, active mind and imagination, displaying intelligence, insight, and an unexpectedly generous range of interest and enthusiasm." Elaborating on this idea, another critic wrote that "the prime importance of *Survival* . . . is . . . not what it says about Canadian books," but rather what it reveals about Atwood's own creative impulses. And, finally, some who appreciated her achievement pointed to her breezy, non-academic style: "It's a terrific book," said one reviewer, "funny, enraging, alive."[6]

Taken, not for its ideas as such, but for its incisive wit, *Survival* is indeed a remarkable entertainment; yet Atwood's humor serves rhetorical purposes also. Through such devices as the seemingly inconsequential parenthetical observation, the theatrical aside, Atwood simultaneously advances her idea even as she deflates the seriousness of its tone. Early in the book, for example, she observes that "you might decide at this point that most Canadian authors with any pretensions to seriousness are neurotic or morbid, and settle down instead for a good read with *Anne of Green Gables* (though it's about an orphan . . . ," 35). On occasion, her humor extends to her textual criticism, where incisively correct analyses may mask themselves as irreverent witticisms: commenting on E. J. Pratt's *Brébeuf and His Brethren,* she remarks that one passage about the Indians "reads like a cross between a slum-clearance proposal and an antacid ad" (94). If such unacademic prose seems unbecoming to a literary critic, yet we may be astonished by the accuracy of Atwood's flippant observation; for, a few lines down the page, she quotes Pratt and we see that he does indeed refer to "that bloated feeling," predating the familiar television commercial by at least a generation.

Atwood's wit, however, serves yet more political purposes in *Survival,* a book she admits is "a personal statement [and] political manifesto" as well as a guidebook for "students and . . . teachers" (13, 11). Late in the book, in what seems merely one more bit of grimly irreverent commentary, she notes (with regard to the characteristic treatment of raw material in Canadian literature) that "the question . . . is not whether boy should meet girl in Winnipeg or in New York; instead it is, What happens in Canadian literature when boy meets girl? And what sort of boy, and what sort of girl? If you've got this far, you may predict that when boy meets girl she gets cancer and he gets hit by a meteorite" (237). Not recanting her thesis that a theme of victimization pervades Canadian literature, but clearly allowing for its possible abuse, she says of the exaggerated application she has provided, "that wasn't just a bad joke; it indicates the dangers of cliché writing once there's a defined tradition"; and she goes on to suggest that, "if you're a writer, you need not discard the tradition, nor do you have to succumb to it. . . . Instead, you can explore the tradition—which is not the same as merely reflecting it— and in the course of the exploration you may find some new ways of writing" (237–38).

Atwood thus anticipated one of the more crucial attacks on her book by one of her more tenacious critical adversaries, Frank Davey, who (in a combined review of *Survival* and *Surfacing*) observed that the "successful popularization of [Atwood's] view of Canadian literature—especially to high schools and universities—could be a disaster for many Canadian writiers [*sic*]: those who haven't expressed the 'right ideas' to make the Atwood canon. Entire regions and movements within Canadian writing could be effectively driven underground. . . . I don't like the implications here, and neither should Atwood." Underscoring Davey's fears, another reviewer wrote, "I understand that young creative writing students have already begun to submit grim stories of Canada victimized."[7]

The battle joined.   It is beyond the scope of this discussion to recount exhaustively all the events or miscellaneous quibbles in the critical melodrama surrounding *Survival* or to list the entire—generally moderate—cast of players who eventually became involved. But the extremes of the debate can be apprehended through a brief review of the remarks of two critics, Davey and the cultural nationalist Robin Mathews, among whose pursuits in the late 1960s and early 1970s was his controversial campaign to reduce the supposedly high proportion of foreigners, particularly Americans, teaching in Canadian universities. Davey's dissent—published in an issue of his formalist critical journal *Open Letter* and elaborated upon in a 1974 address in Toronto—involved his view that thematic criticism, as offered by Atwood in *Survival* and earlier by Northrop Frye and D. G. Jones, was a misguided and destructive approach to literature generally and Canadian literature in particular. Mathews's attack—published in *This Magazine*—was more nearly a nationalistic and vaguely Marxist one. It, too, revealed discontent with Frye (though on prin-

ciples more political and cultural); and it was based largely on Mathews's belief that, despite Atwood's proclaimed anticolonial position
in *Survival*, her treatment of her material in fact advocated a colonial
status for Canadian culture.[8]

According to Davey, Atwood had committed several fatal errors in
Survival. Citing "a series of Canadian culture-fixing books" that had
recently appeared, he observed that Atwood's offered "the narrowest
definition of a Canadian tradition yet attempted," that it "is not
really a guide to all Canadian literature. It could with equal justice
have been subtitled a guide to House of Anansi literature." Davey
accused "Atwood—an Anansi editor—[of giving] the impression that
Anansi has been the dominant press in Canadian literary history."
These and other "distortions," he noted, invalidate her generaliza-
tions about Canadian literature.

It is true that *Survival*, published by Anansi, was influenced by editorial suggestions of Dennis Lee, one of Anansi's founders; at the
same time, Davey was probably neglecting Atwood's point that her
texts were chosen at least partly on the basis of their being available
in paperback edition, and forgetting that *Survival* was written at a
time when few publishing houses were printing Canadian literature
in that format. In any event, "the central and discrediting error of
the book," for Davey, was Atwood's nonevaluative approach to literature, her concern more with ideas contributing to her thematic approach than with formal excellence. This concern "perpetuates and
serves Northrop Frye's crippling remark that evaluation of Canadian
literature can be 'only a huge debunking project.' " With more critical acumen, Davey noted that "no nation . . . can have a monopoly
on any literary theme. . . . Where [Atwood] might have found
unique literary expressions of the Canadian character—in the *form* of
its writings—she fails to look." Davey concluded his catalog of Atwood's "disservices" by noting her "messianic obsession . . . to con-
firm the centrality and ubiquity in Canadian literature of [her]
victim/victimizer theme" and "her ignoring . . . [its] very large and
significant celebratory tradition."

Mathews's comments were more ardently political. Yet, despite a
subsequent attack he made on Atwood in 1974, in which he accused
her of guilt by association ("How could she ally herself with people
symbolically and actively involved in the sell-out of the country?"),
his position on *Survival* in *This Magazine* was reasonably moderate,
more so at least than the anonymous, self-parodying Marxist evalua-

tion that appeared in a 1976 issue of *New Literature and Ideology:* "The section of *Survival* which contains these fascist conclusions is headed in italics 'Canadians don't know which side they're on'. Is it possible that Ms. Atwood does not know that she herself is 100 per cent on the side of the oppressors?"[9]

Like Davey, who had questioned the validity of Atwood's disclaimers and had attacked her association with Frye, so too did Mathews "reject her statement that the book is not evaluative. . . . Because what Atwood puts in she obviously selects as valuable to put in. . . . What she leaves out (or barely mentions) is, for the reader, not there. Selection is a process of evaluation." Proceeding to argue that her selection offered a limited, neocolonial evaluation of Canadian literature and society, and implicating both Frye and philosopher George Grant in his indictment, Mathews asserted that *Survival* dealt with "works of colonial stagnation," that it celebrated the role of "colonial" critics, and that its "inordinate emphasis" on "Anansi Press writers" was culpable because "Anansi . . . , with all its virtues, has been a home for the suffering, rather chic, rather experimental, nicely nationalistic writers of a hand-ringing we'll-probably-lose-so-don't-let's-be-anti-American-or-too-militantly-political type."

Mathews had some of the same targets as Davey, but he rejected Davey's position as well as Atwood's. The mutual attacks published during the decade by Davey and Mathews, in fact, provide a useful perspective with regard to Atwood, by revealing the strong biases underlying their public literary pronouncements. In one exchange, concerning the political implications of Davey's formalist poetics, Mathews asserted that "Davey's position is only the latest in a long line of proto-annexationist and annexationist arguments which begin with a rejection of the English Canadian tradition and go on to seek outside Canada for primary guidance in poetics and poetry," arguments which reject "Canadian poetry" and go "in search of foreign masters." Davey's rejoinder was similarly pointed: "In the guise of anti-Americanism and anti-imperialism, Mathews is covertly asking Canadians to give up their Western literary heritage. This would be a pyrrhic and unnecessary sacrifice. . . . Catch-words will build neither an idiosyncratic national literature nor a distinct poetics; they haven't done so even for the bullies of Mathews' fantasies, Britain and the U.S."[10]

Atwood believed that both Davey and Mathews had viewed *Survival* through a haze of distortion and misrepresentation, yet in her

public response to Mathews and in a private assessment she offered in
1978, we see her position as being, if blunt and a bit extravagant,
situated somewhere between those of her two antagonists. She wrote
in *This Magazine:*

There are a number of things about Mathews' work, in this and other areas,
that are truly admirable. No one could fault his motives or his courageous
university campaign. And I admire the *intention* of his critical work, especially because he is trying to locate a tradition and an ideology with roots
inside the country, rather than . . . trying to cram Canada into some other
country's ideological grid. But when it comes to dealing with the actual literature, as we must if we are to be literary critics, zeal often leads him
astray. His critical behaviour both here and elsewhere suggests he's in danger of becoming a one-man garrison society, walled up in his own paranoia,
scanning the critical and literary scene like a periscope and going Bang at
anything that moves.[11]

Elaborating in 1978, she assessed the debate as follows: ". . . in a
way," she said, Davey and Mathews "epitomize two different approaches to literature which are diametrically opposed. And if I had
to come down on one side or the other, from a political point of view
I'd have to go with Mathews"; but, "being a writer, from a literary
point of view I have to go with Frank Davey, biased as he is. He has
a love for literature and Robin Mathews does not. He's not really interested in literature. He's interested in separating the sheep from the
goats and doing away with the goats."[12]
   We need not dwell on Mathews's and Davey's attacks on *Survival*
or speculate on the accuracy of the mutual recriminations of all three
figures in the drama. Their remarks do suggest, however, the sometimes perverse vitality and tenor of the debate that contributed to the
notoriety of Atwood's "modest literary endeavour." During a 1978
discussion about how the book's success (fostered in part by its notoriety) had contributed to an increased use of Canadian literature in
the schools, Atwood acknowledged that "I knew . . . I was going out
on a limb. I knew that there would be some bad reactions, but I
didn't see anybody else prepared to go out on that limb at that time.
. . . So I knew that there would be fuss. But I wasn't prepared for
the mess . . . the kind of wild-eyed accusations of [my] intending to
take over the entire literary scene."[13]
   Upon reflection, it appears that the "mess" may well have been a
sign of the times, a momentary tempest in Canada's cultural growing

pains, fed by the views of strong-willed, and not always discreet, personalities. In the midst of the controversy, during her 1973 address to the Empire Club of Canada, Atwood herself pointed out that the notoriety accorded *Survival* was a result of its timing, that its publication necessarily fell, for better or worse, at the height of a period of resurgent Canadian nationalism and concern for the health of Canadian culture: "If this book had appeared ten years earlier," she observed, "no one would have noticed it and if it were to appear ten years later it would be obsolete either because Canada will have overcome the problems . . . noted in *Survival* and gone on to other problems or because there won't be a Canada. But right now [it] seems to have hit a tender part of the national consciousness dead centre."[14]

Certainly it is true that by 1976, after other book-length studies of Canadian literature had emerged (e.g., Laurence Ricou's *Vertical Man/Horizontal World,* John Moss's *Patterns of Isolation,* Margot Northey's *The Haunted Wilderness*), the noise surrounding Atwood's book had quieted down; and, by that year too, she and the Canadian literary community had moved on to other matters.

The Critic at Large: *Second Words* and Others

A sampling of Atwood's ephemeral prose writings—many collected in a 1982 Anansi publication, *Second Words*—reveals an eclectic blend: sparkling and sensitive, yet at times merely competent reviews of other writers' works; essays of literary criticism composed, at times, in a typically dry, academic manner; travel articles, derived from Atwood's world journeys and providing (despite their calm, informative demeanor) subtle links with such subsurface horrors facing the travel writer as Atwood depicts in her story "A Travel Piece" and her novel *Bodily Harm;* polemic pieces reiterating the cultural nationalism of *Survival;* a few hesitant discussions of feminism and the role and expectations of woman writers; profiles of other woman writers; and miscellaneous journalistic commentaries. Out of this diverse mix, several predominant themes and intellectual proclivities emerge.

A synthetic vision. In general, Atwood's critical method follows the comparative and synthetic manner she pursues not only in *Survival,* but in the interconnected image patterns of her fiction also. Atwood defines this synthetic vision (one she considers particularly Canadian) in her 1971 article on James Reaney's then recently de-

funct little magazine, *Alphabet:* "there seem to be important differences between the way Canadians think . . . and the way Englishmen
and Americans do. The English habit of mind . . . might be called
empirical; reality for it is the social hierarchy and its dominant literary forms are evaluative criticism and the social novel. It values
'taste.' The American habit of mind . . . is abstract and analytical; it
values 'technique,' and for it reality is how things work. . . . The
Canadian habit of mind . . . is synthetic. 'Taste' and 'technique' are
both of less concern . . . than is the ever-failing but ever-renewed
attempt to pull all the pieces together." Applying this dynamic
model to *Alphabet,* and transcending the thematic definitions of
"Canadian-ness" invoked in *Survival,* Atwood observes that "*Alphabet*
had something much more important than 'Canadian Content'; . . .
it was Canadian in *form,* in how the magazine was put together."[15]

Atwood places *Alphabet*'s form in the context of the "Canadian
preoccupation with . . . documentaries," noting that "the documen-
tarist's (and *Alphabet*'s) stance towards . . . raw material, and thus
towards everyday life, is that it is intrinsically meaningful but the
meaning is hidden; it will only manifest itself if the observer makes
the effort to connect." She elaborates, noting the differing perspectives her model American, Englishman, and Canadian would take toward a commonplace hamburger. "The Canadian," she suggests,
"will be puzzled by it" yet will eventually say, "I don't know what
this hamburger means . . . but if I concentrate on it long enough
[its] meaning"—which resides "in the exchange between the observing and the observed—. . . will reveal itself to me." Atwood observes facetiously that "the Canadian . . . is less sure of himself and
more verbose . . . than the other two." More important, however, is
the fact that "the Canadian's" relation to Atwood's hypothetical hamburger nearly approximates the relationship between reader and
speaker in her poem "This Is a Photograph of Me." It thus suggests,
again, the connection between Atwood's philosophic tendencies, her
ideas about Canadian identity, and her poetic technique. She readily
admits that "such theories" about cultural identity are "questionable,"
but in her case at least they seem to apply.

Atwood's synthetic view of the world—her building of systems
that interlink seemingly disparate entities—carries over into many of
her other prose pieces. In "What's so Funny? Notes on Canadian Humour," for example, a partly polemic, partly literary essay published
in 1974, Atwood again attempts to place the Canadian identity into

the context of other cultures, speaking of the class-conscious humor of the English, the competitive humor of the Americans, and the self-denigrating humor of the Canadians, whose colonial attitudes amount to a kind of "self-hatred" that defines its place in the world. Less direct, her essay on "Canadian Monsters: Some Aspects of the Supernatural in Canadian Fiction,"—originally presented, in 1976, as a lecture at Harvard University—merely flirts with the idea of synthesis, approaching it more circumspectly, letting the reader (or listener) find his own connections. Following a study of several literary works, Atwood suggests that "it is usual for a critic to present some general conclusions at the end of an effusion such as this. I'm not sure that I have any to offer." Before she has concluded her remarks, however, the mind prone to synthesis emerges—teasingly, but clearly—to suggest a coherent pattern and to allow, also, the notion that it is indeed "in the exchange between the observing and the observed" that the pattern becomes manifest: "I've begun with a story which plays upon man's fear of natural power and ended with one illustrating the dangers inherent in his own lust for power. The connection between this pattern and the changes in Canadian society and outlook over the last sixty years is perhaps too obvious to be mentioned. In any case, such a critical pattern exists in the mind of the critic rather than in the external world. Perhaps the critic is himself a kind of magician," a maker of critical observations that are always subject to revision. The only necessary condition of such critical relativism, as Atwood observed in a 1978 conversation, is that the observer be honest, that the synthesis presented be "a view that you think is true."[16]

Neither killer nor victim. Operating within Atwood's synthetic world view are several interrelated themes that seem to preoccupy her thoughts. Her overriding concern—one that comprehends her ideas about the status of women, the abuse of animals, the colonial attitude of Canadians, the exploitation of individuals—is the dilemma posed by a world that allows victors and victims, winners and losers, but seems incapable of providing a way for "the ideal," for the creation of "somebody who would neither be a killer or a victim, who could achieve some kind of harmony with the world, . . . a productive or creative harmony, rather than a destructive relationship."[17]

We see this concern in writings as diverse as her literary profiles, her comments about the Dionne quintuplets, and her observations about the Toronto Zoo. In her 1975 *Maclean's* article about Toronto's new Metro Zoo, designed "for the welfare of the animals as well as that of the viewers," Atwood observes that "zoos make me nervous"; and she hearkens to her childhood, "back in the Forties when it was not unusual to find scruffy, badly nourished, miserable bears, deer, raccoons, porcupines and even skunks used as tourist curiosities" at "roadside gas station[s]." Relating this image to human beings and their victimization, Atwood asks the reader to "imagine yourself in a small dirty cage with little room to move around, no one to talk with and nothing to do." The Toronto Zoo is different, Atwood's commentary amply illustrates; but as she ends the article the niggling doubt remains: "Zoos still make me nervous. There's something about animals in cages, even the luxurious non-cages of the Toronto Zoo, that hints of prison." And she points to the paradox that human beings spend "enormous amounts of money" to preserve animals in zoos, while other humans "are just as busy hunting, killing, skinning, stuffing for trophies and eating" them. "Perhaps," she suggests, our zoos represent our futile "attempt . . . to preserve in artificial form a time when men and animals lived in a more balanced harmony than they share now, a time before the big-headed monkeys invented agriculture and began to crowd the earth."[18]

If caged animals concern Atwood, so too do literally or spiritually caged people, and not only those tortured for political views or incarcerated in prison cells for crimes. The Dionne quintuplets, Atwood observes of the celebrated sisters who became a minor obsession of the 1930s, were exhibited, like caged roadside animals, "for nothing (from behind a one-way wire mesh screen)." As Atwood suggests in her 1977 review of Pierre Berton's book on the quints, the story of the Dionnes is a painful tale of exploitation, of human beings demoted to the status of objects for the gratification of the masses and the financial enrichment of the Dionne sisters' public and private guardians. "What The Dionne Years is about, finally," says Atwood, "is the destructive nature of the public's hunger for two-dimensional images" and the public's ignorance of the multidimensional lives caged by the images forced upon them.[19]

In her profiles of other literary personalities Atwood faces more personally and more directly the question of public image versus private reality. Her tack in these articles is a curious one, given her usually vigorous condemnation of the tendency of press and public to project stereotypical ideas of the writer's life. In two of her major profiles—a 1974 piece on Margaret Laurence and one, in 1975, on Marie-Claire Blais—Atwood places herself in the public camp, characterizing herself as one of the naive and misguided propagators of the stereotyped image. "I first met Margaret Laurence," she writes, "the way most people meet most writers: on the dust jacket of a book. . . . My first reaction was, 'This is not someone I would ever want to get into a fight with.' " Atwood, in this article, quickly demolishes the "straw man" figure she has strategically set herself up to be; when she finally met Laurence, the dust-cover image shattered and it became "clear to me that Margaret Laurence was no bulldozer." An ordinary person, Laurence was not "the least bit interested in being a legendary figure: she was far too involved in the joys and despairs of being human."[20]

In the Blais article Atwood approaches, more directly, her own experiences with an image-propagating public. Here she is both the ardent critic of that public and a victim of the same forces that compel it to see artists as something other than people plying their particular trade. "Talent is frightening," asserts Atwood, "and when you've read a particularly grueling and effective book it's hard to resist the temptation to attribute some of the character's demonic energies to the author. . . . I've had this done to me so often that I should have been well aware of the difference between fictions and those who make them." Looking ahead to her meeting with Blais, however, she observes with helpless complicity, "still, I must have been expecting the waif of the early press coverage or the romantic demon-ess of the more *outré* of the novels." What Atwood meets, of course, as she relates in the remainder of the article, is another human being—"almost as nervous about me as I was about her," tolerantly amused by "the myth that journalists have created of her," "a perceptive and lively professional woman with a sly sense of humor." In its attention to Blais's concern for her craft, to her aspirations about it, and to the nuances of her public image, "Marie-Claire Blais is Not For Burning" becomes as much a profile of Atwood as of Blais herself.[21]

An intellectual and moral landscape. As with her articles on zoos, victims of carnival-like exploitation, and literary personalities, Atwood's few written commentaries on the woman's movement place her immediate subject into the broader, more synthetic context of her most basic concerns. She has acknowledged herself a "feminist" only in the sense that she lived a life, even before the flowering of the woman's movement in the 1970s, that exemplified the ideological aspirations and achievements of that movement ("If feminism is dealing with women as independent entities," she once said, "then I'm a feminist. . . . What the hell, why not?"). As a result, her feminist pieces tend to be "crypto-feminist," her support for the movement submerged beneath or subsumed by the larger picture. She begins "Paradoxes and Dilemmas: The Woman as Writer" (1976), for example, noting "a good deal of reluctance" about writing it. She wishes not to be labeled as a propagandist for the movement and questions the "value of writers, male or female, becoming directly involved in political movements of any sort"; such involvement "may be good for the movement, but it has yet to be demonstrated that it's good for the writer." And expanding this idea, later in the article, she observes that "no good writer wants to be merely a transmitter of someone else's ideology."[22]

So with political movements; so, too, with one's cultural roots. In Atwood's reflections on Canadian nationalism—"Travels Back," for example, a 1973 piece that depicts Atwood on a poetry reading tour—the writer meditates on the Canadian identity and comments on her Nova Scotian roots ("In Deep River I stay with my second cousin, a scientist with the blue inhuman eyes, craggy domed forehead and hawk nose of my maternal Nova Scotian relatives"). Most significant, however, is her warning against espousing the cultural doctrines of another country. "Refusing to acknowledge where you come from," she writes, in language that parallels her words in *Surfacing,* "is an act of amputation: you may become free-floating, a citizen of the world . . . but only at the cost of arms, legs or heart." Expanding into a recognition that "this territory, this thing I have called 'mine,' may not be mine much longer," she concludes the article with a condemnation of foreign exploitation of Canada's resources: "Exploiting resources and developing potential are two different things: one is done from without by money, the other from within, by something I hesitate only for a moment to call love." Earlier, in "Nationalism, Limbo & the Canadian Club" (1971), recalling her experiences with Canadians at Harvard, Atwood elaborated, lamenting those who do refuse to acknowledge their roots, who refuse to "travel back"—all except one "short red-head from Newfoundland who kept trying to sing the Newfoundland National Anthem."[23]

Her travel pieces—as with "Timeless in Afghanistan" (1978)—appear to be merely facile promotions for journeys to exotic places, but they do touch upon at least two of her impulses. There is, for example, though mildly presented, the possibility of terror in such places.

She relates the fact that, "some months before" she visited Afghanistan, "two British girls who had decided to . . . swim in a lake were found dead," victims apparently of overzealous Afghanis who thought the girls had been "exposing too much flesh" in their Western bathing outfits. At the same time, however, Atwood typically sees the Afghanis' maintaining of their roots as a virtue: "if you want to step into another world, a place that has not yet been depilatorized, deodorized and remade into a Disneyland for tourists, Afghanistan is one of the few places left where you can do it." "Atwood Among the Ozzies" (also 1978, and involving the other leg of the journey that took her to Afghanistan) more directly focuses on cultural nationalism, as Atwood comments on the Australians' own striving for a national identity that captures the spirit of the island continent.[24]

The literary essays and reviews fit less directly into this synthesis of Atwood's ideas. Her 1965 *Alphabet* article on Rider Haggard, "Superwoman Drawn and Quartered: The Early Forms of *She*," for example, is essentially an academic essay. It exploits Atwood's lifetime concern with the supernatural, grotesque, and gothic elements in literature—so evident in her own imaginative works and reaching back to her childhood experiences with Grimm's tales. Her approach, though, is typically synthetic: of her study, she says, "the motives . . . are similar to those that connect themselves with jigsaw puzzles: curiosity, an assumption that the pieces can be fitted together somehow, and a desire to see what the total picture looks like." A similar approach operates in "MacEwen's Muse" (1970) where Atwood attempts to define a pervasive thread in Gwendolyn MacEwen's poetry. In her 1980 review of W. D. Valgardson's *Red Dust,* another familiar element emerges, as Atwood focuses on the particular locale of Valgardson's short stories, a "territory" that is his own, that reflects the locale of his spirit. In her 1972 review of an anthology of *Great Canadian Short Stories* she stresses the curious un-Canadianness of the collection, wondering why more local examples had not been chosen by the editor, condemning the internationalism stressed by the stories chosen. The 1971 "Love is Ambiguous . . . Sex is a Bully," a review of a poetry collection by A. W. Purdy, elaborates on the stereotypes that cause men and women to exploit and victimize each other; "Unfinished Women," a review of Adrienne Rich's poetry (1978) deals, in part, with the labels the public attaches to artists.[25]

The point revealed by this sampling—not a surprising one at all—
is that Atwood's concerns pervade her writings; they appear and reappear, echo and reecho throughout her poems, her fiction, and her
criticism. Her prose pieces, like patches of a particolored quilt, stand
alone yet also blend into one another to reveal the texture of her
thought and to capture the continuity and cohesiveness of her intellectual and moral landscape.

Chapter Six

Where is Here?

"Notes From Various Pasts"

When Margaret Atwood began her writing career, the state of both literature and publishing in Canada was something rather short of invigorating. Writing in the *University of Toronto Quarterly* in 1960, at the end of his tenure as poetry editor of the "Letters in Canada" yearly review, Northrop Frye seemed to be making excuses for the stress he had put, during the previous decade, on the provincial quality of Canadian literature: "I have for the most part," he said, "discussed Canadian poets as though no other contemporary poetry were available for Canadian readers. . . . The critic to whom falls the enviable task of studying Canadian poetry in the sixties will, I trust, be dealing with a fully matured culture, no longer preoccupied with the empty unpoetics of Canadianism, but with the genuine tasks of creative power."[1]

As late as 1965, in his "Conclusion" to the first edition of the *Literary History of Canada*, Frye was still observing that "Canada has produced no author who is a classic in the sense of possessing a vision greater in kind than that of his best readers." Yet by 1976, in his remarks for the second edition of the *Literary History*, Frye had altered his tone. Recognizing not only the enormous quantitative growth of Canadian literature but its shift in quality as well, he asserted that "there is much more to come . . . but Canadian literature is here, perhaps still a minor but certainly no longer a gleam in a paternal critic's eye . . . one may say that a population the size of English-writing Canada, subject to all the handicaps which have been chronicled so often in Canadian criticism, does not produce such a bulk of good writing without an extraordinary vitality and morale behind it."[2]

This "vitality and morale" revealed itself in a variety of ways. Before a surge of creative power became a manifest part of the Canadian scene in the early 1960s, Canada was for its writers a place to leave as quickly as possible, to head for the international cultural centers of

London and New York. George Woodcock has noted of his own career that "the scene in 1949," when he had returned to Canada from
many years in England, "was as bleak as a Winnipeg winter."[3] But
if there was, in 1949, little cultural activity in Canada, that year,
too, saw the formation of the Royal Commission on National Development in the Arts, Letters and Sciences. Better known as the Massey
Commission, its major recommendation, in its 1951 report, concerned the creation of the Canada Council, which began operating in
1957, the year Atwood graduated from high school.

The Canada Council, similar to the National Endowment for the
Arts in the United States, contributed generally to Canada's cultural
development. For writers, in particular, it provided grants that allowed poets and novelists to spend their time writing; it also helped
support new publishing ventures that provided outlets for the work
of these writers. Although, as Woodcock has noted, it may be difficult to measure precisely what percentage of Canada's literary growth
was created by the Canada Council and how much the Council's activity merely "coincided with an upsurge in creativity linked with the
general social restiveness of the 1960's," it remains true that the
Council was present when Canada seemed, artistically, "to come of
age."[4]

Woodcock's assessment of this "coming of age" is a compelling
one, appearing as it did in the pages of *Canadian Literature,* a critical
journal whose own vitality illustrated the strengths of the Canadian
literary scene: "When *Canadian Literature* began, twelve years ago,"
he wrote in 1971, "I promised that every book of verse by a Canadian
poet, as well as every novel published in this country, would be re-
viewed in its pages. It was an easy promise in a year—1959—when
twenty-four volumes of poetry were all that the bibliographer who
compiled our checklist of publications could discover." This meager
output of poetry collections "came, in those days, mainly from the
regular publishers, who lost money on good poets to give prestige to
their lists. There were few small presses; amateur publishing hardly
existed; the mimeograph revolution had not begun." The occasion for
Woodcock's writing this capsule history was his receiving for review
"nineteen books of verse . . . in one mail delivery," an "augury" of
perhaps "250 or 300 titles in English" for the year.[5]

The crush of new volumes of poetry, and of fiction, coincided with
the creation of new presses. House of Anansi, founded in 1967 by

Dave Godfrey and Dennis Lee, was only one of several small presses, subsidized by Canada Council funds, formed to accommodate writers whose works were not being picked up by commercially cautious established houses. Sometimes these writers were the publishers themselves. Anansi's first books, for example, included Lee's *Kingdom of Absence* and Godfrey's *Death Goes Better With Coca-Cola*. Other new presses formed during this fertile period were Coach House Press (1965), Oberon Press (1966), Talonbooks (1967), Sono Nis Press (1968), New Press (1969), and Press Porcépic (1971)—all contributing to a flourishing production of new, often experimental, poetry and prose. Older presses also contributed to the promotion of Canadian literature. McClelland and Stewart, for example, began in the 1950s to reprint Canadian classics in its New Canadian Library series and, later, along with other companies, helped expand the Canadian paperback market.

The new Canadian cultural nationalism, manifested in these publishing ventures, in this increased writing output, and in education (with the introduction of Canadian literature courses into the schools), was also marked by an increase in new literary and critical journals, and in an abundance of fresh critical study of Canadian literature. The Canadian section of the annual bibliography published by the *Journal of Commonwealth Literature* listed, in its roster of selected journals, only fourteen for 1965; its 1976 listing contained sixty-four periodicals; and this leaped to 109 in 1978. Though some of these journals produced over the years—such as James Reaney's *Alphabet*—played their role and then departed, many others, like *The Malahat Review, Canadian Literature,* and *Mosaic* remained stable and productive. In full-length books of critical commentary and interpretation, too, there was a flourishing renaissance: D. G. Jones's *Butterfly on Rock*, Atwood's *Survival*, William New's *Articulating West*, Laurence Ricou's *Vertical Man/Horizontal World*, John Moss's *Patterns of Isolation*, Margot Northey's *The Haunted Wilderness*. And surrounding these publications, as we have seen with regard to *Survival*, there arose a critical debate that suggested a coming of age, too, in Canadian literary criticism: a concern with the limits and nature of that critical inquiry, an attempt to discern objective measures of excellence beyond a parochial nationalism. The "Minus Canadian" special issue of *Studies in Canadian Literature,* published in 1977, was only one example of this new view of Canadian criticism.[6]

"Lives of the Poets"

Appearing in the midst of this literary renaissance and intellectual
ferment, Margaret Atwood was at once a paradigm and, for some, a
spiritual leader who, to her own discomfort, soon found herself styled
"the reigning queen of Canadian literature."[7] Considered an established author by 1972, profiled as a celebrity in popular magazines
and daily newspapers, she had by January 1977 achieved sufficient
status that an entire issue of *The Malahat Review* was devoted to her
work, her personality, and her public image. Increasingly her time
was spent, during this period, on reading tours and interviews to promote her books or to advocate the precepts of literary nationalism she
had expressed in *Survival*. In 1973, riding the crest of her notoriety
from that book, which had captured the imagination of a broad spec-
trum of Canadian society, she became the first woman poet to address
the Empire Club of Canada, whose membership consisted of bankers,
lawyers, stockbrokers, and other representatives of the business and
professional community. That same year she was invited to the Soviet
Union—the first Canadian writer to be so honored—in a cultural exchange program (which, for political reasons, she later declined to at-
tend). Late in the decade, discussion of her works became a fixture at
annual meetings of the Modern Language Association of America;
and, earlier, at the 1975 meeting in San Francisco, Atwood herself
gave a reading before an audience of several hundred persons.

By 1976, partly because of the impending birth of her daughter,
Jess, she appeared ready to settle down. Responding to an interview
question about her apparently less public role as an advocate of literary nationalism, she said, "I feel that I made my statement, did my
thing . . . and I'm quite happy to sit back now and watch other people attacking each other." She also noted that year, concerning the
controversial recognition her activities had brought upon her, "some
people love this kind of attention, they revel in it. I don't. And I
don't particularly like being a public figure."[8] Nevertheless, by 1978
she was again voicing, publicly and strongly, her views on such matters as the remainders issue, the gap in Canadian copyright laws that
permitted American publishers to flood the Canadian market with in-
expensive remainders of the works of Canadian authors, in direct
competition with Canadian publishers. And by 1981, asserting her
political role more officially, she became chairman of the Writers'
Union of Canada.

Atwood's literary accomplishments, her political activities, and her fame did not produce unalloyed goodwill. Responding to a certain kind of attack, she suggested on more than one occasion that it was a masculine castration fear—based on confusing Atwood and her Medusa-like personas—that had provoked the sometimes "offensive" characterizations of herself and her work. Fitting into this category, apparently, was the anonymously printed parody of Atwood and her image published in 1974 in *The Canadian Forum.* Subtitled "The Lady of the Lake: Or How the Octopus Got its Tentacles," it depicted Atwood as a little girl transformed into a "leprechaun"-devouring octopus who had taken over "Lake Canada." To Atwood, the caricature was little more than "a personal attack," falsely depicting her "as a very powerful black magic person." Similarly attributing imperialistic motives to her, but less provocatively, was Kildare Dobbs's 1972 observations about Atwood and the Independent Publishers' Association (IPA): "Everyone was watching Margaret Atwood. In the fall she had two new books in the best-seller lists. She was alert for insults to the IPA. She was helping to initiate a writers' union. It was not beyond possibility that [she'd] get herself elected president of the IPA in 1973 and president of the projected writers' union as well. That way she could negotiate with herself."[9] Given Atwood's controversial association with House of Anansi Press—one of Canada's independent publishing ventures—and with the Writers' Union of Canada, Dobbs's quip may not have been too far from the mark.

When Dave Godfrey and Dennis Lee formed Anansi in 1967, Atwood helped initially in two ways: she made *The Circle Game* available as one of the first books Anansi was to publish and, along with the other authors, she contributed money to help the fledgling enterprise. Her next contact came with Anansi's publication of *Power Politics* in 1971. That year, too, she joined the company as editor and member of the board, a position she held until the summer of 1973. She commented later that her association with Anansi had been "one of the more stupid things I've done in my life"; "Dave Godfrey had left, Dennis was on the verge of leaving and the press was embroiled in internal warfare. . . . I thought I was going to be an unpaid and marginal participant, mainly lending my name. I was wrong."[10] The in-house intrigues, later captured (according to some) in Ellen Godfrey's 1976 mystery novel, *The Case of the Cold Murderer,* affected Atwood personally and—in a brief and oblique exchange of letters by

Atwood and Godfrey that appeared during 1977 in the magazine *Saturday Night*—publicly as well. Perhaps more significant, her association with Anansi provided an opportunity for others to attack her objectivity in *Survival* as an observer of the Canadian literary scene.

A yet more public event, provoked at least in part by Atwood herself, was the series of charges and countercharges that became known in Canadian literary circles as "The *Northern Journey* Affair." Reaching scandal proportions, the episode focused on Atwood's dispute with the editors of a little magazine, *Northern Journey*, who in 1973 published a short story by Wil Wigle, entitled "Slow Burn." In a larger context, it involved Atwood's role in the founding of the Writers' Union of Canada and in becoming its first cause célèbre.

Until 1973 there had been little recourse for Canadian writers to protect their professional privileges and to take full economic advantage of the burgeoning demand for Canadian literature. Although one organization, the Canadian Authors' Association, had formed in 1921, it seemed unresponsive to current concerns; even earlier, it had been satirized by F. R. Scott, in his 1936 poem "The Canadian Authors Meet," as a petty, chauvinistic gathering of tea-drinking colonials, loyal to the Royal House of Great Britain. The League of Canadian Poets, established in 1966, concentrated its efforts on sponsoring reading tours to promote poetry in the public schools and universities; lacking a large membership, it was unable to bring pressure on politicians and publishers in such matters as copyright law, royalties, promotion and distribution of books, and other matters of economic concern to Canadian writers. A stronger organization was required.

In late 1972, a group of writers, including Atwood, began a series of embryonic meetings. The first, according to Atwood, involved "about five people, and then there were about ten people at the ones after that, and then we had a conference at which there were about thirty people, and then we had the big one at which there were a lot of people." They met to consider the possibility of forming a union of writers. Some—both publishers and writers—had their doubts. Jack McClelland (of McClelland and Stewart) observed that "very few serious authors will take the time to join and work for a union." Several years later, after Atwood, Graeme Gibson, Marian Engel, and other activist writers had taken the time to establish a viable organization, Atwood observed that "in Canada these things are necessary. You can't afford the luxury of saying writers can't do this and . . .

shouldn't do that and should only write . . . so [many writers do]
feel that they have to do a certain amount" of political work.[11]

The inaugural convention of the Writers' Union of Canada met at
the National Arts Centre in Ottawa, in November 1973. By November 1974, when it held its second annual convention at the University of Ottawa for its almost one hundred members, the Union was
faced with resolving its first major crisis, which involved neither publishers' intransigence, government unconcern, nor writers' apathy.
Rather, for much of the previous year, it seemed that the most per-
plexing issue of the newly formed union had been Margaret Atwood
and her battle with *Northern Journey*. A union representative had earlier said, as the controversy was evolving and the Writers' Union was
becoming enmeshed in its web, "Margaret Atwood . . . has been
made into the unofficial high priestess of Canadian writing and, as a
result[,] she is liable to be attacked by lesser talents who are consumed by jealousy. We feel we should protect her. Besides, she came
to us for help."[12]

What happened was that, in its third issue (October 1973), the
Ottawa-based little magazine had published Wigle's story, in which
a character named Margaret Atwood is conversing with the narrator's
girlfriend during a reception given in "Atwood's" honor after a poetry
reading. The narrator describes the fictional Atwood as seeming "just
a little uncomfortable with her role as the reigning queen of Canadian
literature." Soon the characters leave the reception and, on the way
to her hotel, "Atwood" comments that an earlier reading, in Montreal, had been more satisfying. It had been so, she relates, because
there she had received "a grand compliment": a mildly pornographic
remark attesting to her sexual desirability.[13]

Atwood responded to this use of her name in a fictional construct
by engaging her attorney to request from *Northern Journey* a published
apology and a withdrawal from sale of the offending issue. She also
declined to use space in *Northern Journey*'s next issue for a reply to
Wigle and referred the matter (in February 1974) to the Writers'
Union for its assistance. The Union itself recommended that its
members not offer their work to the magazine, thus contributing to
the debate that engaged many major figures in the Canadian literary
community for many months. The events of the affair, reported fully
(and, Atwood believed, unfairly) by the trade journal *Quill & Quire,*
provoked Atwood (who had remained quietly in the background) to
issue, in July 1974, a public statement explaining the basis of her

distress with *Northern Journey*. She wrote, in a letter to *Quill & Quire,*
that her actions had been based on "something called the concept of
estoppages, which states generally that once a person has committed
an action and you are deemed to have consented to it by failing to
protest, you are in a bad position to protest, effectively[,] should he
do it again. . . . if I permit Wigle to use me as a fictional character
once *without protest,* he [or anyone else] can do it again with virtual
impunity."[14]

However valid Atwood's legal argument and the actions she pursued to establish her position, it is likely that all those involved in
the affair overreacted. Atwood's response may have been conditioned
by prior attacks engendered by her all-too-public career: Wigle's
story provided the proverbial last straw and she simply lashed out at
the nearest target. *Northern Journey,* obstinately facing the protests of
what it perceived to be an arrogant colossus in the world of Canadian
letters, may have believed it had to stand its ground: a David fighting (in one more image Atwood might have objected to) an enormous
Goliath. The magazines that reported the story may also have been
reacting to—and exploiting—Atwood's status as a celebrated literary
figure. And the Writers' Union, perhaps too eager to show its potential power, too young to see its role as mediator, may have taken
sides when it should probably have attempted to resolve the issue am-
icably. It is true, in any event, that during its November meeting in
1974, the Union quietly concluded the ruckus by resolving to establish a committee to deal with any similar future disputes in a less
confrontational manner.

"A Premature Canonization"

The image of Atwood in the 1970s as controversial figure—as Me-
dusa, as queen bee, as octopus, as black magic witch—rather than as
talented writer or ordinary human being did not end with the *Northern Journey* affair. In 1975, before the dust raised by the "Slow Burn"
squabble had fully settled, Atwood's desire to protect herself and others from media distortions—to retain her privacy despite her public
activities—again engaged others in debate. This time it centered on
her demand that she be allowed a certain degree of editorial control
over articles derived from interviews in which she agreed to participate. Acting on her agent's advice, she had prepared a letter, to be
signed by prospective interviewers, before she would consent to an-

swer any questions. As reported in the article that precipitated the controversy, a profile of Atwood by Patrick Conlon in the February 1975 issue of *Toronto Life,* the letter allowed her "the right to correct for accuracy and meaning. And . . . it [gave her] the opportunity to consult on any references to third parties."[15]

Here, as in the *Northern Journey* matter, Atwood's actions hinged on an inherent conflict between individual privacy and free expression. When the magazine appeared on the newsstands, Val Clery wrote in a *Quill & Quire* column that both Conlon and his editor, Alexander Ross, had "signed away" their "independence and integrity merely to add to the already overstuffed Myth Atwood file." Referring obliquely to the *Northern Journey* matter, he observed that "misinterpretation is not confined to reporters," that "imaginative writers too are prone to trifle with fact and meaning." And, insinuating that Atwood was being hypocritical, that she herself had "co-opted" actual people "as characters" in her work, he suggested that he knew "at least one writer in Toronto . . . who would have welcomed the means to control her poetic profile of their relationship."[16]

Responding to these comments, in the next issue of *Quill & Quire,* Conlon suggested that Atwood's letter had simply formalized what should normally be the relationship between interviewer and subject, that it was "a simple plea for respect." Ross wrote that he retained some doubts about the propriety of his agreeing to Atwood's conditions but that he did not see it as a critical problem. And novelist Margaret Laurence, offering similar ideas and asserting the common-sense desirability of ensuring accuracy in interviews, objected as well to Clery's use of "personal gossip" to advance his views. "Atwood," wrote Laurence, "is one of our finest poets and novelists. She deserves better treatment than this."[17]

But Clery's response to these sentiments pointed to a possibility that was voiced more than once as the decade played itself out: "Ms. Atwood's injunction implies control over much more than matters of fact. Far from being vulnerable, she seems lately to have been declared sacrosanct; the vitriol has been reserved for those whose admiration falls even slightly short of idolatry." Similarly, in a 1977 diatribe against what he perceived to be a frigid literary matriarchy in control of the Canadian cultural scene, Scott Symons offered this comment about "the lady Amazons," Marian Engel (whose novel *Bear* he was purportedly reviewing) and Margaret Atwood: "To dare to assess them . . . remains a dangerous occupation. I am told that a

young editor criticized Atwood in print and found his career badly
damaged."[18]

Given the tone of Symons's comments, which Margaret Laurence
(once again getting into the fray) called a "malicious and vitriolic
. . . piece of hysterical ranting," it is not too difficult to credit Atwood's own assessment, voiced on numerous occasions during the decade, that such attacks were the product of a "small-town" Canadian
jealousy of those who had succeeded. Robert Fulford, editor of *Saturday Night,* seemed to agree. Writing in May 1980, he asked
whether the negative criticism Atwood's new novel *Life Before Man*
had received in Canada, despite rave reviews in England and the
United States, illustrated Canadians' fear of excellence, whether it
showed Canadians to be threatened by her success.[19]

There were, however, other voices. Calmer and more moderate
than either Clery or Symons, they were nevertheless concerned with
the effects on Atwood of what appeared to be an unquestioning and
uncritical attitude toward her by her most ardent admirers. Responding to Fulford's bemoaning of the unfavorable Canadian reception of
Life Before Man, Paul Delany asserted that "the real danger to her talent . . . would be the cult of personality that has come to surround
her in recent years." And, earlier, in 1977, a reviewer of the Atwood
issue of *The Malahat Review* observed that "what Atwood needs at this
stage in her brilliant career is not a tribute taking the form of a premature canonization but a criticism which, while acknowledging the
importance of her work, is engaged in a fully critical dialogue with
it."[20]

And so it went. While these discussions billowed around her, Atwood's reactions alternated between chagrin and amusement, at one
time angrily deploring the images attached to her, at another using
reviewers' misconstructions of her poetry as the basis for humorous
anecdotes at her public readings. Her wit, on occasion, suggested her
alternating states of mind, as in a letter she wrote in November 1978
to *Saturday Night* magazine. Reflecting her battles with Robin
Mathews, her defense of third parties (as in the Conlon/Clery dispute), her meditations about human cruelty, and her scientific
knowledge, it involved an attack that Mathews had made upon Fulford: "I write to protest Robin Mathews' use of the phrase 'wartiest
toad' to describe Robert Fulford. Not on behalf of Mr. Fulford. . . ,
but on behalf of a wronged and helpless third party for whom verbal
self-defence is an improbability, namely, the Toad."[21] A response to

Mathews, Atwood's letter, through its wit, also served to deflate her own pretensions in the controversies that had preceded it.

"Foretelling the Future"

By the end of the 1970s, success—not always happily manifested—had apparently come to Margaret Atwood. In "A Statement of My Intellectual Interests, Related Activities, and Future Plans," written while she was a student at Victoria College, Atwood expressed a desire to combine the academic and the creative life: she would continue to write, but she would also obtain her doctorate and become a college teacher.[22] By 1973, she had decided that she was able to support herself with her writing alone. Her doctoral thesis—lying uncompleted—became an unessential avocation. As the 1970s progressed and the corpus of her works grew, her reputation became international: her novels were translated and published in Italy, France, Norway, and Spain, were read in English in Japan, and became best sellers on the Continent as well as in the United States, England, and Canada. By 1982, according to a blurb on the dust jacket of *Second Words,* her work had seen print in fourteen foreign languages.

Thus stands Atwood at midpoint in her life and career. Accommodating herself to a success she insists she had no reason to anticipate, she leads today a life that reflects the doubleness of her poetry and fiction. Traveling to Afghanistan or Australia, traipsing around on extended reading tours, she is often accompanied by her daughter, Jess, who has become part of a life with extraordinary dimensions, swept up in the activities of her very public parents. Wanting to protect her daughter's privacy as well as her own, Atwood—as in one of her "Small Poems for the Winter Solstice"—continues to assert the ordinariness of her life. To continue treading that ambiguous road, in the face of burgeoning popular and critical inquiry, may be Atwood's most difficult task as her career journeys into the coming decades.

Notes and References

Abbreviations for frequently cited source information:
MA/JR: Margaret Atwood in conversation with Jerome Rosenberg
MA to: letter from Atwood
TFRBL, UT: Thomas Fisher Rare Book Library, University of Toronto
N. B.: first citations for Atwood's works, within any chapter, are indicated below; pages for subsequent quotations are cited in text.

Chapter One

1. Margaret Kaminski, "Interview with Margaret Atwood," *Waves* 4 (Autumn 1975): 10.
2. "Rhyming Cats" (unpublished manuscript, *ca*. 1945), Atwood Papers, TFRBL, UT.
3. Linda Sandler, "Interview with Margaret Atwood," *Malahat Review*, no. 41 (Jan. 1977), p. 14.
4. MA to Jerome Rosenberg, 29 Nov. 1981.
5. *Power Politics* (Toronto, 1971), p. 1.
6. John Ayre, "Margaret Atwood and the End of Colonialism," *Saturday Night*, Nov. 1972, p. 26.
7. *The Animals in That Country* (Toronto, 1968), p. 39.
8. MA to Peter Miller, 19 Oct. 1965, Contact Press Papers, TFRBL, UT.
9. Valerie Miner, "Atwood in Metamorphosis: An Authentic Canadian Fairy Tale," in *Her Own Woman: Profiles of Ten Canadian Women* (Toronto, 1975), p. 179; MA/JR, 16 Aug. 1978.
10. Iris Murdoch, *The Unicorn* (New York: Avon, 1964), p. 85.
11. MA/JR, 8 Aug. 1975; see also J. R. (Tim) Struthers, "An Interview with Margaret Atwood," *Essays on Canadian Writing*, no. 6 (Spring 1977), p. 18; subsequent poetry quotations are from *Double Persephone* (Toronto, 1961), unpaginated.
12. Struthers, "Interview," p. 22.
13. Northrop Frye, *The Bush Garden: Essays on the Canadian Imagination* (Toronto: Anansi, 1971), pp. 76, 44–45; reprinted from "Letters in Canada," *University of Toronto Quarterly*, 1958, 1956.
14. Frye, *Bush Garden*, pp. 43–44, 56, 74; reprinted from "Letters in Canada," *University of Toronto Quarterly*, 1955, 1956, 1958.
15. Peter Dale Scott, "Turning New Leaves," *Canadian Forum* 41 (Feb. 1962): 260.
16. "My Poetic Principles on Oct. 29 1962" (ms.), Atwood Papers,

TFRBL, UT; Milton Wilson, "Letters in Canada: 1963, Poetry," *University of Toronto Quarterly* 33 (July 1964): 385.

17. Sandler, "Interview with MA," p. 10; Miner, "Atwood in Metamorphosis," p. 180; Bohemian Embassy advertisement (1961), Atwood Papers, TFRBL, UT.

18. MA to Charles Pachter, 23 Sept. 1964, Atwood Papers, TFRBL, UT; remaining quotations in this chapter, from other Thomas Fisher holdings, are as follows: MA to Pachter, 9 Nov. 1964 and 17 Oct. 1964, Atwood Papers; MA to Peter Miller, 19 Oct. 1965, 13 Feb. 1966, and 9 Mar. 1966, Contact Press Papers.

Chapter Two

1. Quoted in Patrick Conlon, "Margaret Atwood: Beneath the Surface," *Toronto Life,* Feb. 1975, p. 51.

2. Frye, *Bush Garden,* p. 225; reprinted from *Literary History of Canada,* ed. Carl F. Klinck (Toronto: University of Toronto Press, 1965).

3. *The Circle Game* (Toronto, 1967), pp. 74–76.

4. "This Is a Photograph of Me" (ms.), Atwood Papers, TFRBL, UT.

5. Ralph Ellison, *Invisible Man* (New York: Random House, 1952), p. 438.

6. *The Animals in That Country* (Toronto, 1968), pp. 30–31.

7. MA to Wynne Francis, 24 Sept. 1966, Atwood Papers, TFRBL, UT.

8. Frye, *Bush Garden,* p. 220.

9. *Survival: A Thematic Guide to Canadian Literature* (Toronto, 1972), p. 124.

10. "Some Difficulties of a Pioneer" (ms.), Atwood Papers, TFRBL, UT.

11. David Helwig, "Poetry," *Queen's Quarterly* 76 (Spring 1969): 162.

12. *The Journals of Susanna Moodie* (Toronto, 1970), pp. 62–63.

13. Susanna Moodie, *Roughing It in the Bush: Or, Forest Life in Canada* (Toronto: Bell & Cockburn, 1913), p. 112.

14. Moodie, *Roughing It,* pp. 337, 544–45.

15. Susanna Moodie, *Life in the Clearings,* ed. Robert L. McDougall (Toronto: Macmillan, 1959), p. 258; see also George Grant, *Lament for a Nation: The Defeat of Canadian Nationalism* (Toronto: McClelland & Stewart, 1970), and Grant, *Technology and Empire: Perspectives on North America* (Toronto: Anansi, 1969); and John R. Seeley, *The Americanization of the Unconscious* (New York: International Science Press, 1967).

16. Peter Stevens, "Books in Review: Dark Mouth," *Canadian Literature,* no. 50 (Autumn 1971), p. 92.

17. Sandler, "Interview with MA," p. 18; MA to William Toye, 27 Jan. 1970 (draft letter), Atwood Papers, TFRBL, UT.

18. *Procedures for Underground* (Toronto, 1970), pp. 24–25.

Chapter Three

1. *Power Politics* (Toronto, 1971), p. 36.
2. See, for example, Miner, "Atwood in Metamorphosis," p. 185.
3. Quoted in Joan Larkin, "Soul Survivor," *Ms.,* May 1973, p. 35.
4. "Love is Ambiguous . . . Sex is a Bully," *Canadian Literature,* no. 49 (Summer 1971), p. 74.
5. "Notes on Power Politics," *Acta Victoriana* 97 (Apr. 1973): 7.
6. Harriet Zinnes, "Reviews: Seven Women Poets," *Carleton Miscellany* 14 (Spring-Summer 1974): 124; Joan Harcourt, review of *Power Politics, Quarry* 20 (Year End 1971): 71.
7. *You Are Happy* (Toronto, 1974), pp. 8–9.
8. Maureen Dilliott, "Emerging from the Cold: Margaret Atwood's *You Are Happy,*" *Modern Poetry Studies* 8 (Spring 1977): 90; regarding Atwood's duplicity at the end of *You Are Happy,* see Sherrill Grace, *Violent Duality: A Study of Margaret Atwood* (Montreal, 1980), pp. 77–78.
9. *Two-Headed Poems* (Toronto, 1978), pp. 24–25, 21, 13.
10. Julian Jaynes, *The Origin of Consciousness in the Breakdown of the Bicameral Mind* (Boston: Houghton Mifflin, 1977), *passim;* Gershom G. Scholem, *Major Trends in Jewish Mysticism,* 2d ed. (New York: Schocken, 1946), p. 7.
11. *The Circle Game* (Toronto, 1967), p. 80; and *Surfacing* (Toronto, 1972), p. 189.
12. *Procedures for Underground* (Toronto, 1970), pp. 50–51.
13. Quoted in Graeme Gibson, *Eleven Canadian Novelists* (Toronto, 1973), p. 8; and Karla Hammond, "An Interview with Margaret Atwood," *American Poetry Review* 8 (Sept.-Oct. 1979): 29.
14. *True Stories* (Toronto, 1981), p. 46.

Chapter Four

1. Gordon R. Elliott, "Book Reviews," *West Coast Review* 5 (Oct. 1970): 69; "Way of the Wild," (London) *Times Literary Supplement,* 1 June 1973, p. 604; Frank Davey, *From There to Here: A Guide to English-Canadian Literature Since 1960* (Erin, Ont.: Press Porcépic, 1974), p. 30.
2. "New Books: Five for Fall," *Time* (Canada), 21 Nov. 1969, p. 18; Edward Weeks, review of *Surfacing, Atlantic,* Apr. 1973, p. 127.
3. Quoted in Raymond Gardner, "In a Strange Land," *The Guardian,* 14 Oct. 1970, p. 9.
4. *The Edible Woman* (Toronto, 1969), p. 40.
5. Sandler, "Interview with MA," pp. 13–14.
6. Blurbs quoted from *Surfacing* (New York: Popular Library, 1974), front cover, p. [ii], back cover; Cynthia Griffin Wolff, "Thanatos and Eros: Kate Chopin's *The Awakening,*" *American Quarterly* 25 (Oct. 1973): 450.

7. Susan Fromberg Schaeffer, " 'It Is Time That Separates Us': Margaret Atwood's *Surfacing*," *Centennial Review* 18 (Fall 1974): 335.

8. *Surfacing* (Toronto, 1972), pp. 189, 191.

9. See, for example, Rosemary Sweetapple, "Margaret Atwood: Victims and Survivors," *Southern Review* 9 (Mar. 1976): 52; and Roberta Rubenstein, "*Surfacing:* Margaret Atwood's Journey to the Interior," *Modern Fiction Studies* 22 (Autumn 1976): 388; cf. Atwood's own remark that the protagonist's "marriage isn't real. She made it up," in Gibson, *Eleven Canadian Novelists*, p. 21.

10. Even the lengthy segment comprising most of part 2, seemingly given in past tense, is a recapitulation of six days' events, told by the narrator as she sits in the cabin (in the present tense) at the end of those six days, listening to the voices of her companions in the next room. A memory, it records experiences that occurred during her escape from her own time—from her first dive into the lake at the end of part 1, to her entering and then surfacing from her mystical experience in the chapters gapping parts 2 and 3.

11. Rosemary Sullivan, "Breaking the Circle," *Malahat Review*, no. 41 (Jan. 1977), pp. 40–41.

12. MA/JR, 31 July 1976; Patricia Morley, "The Gothic as Social Realism," *Canadian Forum* 56 (Dec.-Jan. 1976–77); 49: cf "Letters: Royal Porcupine's Identikit," *Saturday Night*, Jan.-Feb. 1977, p. 3.

13. *Lady Oracle* (Toronto, 1976), p. 7.

14. Struthers, "Interview," p. 24.

15. *Dancing Girls and Other Stories* (Toronto, 1977), p. 13.

16. Alicia Metcalf Miller, "Margaret Atwood Falters in Elaborate Soap Opera," *Cleveland Plain Dealer*, 24 Feb. 1980; Doris Grumbach, "Men Without Women, Women Without Men," *Books & Arts*, 7 Mar. 1980, p. 7.

17. *Life Before Man* (Toronto, 1979), p. 290.

18. Sherrill E. Grace, " 'Time Present and Time Past': *Life Before Man*," *Essays on Canadian Writing*, no. 20 (Winter 1980–81), p. 168.

19. *Bodily Harm* (Toronto, 1981), p. 295.

20. Grace, "Time Present and Time Past," p. 166.

21. Urjo Kareda, "Atwood on Automatic," *Saturday Night*, Nov. 1981, p. 72.

Chapter Five

1. "Getting Out from Under," in *The Empire Club of Canada: Addresses 1972–73* (Toronto: Empire Club Foundation, 1973), p. 357; Dennis Lee to Jerome Rosenberg, 20 Jan. 1978.

2. T. D. MacLulich, "The *Survival* Shoot-Out," *Essays on Canadian*

Writing, no. 1 (Winter 1974), p. 14; "Getting Out from Under," p. 358; Lee to Rosenberg, 1978.

3. *Survival: A Thematic Guide to Canadian Literature* (Toronto, 1972), p. 31.

4. D. G. Jones, *Butterfly on Rock: A Study of Themes and Images in Canadian Literature* (Toronto: University of Toronto Press, 1970), p. 4.

5. Stephen Scobie, review of *Survival, Canadian Fiction Magazine,* no. 10 (Spring 1973), pp. 117, 119; George Jonas, "Maggie Is a Thing Apart," *Maclean's,* 14 Aug. 1973, p. 14.

6. Christopher Driver, "Hastings Owl," *The Listener,* 14 Mar. 1974, p. 342; Germaine Warkentin, review of *Survival, Quill & Quire,* 38, no. 9 (1972): 8; Walter E. Swayze, "Survey and Survival," *Journal of Canadian Fiction* 3 (Winter 1974): 112; F. W. Watt, "Letters in Canada 1972: Humanities," *University of Toronto Quarterly* 42 (Summer 1973): 441; George Woodcock, "Surfacing to Survive: Notes of the Recent Atwood," *Ariel* 4 (July 1973): 22; Christina Newman, "Books," *Maclean's,* Dec. 1972, p. 104.

7. Frank Davey, "Atwood Walking Backwards," *Open Letter,* 2d Series, no. 5 (Summer 1973), p. 84 (unless otherwise cited, all Davey quotations are from this source, pp. 81–84); Richard T. Harrison, "The Literary Geography of Canada," *Lakehead University Review* 6 (Fall–Winter 1972): 276.

8. Davey's address was published as "Surviving the Paraphrase," *Canadian Literature,* no. 70 (Autumn 1976), pp. 5–13; Mathews's article, "Survival and Struggle in Canadian Literature: A Review of Margaret Atwood's *Survival,*" appeared in *This Magazine Is About Schools* 6 (Winter 1972–73): 109–24 (unless otherwise cited, all Mathews's quotations are from this source).

9. Robin Mathews, "*Survival* and the Canadian Sell-Out," *It Needs To Be Said* 1 (Feb. 1974): 8; "Margaret Atwood: The Historical Role and Destiny of the 'Creative Non-Victim,' " *New Literature and Ideology,* no. 20 (1976), p. 78.

10. Robin Mathews, "Poetics: The Struggle for Voice in Canada," *CV/II* 2 (Dec. 1976): 6–7; Frank Davey, "Robin Mathews' Fantasies," *CV/II* 3 (Spring 1977): 50.

11. "Surviving the Critics: Mathews and Misrepresentation," *This Magazine* 7 (May/June 1973): 33; reprinted in *Second Words: Selected Critical Prose* (Toronto, 1982), pp. 129–50 (hereafter cited as *SW*).

12. MA/JR, 16 Aug. 1978.

13. Ibid.

14. "Getting Out from Under," pp. 358–59.

15. "Eleven Years of *Alphabet,*" *Canadian Literature,* no. 49 (Summer 1971), p. 62; subsequent quotations, p. 63 (*SW,* pp. 90–96). Although I

arrived at my ideas regarding Atwood's synthetic approach independently, readers may wish to refer to George Woodcock's similar conclusions; see "Bashful but Bold: Notes on Margaret Atwood as Critic," in *The Art of Margaret Atwood,* ed. Arnold E. and Cathy N. Davidson (Toronto, 1981), pp. 223–41.

16. "What's So Funny? Notes on Canadian Humour," *This Magazine* 8 (Aug./Sept. 1974): 27 (*SW,* pp. 175–89); and "Canadian Monsters: Some Aspects of the Supernatural in Canadian Fiction," in *The Canadian Imagination: Dimensions of a Literary Culture,* ed. David Staines (Cambridge, Mass.: Harvard University Press, 1977), pp. 121–22 (*SW,* pp. 229–53); MA/JR, 16 Aug. 1978.

17. Quoted in Gibson, *Eleven Canadian Novelists,* p. 27.

18. "Don't Expect the Bear to Dance," *Maclean's,* June 1975, pp. 68, 71.

19. "The Berton Quintuplets Meet the Dionne Quintuplets," *Saturday Night,* Oct. 1977, pp. 62–63.

20. "Face to Face: Margaret Laurence, as Seen by Margaret Atwood," *Maclean's,* May 1974, p. 38.

21. "Marie-Claire Blais is Not for Burning," *Maclean's,* Sept. 1975, p. 26.

22. Ellen Coughlin, "Margaret Atwood," *Books & Arts,* 7 Mar. 1980, p. 6; "Paradoxes and Dilemmas: The Woman as Writer," in *Women in the Canadian Mosaic,* ed. Gwen Matheson (Toronto: Peter Martin, 1976), pp. 257, 270 (*SW,* pp. 190–204).

23. "Travels Back," *Maclean's,* Jan. 1973, pp. 31, 48 (*SW,* pp. 107–13); and "Nationalism, Limbo & the Canadian Club," *Saturday Night,* Jan. 1971, p. 11 (*SW,* pp. 83–89).

24. "Timeless in Afghanistan," *Toronto Life,* Aug. 1978, pp. [76, 79]; and "Atwood Among the Ozzies," *Saturday Night,* June 1978, pp. 45–51 (*SW,* pp. 296–306).

25. "Superwoman Drawn and Quartered: The Early Forms of *She,*" *Alphabet,* no. 10 (July 1965), p. 66 (*SW,* pp. 35–54); "MacEwen's Muse," *Canadian Literature,* no. 45 (Summer 1970), pp. 24–32 (*SW,* pp. 67–78); "Valgardsonland," *Essays on Canadian Writing,* no. 16 (Fall/Winter 1979–80), p. 190 (*SW,* pp. 320–24); review of *Great Canadian Short Stories, World Literature Written in English* 11 (Apr. 1972): 63–64; "Love is Ambiguous . . . Sex is a Bully," *Canadian Literature,* no. 49 (Summer 1971), pp. 71–75 (*SW,* pp. 97–102); and "Unfinished Women," *New York Times Book Review,* 11 June 1978, pp. 7, 42–43.

Chapter Six

1. Frye, *Bush Garden,* pp. 126–27; reprinted from "Letters in Canada," *University of Toronto Quarterly,* 1960.

2. Ibid., p. 213; reprinted from *Literary History of Canada,* ed. Carl F. Klinck; and Frye, "Conclusion," in *Literary History of Canada,* 2d ed., ed. Carl F. Klinck (Toronto: University of Toronto Press, 1976), vol. 3, p. 319.

3. George Woodcock, "Massey's Harvest," *Canadian Literature,* no. 73 (Summer 1977), p. 2.

4. Ibid., p. 4.

5. George Woodcock, "Swarming of Poets: An Editorial Reportage," *Canadian Literature,* no. 50 (Autumn 1971), p. 3.

6. For a more detailed examination of the history outlined in the previous paragraphs, see Claude Bissell, "Politics and Literature in the 1960s," in *Literary History of Canada,* 2d ed., vol. 3, pp. 10–15.

7. Wil Wigle, "Slow Burn," *Northern Journey,* no. 3 (Oct. 1973), p. 17.

8. Helen Slinger, "Interview with Margaret Atwood," *Maclean's,* 6 Sept. 1976, p. 6; Sandler, "Interview with MA," p. 9.

9. Joyce Carol Oates, "A Conversation with Margaret Atwood," *Ontario Review,* no. 9 (Fall-Winter 1978–79), p. 12; [Ioan Davies], "Fairy Tales of Canada," *Canadian Forum* 54 (May-June 1974): 68–69; MA/JR, 31 July 1976; Kildare Dobbs, "Books in English Canada: 1972," *Books in Canada* 2 (Jan.-Feb. 1973): 11.

10. MA/JR, 31 July 1976; Sandler, "Interview with MA," p. 26.

11. MA/JR, 8 Aug. 1975; Jack McClelland, quoted in Charles Taylor, "Writers' Plight: Slim Pickings from Publishers' Bonanza," *Toronto Globe & Mail,* 7 Apr. 1973, p. 23; for additional history on the formation of the Writers' Union, see *Canada Writes!,* ed. K. A. Hamilton (Toronto: Writers' Union of Canada, 1977), pp. xii–xiii.

12. " 'Slow Burn' Still Smoldering," *Quill & Quire* 40 (May 1974): 10.

13. Wigle, "Slow Burn," p. 17.

14. "Letters: Is Any Name Fair Game?" *Quill & Quire* 40 (July 1974): 2.

15. Patrick Conlon, "Margaret Atwood: Beneath the Surface," *Toronto Life,* Feb. 1975, p. 47.

16. Val Clery, "Backwords & Forewords: Official Portrait," *Quill & Quire* 41 (Feb. 1975): 8.

17. Patrick Conlon, Alexander Ross, Margaret Laurence, "Letters: A Simple Plea for Respect," *Quill & Quire* 41 (Mar. 1975): 2.

18. Val Clery, reply following above letters; Scott Symons, "The Canadian Bestiary: Ongoing Literary Depravity," *West Coast Review* 11 (Jan. 1977): 15.

19. Margaret Laurence, "Letters: Hysterical Ranting," *Canadian Forum* 57 (Nov. 1977): 31; Oates, "A Conversation," p. 13; Robert Fulford, "Notebook," *Saturday Night,* May 1980, p. 12.

20. Paul Delany, "Letters: Atwood and the Reviewers," *Saturday*

Night, July-Aug. 1980, p. 11; Sam Solecki, "Anniversary Waltz," *Canadian Forum* 57 (June-July 1977): 44.

21. "Letters: In Defence of Toads," *Saturday Night,* Nov. 1978, p. 12.

22. "A Statement of My Intellectual Interests, Related Activities, and Future Plans" (undergraduate essay), Atwood Papers, TFRBL, UT.

Selected Bibliography

PRIMARY SOURCES

With several exceptions, primary sources are limited to hardcover first editions only; not indicated are paperbound reprints or individual poems, stories, reviews, and essays Atwood has published in various periodicals and anthologies; for a complete list of these and other items, see Alan J. Horne's bibliographies cited below.

1. Poetry

The Animals in That Country. Toronto: Oxford University Press, 1968; Boston: Little, Brown, 1968.

The Circle Game. Toronto: Contact Press, 1966; Toronto: House of Anansi Press, 1967; Toronto: House of Anansi Press, 1978.

Double Persephone. Toronto: Hawkshead Press, 1961.

The Journals of Susanna Moodie. Toronto: Oxford University Press, 1970.

Power Politics. Toronto: House of Anansi Press, 1971; New York: Harper & Row, 1973.

Procedures for Underground. Toronto: Oxford University Press, 1970; Boston: Little, Brown, 1970.

Selected Poems. Toronto: Oxford University Press, 1976; New York: Simon and Schuster, 1978.

True Stories. Toronto: Oxford University Press, 1981; New York: Simon and Schuster, 1982; London: Jonathan Cape, 1982.

Two-Headed Poems. Toronto: Oxford University Press, 1978; New York: Simon and Schuster, 1980.

You Are Happy. Toronto: Oxford University Press, 1974; New York: Harper & Row, 1975.

2. Novels and Short Stories

Bluebeard's Egg. Toronto: McClelland & Stewart, 1983.

Bodily Harm. Toronto: McClelland & Stewart, 1981; New York: Simon & Schuster, 1982; London: Jonathan Cape, 1982.

Dancing Girls and Other Stories. Toronto: McClelland & Stewart, 1977; New York: Simon & Schuster, 1982; London: Jonathan Cape, 1982.

The Edible Woman. Toronto: McClelland & Stewart, 1969; London: André Deutsch, 1969; Boston: Little, Brown, 1970.

Lady Oracle. Toronto: McClelland & Stewart, 1976; New York: Simon & Schuster, 1976; London: André Deutsch, 1977.

Life Before Man. Toronto: McClelland & Stewart, 1979; New York: Simon & Schuster, 1980; London: Jonathan Cape, 1980.

Murder in the Dark. Toronto: Coach House Press, 1983.

Surfacing. Toronto: McClelland & Stewart, 1972; New York: Simon & Schuster, 1973; London: André Deutsch, 1973.

3. Non-Fiction

Days of the Rebels: 1815/1840. Canada's Illustrated Heritage Series. Toronto: McClelland & Stewart, 1977.

Second Words: Selected Critical Prose. Toronto: House of Anansi Press, 1982.

Survival: A Thematic Guide to Canadian Literature. Toronto: House of Anansi Press, 1972.

4. Books for Children

Anna's Pet (co-authored with Joyce Barkhouse). Toronto: James Lorimer, 1982.

Up in the Tree. Toronto: McClelland & Stewart, 1978.

SECONDARY SOURCES

1. Bibliographies

Fairbanks, Carol. "Margaret Atwood: A Bibliography of Criticism." *Bulletin of Bibliography* 36 (April–June 1979): 85–90, 98. Intended as an update and supplement for Horne's "Preliminary Checklist" cited below.

Horne, Alan J. "Margaret Atwood: An Annotated Bibliography (Poetry)." *The Annotated Bibliography of Canada's Major Authors,* vol. 2, edited by Robert Lecker and Jack David. Downsview, Ont.: ECW Press, 1980, pp. 13–53. Complete listing of Atwood's poetry publications, including books, contributions to periodicals and anthologies (cross-referenced to book publication), audiovisual materials, graphic work; also selected secondary listing, including books, articles, theses and dissertations, interviews, book reviews.

————. "Margaret Atwood: An Annotated Bibliography (Prose)." *The Annotated Bibliography of Canada's Major Authors,* vol. 1, edited by Robert Lecker and Jack David. Downsview, Ont. ECW Press, 1979, pp. 13–46. Complete listing, as above, for Atwood's prose works; a combined, less fully annotated version of these two listings (prose and poetry) appears in *The Art of Margaret Atwood,* cited below.

————. "A Preliminary Checklist of Writing By and About Margaret Atwood." *The Malahat Review*, no. 41 (January 1977), pp. 195–222. An unannotated version of the above, containing some entries deleted from the later listings; supersedes earlier checklist in *Canadian Library Journal*, November–December 1974.

2. Books and Journal Issues Devoted to Atwood
Davidson, Arnold E., and Cathy N. Davidson, eds. *The Art of Margaret Atwood: Essays in Criticism.* Toronto: House of Anansi Press, 1981. Thirteen essays on Atwood's work and literary roots.
Grace, Sherrill. *Violent Duality: A Study of Margaret Atwood.* Montreal: Véhicule Press, 1980. Exploratory survey of Atwood's work, focusing on the theme of duplicity.
Grace, Sherrill E., and Lorraine Weir, eds. *Margaret Atwood: Language, Text, and System.* Vancouver: University of British Columbia Press, 1983. Nine essays examining Atwood's "system," including a computer analysis of syntax in *Surfacing.*
Sandler, Linda, ed. *Margaret Atwood: A Symposium,* special issue of *The Malahat Review,* no. 41 (January 1977). Informal pieces, photographs, and critical essays on Atwood's work and image, including an informative interview conducted by Sandler.

3. Books with Chapters on Atwood
Cappon, Paul, ed. *In Our Own House: Social Perspectives on Canadian Literature.* Toronto: McClelland & Stewart, 1978. Essay by James Steele, "The Literary Criticism of Margaret Atwood," pp. 73–81.
Cude, Wilfred. *A Due Sense of Differences: An Evaluative Approach to Canadian Literature.* Lanham, Md.: University Press of America, 1980. Extended commentary on *Lady Oracle,* pp. 133–71, 203–6.
Gibson, Graeme. *Eleven Canadian Novelists.* Toronto: House of Anansi Press, 1973. Interview with Atwood, focusing on first two novels, pp. 1–31.
Her Own Woman: Profiles of Ten Canadian Women. Toronto: Macmillan, 1975. Biographical essay by Valerie Miner, "Atwood in Metamorphosis: An Authentic Canadian Fairy Tale," pp. 173–94.
Moss, John, ed. *The Canadian Novel: Here and Now.* Toronto: NC Press, 1978. Three essays, pp. 19–50: John Lauber, "Alice in Consumer-Land: The Self-Discovery of Marian MacAlpine [*sic*]"; Catherine McLay, "The Divided Self: Theme and Pattern in *Surfacing*"; Wilfred Cude, "Bravo Mothball! An Essay on *Lady Oracle.*"
Northey, Margot. *The Haunted Wilderness: The Gothic and Grotesque in Canadian Fiction.* Toronto: University of Toronto Press, 1976. Chapter on "Sociological Gothic: *Wild Geese* and *Surfacing*," pp. 62–69.

Rigney, Barbara Hill. *Madness and Sexual Politics in the Feminist Novel: Studies in Brontë, Woolf, Lessing, and Atwood.* Madison, Wis.: University of Wisconsin Press, 1978. A chapter, " 'After the Failure of Logic': Descent and Return in *Surfacing*," pp. 91–115.

Woodcock, George. *The World of Canadian Writing: Critiques and Recollections.* Vancouver: Douglas & McIntyre; Seattle: University of Washington Press, 1980. "Margaret Atwood: Poet as Novelist," pp. 149–73, combines and updates several earlier Woodcock essays.

4. Interviews and Biographical Essays

Ayre, John. "Margaret Atwood and the End of Colonialism." *Saturday Night,* November 1972, pp. 23–26.

Conlon, Patrick. "Margaret Atwood: Beneath the Surface." *Toronto Life,* February 1975, pp. 44–51.

Coughlin, Ellen. "Margaret Atwood." *Books & Arts,* 7 March 1980, pp. 4–6.

Davidson, Jim. "Interview: Margaret Atwood." *Meanjin Quarterly* 37 (July 1978): 189–205.

Gibson, Mary Ellis. "A Conversation with Margaret Atwood." *Chicago Review* 27 (Spring 1976): 105–13.

Hammond, Karla. "An Interview with Margaret Atwood." *American Poetry Review* 8 (September-October 1979): 27–29.

———. "A Margaret Atwood Interview." *Concerning Poetry* 12, no. 2 (1979): 73–81.

Kaminski, Margaret. "Interview with Margaret Atwood." *Waves* 4 (Autumn 1975): 8–13.

Levenson, Christopher. "Interview with Margaret Atwood." *Manna,* no. 2 (1972), pp. 46–54.

Oates, Joyce Carol. "A Conversation with Margaret Atwood." *Ontario Review,* no. 9 (Fall-Winter 1978–79), pp. 5–18.

———. "Margaret Atwood: Poems and Poet." *New York Times Book Review,* 21 May 1978, pp. 15, 43–45.

Schiller, William. "Interview with Margaret Atwood." *Poetry Windsor Poésie* 2 (Fall 1976): 2–15.

Slinger, Helen. "Interview with Margaret Atwood." *Maclean's,* 6 September 1976, pp. 4–7.

Struthers, J. R. (Tim). "An Interview with Margaret Atwood." *Essays on Canadian Writing,* no. 6 (Spring 1977), pp. 18–27.

Swan, Susan. "Margaret Atwood: The Women as Poet." *Communiqué,* no. 8 (May 1975), pp. 8–11, 45–46.

Varseveld, Gail van. "Talking with Atwood." *Room of One's Own* 1 (Summer 1975): 66–70.

5. Articles: Poetry

Allen, Carolyn. "Margaret Atwood: Power of Transformation, Power of Knowledge." *Essays on Canadian Writing,* no. 6 (Spring 1977), pp. 5–17. Discusses transformation motif in Atwood's poetry.

Bilan, R. P. "Margaret Atwood's 'The Journals of Susanna Moodie.' " *Canadian Poetry,* no. 2 (Spring-Summer 1978), pp. 1–12. Discusses the organizational pattern in *The Journals.*

Davey, Frank. "Atwood's Gorgon Touch." *Studies in Canadian Literature* 2 (Summer 1977): 146–63. Discusses time versus space, movement versus stasis, in Atwood's poetry.

Davidson, Arnold E. "The Different Voices in Margaret Atwood's *The Journals of Susanna Moodie.*" *CEA Critic* 43 (November 1980): 14–20.

Foster, John Wilson. "The Poetry of Margaret Atwood." *Canadian Literature,* no. 74 (Autumn 1977), pp. 5–20. Comprehensive discussion of space, landscape, and self in Atwood's first six volumes.

Glicksohn, Susan Wood. "The Martian Point of View." *Extrapolation* 15 (May 1974): 161–73. Comments on science fiction motifs as artistic device in Atwood's poetry.

Irvine, Lorna. "The Red and Silver Heroes Have Collapsed." *Concerning Poetry* 12, no. 2 (1979): 59–68. Surveys Atwood's attempt in the poems "to demythicize sexual relationships."

Johnston, Gordon. " 'The Ruthless Story and the Future Tense' in Margaret Atwood's 'Circe/Mud Poems.' " *Studies in Canadian Literature* 5 (1980): 167–76. Discusses Circe's attitudes toward time and the future.

McCombs, Judith. "Power Politics: The Book and Its Cover." *Moving Out* 3, no. 2 (1973): 54–69. Comprehensive, multi-faceted reading of the text.

Onley, Gloria. "Power Politics in Bluebeard's Castle." *Canadian Literature,* no. 60 (Spring 1974), pp. 21–42. Comments on sexual politics in *Power Politics, The Edible Woman,* and *Surfacing.*

Ross, Gary. "The Circle Game." *Canadian Literature,* no. 60 (Spring 1974), pp. 51–63. Discusses the theme of achieving harmony with the wilderness as a structuring device in *The Circle Game.*

Sillers, Pat. "Power Impinging: Hearing Atwood's Vision." *Studies in Canadian Literature* 4 (Winter 1979): 59–70. Discusses style and rhetorical force in *Selected Poems.*

6. Articles: Fiction

Bjerring, Nancy E. "The Problem of Language in Margaret Atwood's 'Surfacing.' " *Queen's Quarterly* 83 (Winter 1976): 597–612.

Broege, Valerie. "Margaret Atwood's Americans and Canadians." *Essays on Canadian Writing,* no. 22 (Summer 1981), pp. 111–35. Comments on

Atwood's attitudes toward and use of the Canadian-American relationship in her fiction and poetry.

Brown, Russell M. "Atwood's Sacred Wells." *Essays on Canadian Writing,* no. 17 (Spring 1980), pp. 5–43. Intelligent, comprehensive study of the well as mystic symbol in Atwood's fiction and poetry.

Campbell, Josie P. "The Woman as Hero in Margaret Atwood's *Surfacing.*" *Mosaic* 11 (Spring 1978): 17–28. Discusses quest myth in the novel.

Carrington, Ildikó de Papp. " 'I'm Stuck': The Secret Sharers in *The Edible Woman.*" *Essays on Canadian Writing,* no. 23 (Spring 1982), pp. 68–87. Comments on Atwood's allusions to Conrad's "The Secret Sharer" and on Duncan's role as Marian's double.

Christ, Carol P. "Margaret Atwood: The Surfacing of Women's Spiritual Quest and Vision." *Signs* 2 (Winter 1976): 316–30. Offers a feminist theological reading of *Surfacing;* followed by Judith Plaskow's "On Carol Christ on Margaret Atwood: Some Theological Reflections," pp. 331–39, and "A Reply," pp. 340–41, by Atwood.

Colman, S. J. "Margaret Atwood, Lucien Goldmann's Pascal, and the Meaning of 'Canada.' " *University of Toronto Quarterly* 48 (Spring 1979): 245–62. Discusses *Surfacing* as an expression of "Goldmann's tragic world-view."

Davidson, Arnold E., and Cathy N. Davidson. "Margaret Atwood's *Lady Oracle:* The Artist as Escapist and Seer." *Studies in Canadian Literature* 3 (Summer 1978): 166–77.

Freibert, Lucy M. "The Artist as Picaro: The Revelation of Margaret Atwood's 'Lady Oracle.' " *Canadian Literature,* no. 92 (Spring 1982), pp. 23–33.

Garebian, Keith. "*Surfacing:* Apocalyptic Ghost Story," *Mosaic* 9 (Spring 1976): 1–9.

Hutcheon, Linda. "Atwood and Laurence: Poet and Novelist." *Studies in Canadian Literature* 3 (Summer 1978): 255–63. Discusses effect of image patterns on readers' response to *The Edible Woman.*

Maclean, Susan. "*Lady Oracle:* The Art of Reality and The Reality of Art." *Journal of Canadian Fiction,* nos. 28/29 (1980), pp. 179–97. Comprehensive study of the novel's "reflexive narrative technique."

MacLulich, T. D. "Atwood's Adult Fairy Tale: Levi-Strauss, Bettelheim, and *The Edible Woman.*" *Essays on Canadian Writing,* no. 11 (Summer 1978), pp. 111–29. Applies psychoanalytic and structuralist theories toward an understanding of Atwood's first novel.

Mansbridge, Francis. "Search for Self in the Novels of Margaret Atwood." *Journal of Canadian Fiction,* no. 22 (1978), pp. 106–17. Deals with *The Edible Woman, Surfacing,* and *Lady Oracle.*

Nodelman, Perry. "Trusting the Untrustworthy." *Journal of Canadian Fiction,* no. 21 (1977–78), pp. 73–82. Discusses first-person narrative and image patterns in *The Edible Woman.*

Ross, Catherine Sheldrick. " 'Banished to This Other Place': Atwood's *Lady Oracle.*" *English Studies in Canada* 6 (Winter 1980): 460–74. Discusses the tension between art and life in *Lady Oracle.*

————. "Nancy Drew as Shaman: Atwood's *Surfacing.*" *Canadian Literature,* no. 84 (Spring 1980), pp. 7–17.

Rubenstein, Roberta. *"Surfacing:* Margaret Atwood's Journey to the Interior." *Modern Fiction Studies* 22 (Autumn 1976): 387–99.

Schaeffer, Susan Fromberg. " 'It Is Time That Separates Us': Margaret Atwood's *Surfacing.*" *Centennial Review* 18 (Fall 1974): 319–37. Discusses theme of mortality and human limitation.

Sullivan, Rosemary. "Surfacing and Deliverance." *Canadian Literature,* no. 67 (Winter 1976), pp. 6–20. Comments on the divergent cultural preoccupations of Atwood's and Dickey's novels.

7. Articles: Criticism

Davey, Frank. "Atwood Walking Backwards." *Open Letter,* 2d Series, no. 5 (Summer 1973), pp. 74–84. Attacks the objectivity and critical accuracy of *Survival.*

Gutteridge, Don. "Surviving the Fittest: Margaret Atwood and the Sparrow's Fall." *Journal of Canadian Studies* 8 (August 1973): 59–64. Questions the credibility of *Survival.*

MacLulich, T. D. "The *Survival* Shoot-Out." *Essays on Canadian Writing,* no. 1 (Winter 1974), pp. 14–20. Reviews the critical dialogue surrounding *Survival.*

Macri, F. M. "Survival Kit: Margaret Atwood and the Canadian Scene." *Modern Poetry Studies* 5 (Autumn 1974): 187–95. Offers a negative assessment of Atwood's poetry and sees *Survival* as a potentially misleading book.

Mathews, Robin. "Survival and Struggle in Canadian Literature." *This Magazine Is About Schools* 6 (Winter 1972–73): 109–24. Questions the accuracy and the intent of *Survival.*

Morley, Patricia. "Survival, Affirmation, and Joy." *Lakehead University Review* 7 (Summer 1974): 21–30. Finds *Survival* biased, but witty and provocative as well.

Index

818.54
at 887

116 985